M000086344

How Do I
Save My Honor?

To Daryl,

With Warmest Regards,

William Felix

Jan. 2015

How Do I Save My Honor?

War, Moral Integrity, and Principled Resignation

William F. Felice

ROWMAN & LITTLEFIELD PUBLISHERS, INC.
Lanham • Boulder • New York • Toronto • Plymouth, UK

Published by Rowman & Littlefield Publishers, Inc.
A wholly owned subsidiary of The Rowman & Littlefield Publishing Group, Inc.
4501 Forbes Boulevard, Suite 200, Lanham, Maryland 20706
http://www.rowmanlittlefield.com

Estover Road, Plymouth PL6 7PY, United Kingdom

Copyright © 2009 by Rowman & Littlefield Publishers, Inc.
First paperback edition 2009

All rights reserved. No part of this book may be reproduced in any form or by
any electronic or mechanical means, including information storage and retrieval
systems, without written permission from the publisher, except by a reviewer
who may quote passages in a review.

British Library Cataloguing in Publication Information Available

The hardcover edition of this book was previously cataloged by the Library of
Congress as follows:

Felice, William F., 1950–
  How do I save my honor? : war, moral integrity, and principled resignation /
William F. Felice.
   p.   cm.
  Includes index.
   1. War—Moral and ethical aspects—Case studies. 2. Military ethics—Case
studies. 3. Integrity—Case studies. 4. Responsibility—Case studies. 5. Iraq War,
2003– —Moral and ethical aspects. 6. Soldiers—United States—Biography.
7. Civil service—United States—Biography. 8. Soldiers—Great Britain—
Biography. 9. Civil service—Great Britain—Biography. I. Title.
U22.F45 2009
172'.42—dc22

                                                                    2008048443

   ISBN: 978-0-7425-6666-8 (cloth : alk. paper)
   ISBN: 978-0-7425-6667-5 (pbk. : alk. paper)
   ISBN: 978-0-7425-6668-2 (electronic)

∞™ The paper used in this publication meets the minimum requirements of
American National Standard for Information Sciences—Permanence of Paper
for Printed Library Materials, ANSI/NISO Z39.48-1992.

Printed in the United States of America

"Demosthenes: 'Whereas the slave fears only pain, what the free man fears most is shame.' If we grant the truth [that the Bush administration sanctioned torture] then the issue for individual Americans becomes a moral one: how, in the face of this shame to which I am subjected, do I behave? How do I save my honour?"

—J. M. Coetzee, *Diary of a Bad Year*

Contents

Acknowledgments

After a meeting at the Carnegie Council for Ethics in International Affairs (CCEIA), Alexander Platt raised Brady Kiesling's powerful letter of resignation and recommended that "someone should write a book" about the courageous individuals in the Foreign Service and military who resigned from the government due to their moral disagreements with U.S. foreign policy. I am grateful to Alix for this suggestion, as it planted a seed in my mind that eventually grew into this book. CCEIA president Joel Rosenthal has also been a source of ongoing support and encouragement throughout this entire project.

You will be introduced in this book to a pantheon of true American and British patriots who struggled to protect their honor and moral integrity in a time of war: John H. Brown, Aidan Delgado, John Denham, Brady Kiesling, Andy Reed, Carne Ross, Clare Short, Ehren Watada, Wayne White, and Ann Wright. Each of these individuals agreed to spend hours with me as I interviewed them about their personal journeys and ethical struggles. This book is fundamentally a product of their willingness to share their stories and struggles. It is impossible for me to fully express the depths of my gratitude to each of them, as it is only their cooperation that made this project possible.

One of the country's stellar scholars of political theory, Dr. Brent Pickett, read each chapter of this book with great attention and care. Brent's thoughtful suggestions and feedback were indispensible in helping me to conceptualize and articulate an ethic of principled resignation. I am extremely indebted to him and hope to be able to someday return the favor.

My colleague at Eckerd College, Prof. Anthony Brunello, listened patiently to my explanations of the core concepts of the book and provided vital feedback and advice. I am privileged to be able to work every day with Tony, a caring teacher of vast integrity.

In the initial phase of this project, Prof. Al Pierce provided extremely valuable suggestions on key resources which helped me to formulate a clear research plan. Prof. Peter Singer was very generous with his time and thoughts on issues of moral integrity in a time of war. As always, my friend Prof. Michael J. Smith gave his unflinching support and helpful advice at key moments during this difficult project. Greg Shank, the editor of the journal *Social Justice*, provided particularly useful comments and feedback on the ethics chapter.

Todd Germann not only designed and developed the dramatic graphic design for the cover but also gave me valuable computer assistance and technical help throughout the interview process. I deeply appreciate not only his professional help but, more importantly, his friendship. I am most grateful to Linda Krohn for her hard work in transcribing the many hours of interviews. These transcriptions were absolutely essential to the success of this project. I am also very appreciative to Eckerd College for providing me with a series of faculty development grants which made the research interviews for this book possible.

I wish to thank the two people at Rowman & Littlefield Publishers who were instrumental in bringing this book to press. Editorial Director Susan McEachern has been a tremendous source of support, and this project benefited greatly from her professionalism and skilled editorial supervision. Editorial Assistant Carrie Broadwell-Tkach guided the manuscript through the final production process. I am grateful to both Susan and Carrie for their commitment to this project.

I wish to acknowledge with gratitude permission to draw on the following previously published work: "Individual Moral Responsibility in a Time of War," *Social Justice*, Vol. 35, No. 3 (2008).

In 1975, Edward Weisband and Thomas Franck published *Resignation in Protest: Political and Ethical Choices Between Loyalty to Team and Loyalty to Conscience in American Public Life*. This path-breaking book critiqued the difficulties of public civil servants in maintaining individual moral autonomy during the Vietnam War. In many respects, *How Do I Save My Honor?* picks up the questions asked by Weisband and Franck and applies them to international relations today. The issues surrounding individual moral responsibility in a time of war are unfortunately timeless. As long as war continues as a central instrument of foreign policy, all citizens must struggle to protect their individual honor and moral integrity. As during the Vietnam War, these issues are once again paramount to the protection of individual personal honor during the current war in Iraq.

Finally, and most importantly, I want to acknowledge the patience and support of my partner, Dale Lappe. Dale's ongoing feedback, encouragement, and love give me great strength and joy.

Interview List

The following individuals were interviewed for this book. Unless otherwise indicated, all quotes in the text from these individuals are drawn from the transcriptions of these one-on-one discussions with the author.

John H. Brown
U.S. Foreign Service Officer
Resignation: March 10, 2003
Interview: October 1, 2005

Aidan Delgado
U.S. Army Reserves
Military Service: 2001–2004
Interview: October 27, 2007

John Denham
Member of the British Parliament
Cabinet Minister
Interview: June 11, 2007

Michael J. Foster
Member of the British Parliament
Interview: June 12, 2007

John Brady Kiesling
U.S. Foreign Service Officer
Resignation: February 27, 2003
Interview: September 30 and October 2, 2005

Ken Purchase
Member of the British Parliament
Interview: June 12, 2007

Andy Reed
Member of the British Parliament
Interview: June 12, 2007

Carne Ross
British Foreign Service
Resignation: September 2004
Interview: June 8, 2007

Clare Short
Member of the British Parliament
Former Secretary of State for International Development
Interview: June 12, 2007

Peter Singer
The Ira W. DeCamp Professor of Bioethics
Princeton University
Interview: September 14, 2006

Ehren Watada
U.S. Army First Lieutenant
Military Service: 2003–
Interview: September 12, 2007

Wayne White
U.S. Foreign Service
State Department Intelligence, retired
Interview: August 14, 2007

Mary Ann Wright
Colonel, U.S. Army
U.S. Foreign Service Officer
Resignation: March 19, 2003
Interview: August 22, 2005

Author's Note

How Do I Save My Honor? was written during the presidency of George W. Bush. References in the text to the U.S. executive branch and the U.S. administration thus refer to that of President Bush and not the current Obama presidency.

1

⟨∞⟩

Introduction

On a daily basis, most of us make moral and ethical judgments all the time in relation to private action.[1] We make moral judgments about individuals who murder, cheat, lie, and steal. We expect that individuals will act on "universal" principles in their treatment of others independent of race, gender, sexuality, and class. At the national level, appeals to the public good and the responsibilities and duties of public office are also based on ethical deliberations and moral judgments.

I am concerned with levels of moral responsibility and accountability. In large bureaucracies (corporations, governments, universities) it is often difficult to attribute moral responsibility to anyone. Dennis Thompson calls this the problem of "many hands." When an action of the government causes harm to innocents, it is often difficult to trace the "fingerprints of responsibility" to individual actors. There is a tendency to deny the responsibility of an individual person, instead attributing blame abstractly to "the system" or the government or "the state." Citizens often feel unable to connect criticisms of the government with the actions of individuals inside the structures of the state.[2]

The decisions leading to the war and occupation of Iraq were ultimately made at the highest levels of the U.S. and British governments. Legal and moral responsibility lies with the president, prime minister, and their cabinets, as hierarchical responsibility does coincide with moral responsibility. Yet can an ethical analysis of the war stop with the actions of the president, prime minister, and their principal advisers? Should others in the government and military also be held to standards of moral accountability? Do individual citizens have any moral duties in regard to the war?

1

This book explores the degrees of moral responsibility that government employees, soldiers, and citizens bear for the actions of the U.S. and British governments for the 2003 invasion and ongoing occupation of Iraq. Moral responsibility for an outcome is largely dependent upon the contribution an individual actually made, or could have made, to the policy outcome.

The actions of Colin Powell are examined in depth in chapter 4 because of his position as secretary of state. From an ethical point of view, should he have acted differently? If he objected, for example, to the Pentagon's preventive war plans in Iraq and U.S. policy in Guantanamo Bay and Abu Ghraib, should he have resigned? Some argue in Powell's defense, believing that he did the right thing by fighting within the administration to correct certain ethically troublesome policies. Yet, for many other observers, it was painful to watch former Secretary Powell appear to sacrifice his moral principles with his strident and vigorous public campaigning for the war. Did his failure to resign give the green light to the administration to continue questionable ethical policies?

These issues go beyond the office of the secretary of state. What is the moral responsibility of others in the U.S. and British governments? If an individual believes that the U.S. or British government violated basic norms of morality and justice, what is he or she to do? If the individual's voice is ignored inside the government, does this person have an ethical duty to resign?

In Britain, taking moral responsibility often means resigning from office in protest of policies the official finds ethically dubious. As described in detail in chapter 7, in the British parliamentary system, ministers have more political independence from the executive branch than their counterparts in the United States. The list of British government leaders who resigned from office to protest Blair's decision to align with the United States and invade Iraq is impressive, including the following: Bob Blizzard, Anne Campbell, Robin Cook, John Denham, Michael Jabez Foster, Lord Hunt, Ken Purchase, Andy Reed, Carne Ross, Clare Short, and Elizabeth Wilmshurst. Most of these individuals were elected representatives to the British Parliament and remained in the House of Commons after resigning from their posts in the Blair administration. Yet others who resigned, like Carne Ross and Elizabeth Wilmshurst, were members of the British civil service, not the Parliament. With their resignations, these individuals gave up their careers in the government and financial security in an attempt to protect their moral integrity.

In the United States, on the other hand, accepting moral responsibility for American foreign policy decisions has, for the most part, not included resignation. In the entire history of the United States, only two secretaries of state, Williams Jennings Bryan and Cyrus Vance, have resigned for ethical reasons, as documented in the case studies of Bryan and Vance in chapter 2. Certain individuals in the U.S. Foreign Service, however, did resign over Iraq, including career diplomats John H. Brown, John Brady Kiesling, and Mary Ann Wright. Were these officials correct in their actions? Or were these flamboyant resignations examples of "moral self-indulgence," that is, an effort to appear as a "moral" person and keep one's hands clean, no matter what happens to the rest of society?[3] Would it have been better for these diplomats to work from the inside and fight for their moral beliefs within the government? Is this more effective than resignation? These questions are pursued in detail in chapter 5.

And what about the rest of us who aren't in the government? What are our moral duties in a time of war? By not speaking out and actively working to stop our government from committing torture, Mark Danner asserts that "we are all torturers now."[4] It is now impossible for individual Americans to deny knowledge of human rights abuses by their own government. What moral responsibility do we have to speak up and publicly oppose these policies?

The occupation of Iraq submerged the American people into an ethical morass that led many to conclude, on the basis of two overriding factors, that this was not a "just war." First, the UN system for peace established after World War II banned aggressive war. No nation can attack another nation unless it has been attacked or it is faced with an "imminent threat." Former CIA Director George Tenet has made it clear that intelligence analysts "never said there was an imminent threat."[5] The "Downing Street Memo,"[6] combined with the "Butler Report," the official British inquiry into the use of intelligence on Iraq's weapons of mass destruction (WMD),[7] documents that by the late 1990s and into 2002 it had become crystal clear to most experts that Iraq was not rearming and that the policy of containment was working. There was nothing in this intelligence to suggest that Saddam Hussein was either engaged in a successful rearmament effort or intended to attack Iraq's neighbors, Britain, or the United States. In fact, according to the chief of analysis at the CIA's counterterrorist center, the Bush administration invaded Iraq "without requesting—and evidently without being influenced by—any strategic-level intelligence assessments on any aspect of Iraq . . . the intelligence was misused publicly to justify decisions already made."[8] As a result, many American and British citizens felt that the legal and moral justification for the invasion of Iraq withered on the vine. Second, the foundational principles of international human rights law include prohibition against torture, arbitrary arrest, and cruel, inhumane, and degrading treatment. Furthermore, the laws of war require at a minimum that all those arrested and captured in wartime be treated humanely. The images of Abu Ghraib and Guantanamo seemed to announce to the world that the United States no longer considered these human rights sacrosanct. The intentional humiliation and torture at Abu Ghraib, combined with the large numbers of people held at Guantanamo for years with no access to attorneys, no charges filed, and no access to families, led many in America and Britain to conclude that U.S. actions were unethical and in violation of the minimal standards of decency codified in U.S. and international law.[9]

Individual "moral autonomy" is understood "to refer to the capacity to be one's own person, to live one's life according to reasons and motives that are taken as one's own and not the product of manipulative or distorting external forces."[10] This key value of moral autonomy is found in both the Kantian tradition of moral philosophy and the utilitarian liberalism of John Stuart Mill. Weisband and Franck describe this central norm as "the willingness to assert one's own principled judgment, even if that entails violating rules, values, or perceptions of the organization, peer group, or team."[11] Moral responsibility can be defined as the assertion of one's moral autonomy and the ability to resist "groupthink"[12] in governmental service. As will be seen, it remains very difficult for citizens in and out of the government to protect their moral autonomy and assume moral responsibility in a time of war.

Levels of moral responsibility often clearly correspond to hierarchical power. Those with an ability to directly influence the decision-making surrounding the choice to invade and occupy Iraq bear a higher level of moral responsibility than those with no direct power. Yet, in addition to those who made the decisions, all individuals in the military and the Foreign Service who are called on to publicly support and enact the government's policies bear a degree of responsibility as well. Through carrying out the responsibilities of their jobs, these individuals help to promote the government's war policies. If these individuals in the government or the military come to the conclusion that the war in Iraq is immoral and illegal, what are they to do? Do employees of the State Department, when called on to publicly defend U.S. war policies, have a moral duty to step aside if their ethical disagreement is profound? Or is it ethical to "work from within" and try to change, or at least moderate, a disturbing policy? Do military personnel who disagree with the war have an ethical duty to speak up and put down their rifles? How does an individual in the Foreign Service or in the military protect his or her moral autonomy in a time of war?

Many members of the Foreign Service and the military, often due to misplaced feelings of patriotic duty or fear of losing a job, do not even raise issues of personal moral conflict and bury ethical concerns about war policies. Some of these individuals choose not to reason morally and instead merely follow the orders and instructions of their superiors. In the nineteenth century, Henry David Thoreau heaped scorn on those who sacrifice individual moral integrity in the service of the state. Thoreau wrote,

> The mass of men serve the State . . . not as men mainly, but as machines, with their bodies. . . . In most cases there is no free exercise whatever of the judgment or of the moral sense; but they put themselves on a level with wood and earth and stones. . . . Such command no more respect than men of straw, or a lump of dirt. They have the same sort of worth only as horses and dogs. Yet such as these even are commonly esteemed good citizens. . . . A very few, as heroes, patriots, martyrs, reformers in the great sense, and *men*, serve the State with their consciences also, and so necessarily resist it for the most part; and they are commonly treated by it as enemies.[13]

The focus of this book is on the actions of those individuals in the government and the military who accepted Thoreau's challenge to "serve[d] the State with their consciences" and struggled with the ethical issues surrounding the Iraq war. Some of these individuals stayed inside the government and tried to "work from within" to change foreign policy. Others resigned from their positions to protest policies in Iraq that they considered to be illegal and immoral. And, unfortunately, as Thoreau warned, some of these brave individuals have been treated like the "enemy" and have been prosecuted for their actions. All of these persons have lessons to teach all of us about individual moral responsibility in a time of war. No matter where we are in society—teachers, community leaders, janitors, nurses, and so on—we all have a responsibility to the truth and our personal integrity and moral autonomy.

Karl Jaspers wrote clearly about individual moral responsibility and the danger of passivity, silence, and inaction. "But each of us is guilty insofar as he remained inactive. . . . But passivity knows itself morally guilty of every failure, every neglect to act whenever possible, to shield the imperiled, to relieve wrong, to countervail. Impotent submission always left a margin of activity which, though not without risk, could still be cautiously effective."[14]

This book is about certain individuals who took personal risks in the hope that their actions would be "cautiously effective" in changing U.S. and British foreign policy in the Middle East. The focus here is on those individuals in the government and military who had moral qualms about the Iraq war policies. Attention is paid to those who came to question, reevaluate, and ultimately challenge the justifications for the bloodshed. The views of those who had no doubt about the correctness of these policies, expressed, for example, with fundamentalist certainty by Wolfowitz and Cheney, have been fully documented and analyzed elsewhere.[15] On the other side, the legal and moral criticisms of the Iraq invasion and occupation have also been well documented.[16] Yet there has not been similar attention paid to the actions of those individuals who took personal risks to challenge Iraq policies. This book attempts to fill that gap and tell the story of those individuals who came to the point of saying to their government, "Not in my name."

Individuals acting to uphold their personal integrity and moral autonomy have, throughout history, played a significant role in correcting the often immoral behavior of government. Ultimately, in fact, the direction of an entire society is determined by such actions, as Socrates noted so long ago: "Societies are not made of sticks and stones, but of men whose individual characters, by turning the scale one way or another, determine the direction of the whole."[17]

How Do I Save My Honor? is an exploration of the personal responsibility of Foreign Service officers and military personnel during the Iraq war. Following this introduction, chapter 2 evaluates the myriad of issues surrounding "public integrity." In a democracy, civil servants and military personnel are to carry out the decisions of the officials elected by the people. Loyalty is the primary normative value promoted by the government. Individuals in the Foreign Service and the military are expected to advance the nation's interests and set aside personal goals. It is within this context that the moral responsibility of civil servants and military personnel is explored. When an individual's personal ethics conflict with government policy, does the civil servant or soldier resign or "work from within"? The ethics of "staying in" versus "getting out" are fully evaluated. The chapter concludes with an argument in favor of an "ethic of principled resignation." Such an ethic could help a democracy build up individual habits of personal integrity and personal moral autonomy. Such behavioral patterns of individual personal responsibility are crucial to breaking the engrained patterns of conformity and loyalty that accompany large bureaucracies. The pressure to conform and be a "team player" has often stifled open discussion, silenced dissent, and contributed to the phenomenon of groupthink which has led to disastrous foreign policy decisions. Even the "threat" of principled resignation alone could serve to help keep a government's internal decision-making process honest and be a healthy development for a democracy. Included at the end of the chapter are three case studies of individuals who in their public service struggled with the ethics of principled resignation: Williams Jennings Bryan, Cyrus Vance, and Gen. Harold Johnson.

Chapter 3 explores whether ethical theory can help us to sort through these issues of individual moral responsibility and public service. Do the leading ethical theories help us to better understand individual and collective responsibility in a time of war? Are there absolute moral boundaries that can never be crossed? Is there an ethical line that, once traversed, will compel a moral person to act? These questions are analyzed through the following theories and approaches: political realism, deontology, utilitarianism, and the neoconservative values of the Bush administration. Included in this discussion is an interview with Peter Singer, one of the world's leading utilitarian philosophers. These ethical theories and approaches are very helpful for clarifying the many moral issues surrounding intervention and war. However, in the application of theory to the real world, a huge door often opens for consequentialist reasoning with the "ends justifying the means." To the Bush administration, for example, freedom for Iraq justified the horrible means of war and violence. Politicians are expected to have "dirty hands" and sacrifice individual moral autonomy for the interests of the state. The perceived morality of the state too often overwhelms the moral autonomy of the individual.

Chapter 4 analyzes the actions of two individuals who "stayed in" the government and tried from within to moderate or change U.S. policy in Iraq: Colin Powell and Wayne White. Former Secretary of State Colin Powell declined my request for an interview. However, his correspondence with me (reproduced in this chapter) is extremely revealing. Powell viewed the decision to go to war with Iraq as a "policy" and not an "ethical" choice. Since there was no moral dilemma for him, he never considered resigning, and instead he became the administration's chief salesman for the war. Powell's actions can be contrasted to those of Cyrus Vance. When an ethical line regarding the use of force was crossed for Vance, he resigned and maintained his moral autonomy. Powell, on the other hand, even though he remained loyal to the president, was marginalized inside the administration and had little impact on war policy. If Powell did have strong objections to the war, it is hard not to conclude that he would have been more effective raising these views outside the government and publicly speaking out. Instead, by continuing in office and selling the war, many concluded that his actions contributed more harm than good.

Wayne White retired as deputy director of the Office of Analysis for the Near East and South Asia in the State Department's Bureau of Intelligence and Research (INR) in March 2005. White remained in his job despite his serious misgivings about the Bush administration's war planning in Iraq. He felt that the pre-war decision-making policy-makers "often turned a blind eye to intelligence inconsistent with their Middle East agenda." His formal February 2003 INR analysis warned of both military and political dangers for the United States, even with a "successful" occupation of Iraq. He states that the administration refused to allocate adequate forces to the Iraqi campaign. Yet, despite these major differences, White remained in his job in the State Department because he felt he could make a difference from within. As can be seen, White feels that he was able to maintain his moral integrity by consistently pushing alternative analysis and perspectives during the Iraq imbroglio.

Chapter 5 analyzes the actions of three individuals in the U.S. government who "got out" and resigned due to ethical disagreements with the Iraq war: Brady Kiesling, John Brown, and Ann Wright. In February 2003, Brady Kiesling became the first American diplomat to resign over Iraq. Kiesling describes himself as a "State Department realist" and views the failures of the Bush administration's foreign policy as a result of misguided idealism. Kiesling gave up his twenty-year career in the State Department because he felt that the Bush administration's foreign policies were "incompatible not only with American values but also with American interests." John Brown also resigned from the government in 2003 after more than twenty years as a U.S. Foreign Service officer in public diplomacy. Brown came to believe that the war in Iraq was "totally unjustified" and resigned because he could not in good conscience publicly endorse this dangerous foreign policy. When the United States went ahead with the war in Iraq, despite the pleas from the United Nations and the global public in massive demonstrations, Brown felt the administration had betrayed the principles of public diplomacy, and he had no choice but to quit. The final diplomat to resign in 2003, Ann Wright spent thirty-five years of combined service in the military and the State Department. The Bush administration's preventive war strategy in Iraq crossed some basic moral boundaries for Wright. She could no longer publicly support these policies and, to protect her moral integrity, she felt that she had to resign. Wright is now a prominent figure in the antiwar movement. These three former diplomats exemplify the utility of an "ethic of principled resignation" as a means to maintain one's personal moral integrity and to regain one's voice in the public domain.

Chapter 6 examines the actions of two U.S. soldiers who refused to fight in Iraq: Ehren Watada and Aidan Delgado. On June 22, 2006, U.S. Army 1st Lt. Ehren Watada became the first commissioned officer to refuse deployment to the Iraq war. Watada had come to the conclusion that the Iraq war was immoral and illegal. Watada was not a conscientious objector and, in fact, offered to serve in Afghanistan. The U.S. Army denied this request and instead decided to prosecute Watada for deliberately missing the order to deploy and for publicly making antiwar statements. Watada faces a potential jail sentence of two to six years. Aidan Delgado, a former member of the army reserve, served a yearlong tour of Iraq in 2003. His unit, the 320th Military Police Company, spent six months in the southern city of Nasiriyah and another six months at Abu Ghraib prison. During this time, Delgado witnessed U.S. soldiers abusing Iraqi civilians and prisoners. He has stated that the prison abuse at Abu Ghraib was just the tip of the iceberg and that racist brutality infected the entire military operation in Iraq. Delgado's Buddhist beliefs led him to embrace pacifism and nonviolence as a means of conflict resolution. While in Iraq, Delgado turned in his rifle and declared himself a conscientious objector.

In Britain, Prime Minister Tony Blair faced turmoil in his government over his decision to join forces with the United States and invade and occupy Iraq. The actions of key members of the British government who resigned to protest the Iraq war are analyzed in chapter 7. Carne Ross resigned after more than fifteen years in the Foreign Service after concluding that the British government had been systematically misrepresenting the situation in Iraq. Clare Short attempted to use her position as a member of the cabinet to pressure Bush and Blair to internationalize the Iraq occupation and reinvigorate the "road map" between the Israelis and Palestinians. When these efforts failed, she, too, felt that she had no choice but to resign. Andy Reed resigned as a parliamentary private secretary after he came to the conclusion that the Iraq war violated his strong Christian beliefs. He did not believe that the invasion of Iraq was a "just war." Finally, John Denham resigned from the Blair government because he felt that the Iraq invasion would create greater insecurity and deepen problems of extremism and terrorism. Denham, however, kept his resignation within the bounds of accepted discourse in British politics. In June 2007, Britain's new prime minister, Gordon Brown, appointed him to a new cabinet-level post.

The final chapter summarizes some of the broader issues of individual moral responsibility in a time of war. One key conclusion is the centrality of moral autonomy to effective democratic governance. Thoreau perhaps made this point most eloquently:

> Must the citizen ever for a moment, or in the least degree, resign his conscience to the legislator? Why has every man a conscience, then? I think that we should be men first, and subjects afterward. . . . The only obligation which I have a right to assume, is to do at any time what I think right. It is truly enough said, that a corporation has no conscience; but a corporation of conscientious men is a corporation *with* a conscience.[18]

The individuals interviewed for this book refused to sign over their conscience to the government and instead maintained their ethical balance during a difficult time in world history. Thoreau is right. Only when individuals assert their moral autonomy do we have the possibility of creating and maintaining a government with a conscience.

2

⌀

The Moral Obligations of Civil Servants and Soldiers

On December 14, 2004, George W. Bush awarded the Presidential Medal of Freedom to Envoy Paul Bremer, General Tommy Franks, and CIA Director George Tenet. On June 1, 2005, U.S. Deputy Secretary of Defense Paul Wolfowitz, one of the chief architects of the Iraq war, was promoted to the presidency of the World Bank. Through these actions, the Bush administration seemed to be declaring that whatever moral and political failures may have occurred in Iraq, these four individuals were not culpable. Instead, Bush loudly proclaimed that these military and civilian leaders, by carrying out their functions to the best of their abilities, should not only not be held accountable for the growing chaos and suffering engulfing Iraq but also should be rewarded for loyalty to the administration during a difficult war.

The public record of each of these powerful actors, however, challenges that conclusion and raises several troubling ethical issues. In the case of Bremer, the Special Inspector General for Iraq Reconstruction reported that more than nine billion dollars in reconstruction aid to Iraq disappeared through fraud, corruption, or other misbehavior during his tenure as head of the reconstruction of Iraq from 2003 to 2004.[1] Also controversial was Bremer's official decision to disband the former Iraqi army, which put four hundred thousand former Iraqi soldiers out of work. This action was widely criticized for creating a large pool of angry and armed young men from which the insurgency might draw recruits.[2] Franks has been heavily criticized for failing to recognize the threat of irregular fighters, for not demanding enough troops to maintain order following the invasion, and for failing to plan the long-term post-invasion military needs in

Iraq.³ Tenet is the individual most responsible for the misleading intelligence reporting on Iraq's weapons of mass destruction (WMD) and ties to al-Qaeda. And Wolfowitz has openly admitted the Bush administration's underhanded plan to "sell the war" to the American public, stating, "For bureaucratic reasons, we settled on one issue, weapons of mass destruction, because it was the one reason everyone could agree on."⁴ Furthermore, Wolfowitz was notoriously wrong on almost all of his prewar predictions. He loudly declared in early 2003 that Iraqi oil revenues would pay for all costs of reconstructing the country. During this time, he famously dismissed Gen. Eric K. Shinseki's estimates on the size of the post-war occupation force as "wildly off the mark" and, instead, estimated that fewer than one hundred thousand troops would be necessary. There were more than one hundred seventy thousand U.S. troops still in Iraq five years after the invasion.⁵

The same phenomenon occurred after the Vietnam War. Those individuals most responsible for the failed policies in Vietnam were promoted and rewarded and not held accountable for their misjudgments and deceits. The architects of the unsuccessful and deadly U.S. policy in Vietnam included Robert McNamara, McGeorge Bundy, and Henry Kissinger. McNamara, blazing the way for Wolfowitz, was appointed to the presidency of the World Bank. Bundy became president of the Ford Foundation. And Kissinger remains held in high esteem and continues to advise Democrats and Republicans, including George W. Bush, on U.S. foreign policy.

Clearly, not everyone will agree with the criticisms raised here of Bremer, Franks, Tenet, or Wolfowitz (let alone the critique of McNamara, Bundy, and Kissinger). To the supporters of the Iraq occupation, these men were true patriots and deserve promotions and awards. The problem, however, is that even those who are critical of the actions of these individuals in pushing the United States into the Iraq war, and thus think that they should not have been promoted or rewarded, still have a great deal of difficulty placing "moral responsibility" on their shoulders. Thomas Nagel made this point in regard to the Vietnam War. He noted that those who agreed that war crimes had been committed in Vietnam had trouble "attach[ing] the crimes to the criminals, in virtue of the official role in which they were committed." Nagel describes this as a "problem about the moral effects of public roles and offices." There is a "moral insulation" that comes with a position in the civil service or the military.⁶

This moral insulation affects how individuals working for the government view their responsibilities and also how these people are evaluated by the public. The individual civil servant or member of the armed forces often comes to the conclusion that his or her role is simply to do the job,

follow orders, and meet responsibilities. This employee does not see himself or herself as morally responsible for policy outcomes. And the public
seems to agree that these individuals should be released from moral responsibility. There is no historical tradition in the United States of holding
civil servants or soldiers—at all levels of the chain of command—responsible for failed or unethical policies. As Nagel writes:

> Not only are ordinary soldiers, executioners, secret policemen, and bom-
> bardiers morally encapsulated in their roles, but so are most secretaries of
> defense or state, and even many presidents and prime ministers. They act as
> office-holders or functionaries, and thereby as individuals they are insulated
> in a puzzling way from what they do: insulated both in their own view and
> in the view of most observers. Even if one is in no doubt about the merits of
> the acts in question, the agents seem to have a slippery moral surface, pro-
> duced by their roles or offices.[7]

Public civil servants and military personnel are expected to pursue
the public interest and loyally carry out the priorities of the government
efficiently and effectively. These public duties arise from their positions
as agents of the state. They are given resources and authority to do what
they can to help advance the national interest of their country. In a time
of war, the demands of loyal service accelerate (and dissent is not only
discouraged but often also seen as treasonous). These individuals have
special obligations to advance the state's interests, not their own individual interests. To a large extent, these positions have an impersonal
character in the sense that the function to be carried out is not determined
by the individual in the job. Rather, the individual finds himself or herself
as part of a large bureaucratic and institutional structure which, in theory,
exists to carry out the priorities of the elected government officials. All of
this dictates against the idea of public civil servants or military personnel
having individual moral responsibility for policy decisions and policy
outcomes. Those working for the government are expected to pursue the
public good and not individual self-interest.

Those of us who do not serve in the military or in the government do
not face the same types of pressure. Our major moral duty is primarily
to ourselves and our families and not the overall public good. Liberal
capitalism encourages the individual pursuit of self-interest. Each of us
has a personal duty to act with integrity and protect our individual moral
autonomy. Yet, for most of us, our actions are not directly related to promoting or implementing our elected representatives' determination of the
nation's priorities. We do not have power over policy implementation,
and thus our impact on policy outcomes is limited. Our ability to impact
the government's policies during a time of war is circumscribed. We can

express our displeasure with the occupation of Iraq with our votes. It is true that as private individuals we have more freedom than government employees and military personnel to speak up and publicly oppose policies that seem unjust or immoral. Such acts of protest are often critical for an individual to save his or her honor and moral integrity.

The problem for the soldier and the statesman is determining how best to serve the public good. Some argue that in a democratic country, civil servants and military personnel do not have either a duty or a right to develop their own conception of what the public interest requires in particular situations. Those who believe this argue that in a democracy the duties and obligations of civil servants and military personnel are established by the elected officials above them and the law of the land. Furthermore, the government and the military would cease to function if every employee would only participate in those programs in which they had total agreement.

However, in a time of moral extremity, it is difficult to maintain this line of argument. Since the judgment at Nuremberg, it is no longer a credible legal defense or convincing moral argument to maintain that one was merely "following orders" and therefore innocent despite his or her individual participation in war crimes or a war of aggression. In fact, many argue that the opposite is the case and that individual ethical duty increases during a time of war. It is no longer sufficient to accept the argument that in a democracy, the elected officials solely determine the national interest. In fact, moral conduct means that these individuals in the government are not relieved from taking some initiative for conceiving and proposing alternatives to programs they find ethically troublesome.

Joel Fleishman's useful definition of integrity is to have "a genuine, wholehearted disposition to do the right and just thing in all circumstances, and to shape one's actions accordingly." Fleishman points out that there is no code of conduct "declaring society's view of the right course of action in every situation, so each of us must puzzle out for ourself the moral solution to each dilemma we face." This means that for civil servants and military personnel to have integrity, "they must therefore act ethically insofar as they are able to know what is right, in each circumstance."[8] Ultimately, every individual in the government and the military must develop a conception of the moral duties tied to his or her position to best serve the public interest.

Certain categories of moral integrity are clear across the political spectrum. Most would agree, for example, that it is clearly not acceptable behavior for a person to use his or her public position for illegal personal gain or to advance a friend over a more qualified candidate for a particular job. Most would agree that it is unethical to utilize the public trust to advance one's wealth or position to the detriment of the overall public good. Most of us would agree that it is obviously unethical to cheat or steal or kill to advance one's personal fortunes. Unfortunately, these basic ethics in public service are not always upheld. Personal ambition and rationalization often override an individual's judgment and lead to this type of corrupt and illegal behavior. And, in order to protect one's job or advance in the organization, a "blind eye" is often taken toward the observation of such corrupt behavior in one's superiors. The numerous varieties of rationalization of this type of unethical conduct are dangerous and profound.

Yet other categories of moral integrity are not clear across the political spectrum. There is definitely not agreement on the moral duties of civil servants and soldiers during a time of war. As we have seen, some argue that in a democracy one's duty is simply to carry out the public policies determined by superiors. Others claim the opposite, arguing for individual accountability to the use and non-use of violence in our foreign policy. How is an individual to sort out these difficult moral dilemmas?

Unfortunately, it is extremely difficult to even raise these questions. First of all, it is quite natural for an individual to want to succeed in the military or the State Department. Speaking out and raising disagreements to the government's policies, especially in a time of war, is rarely the best avenue for promotion in either bureaucracy. As a result, many individuals who have moral qualms about war policies give up, bury their disagreements, and rationalize their actions. Personal ambition and rationalization again dictate against even raising issues of morality in warfare.

Second, our lives are morally complex. Most of us feel that our first ethical duty is to take care of ourselves and our families. We cause harm to others if we become a burden to society by taking actions which jeopardize our livelihood and well-being. During a time of war, members of the armed forces and the civil service can risk losing not only a promotion but ultimately their jobs as well. What then happens to their moral duties to their families? And how is this effective? Brady Kiesling, for example, gave up a promising career and the security such a job held for his family (in terms of pension and benefits) by resigning to protest the war in Iraq. Ehren Watada not only gave up his career in the military but also risked three to six years in jail for speaking out against the war and refusing to fight in Iraq. Were these responsible actions?

Third, profound feelings of uncertainty and inadequacy often arise when one takes a stand against the government in a time of war. An honest historical analysis of human affairs will acknowledge that there is rarely an easy road to resolving war and conflict and often no clear path to end human suffering. Who am I to stand up and say that all the experts in the government and the military, immersed in the details of the war, are wrong in their policies? How can I possibly have a better understanding of this war than they do? Additionally, in this information age, we are bombarded with conflicting data and contradictory conclusions about basic issues, such as progress in the war on terror. How does one decide which perspective is the correct path for our country to follow? Anyone with a little humility and knowledge of human affairs is undoubtedly a bit unsure about the best path to end the bloodshed in Iraq.[9]

Fourth, above all other ethical norms, the central moral value prized in the American political system is "loyalty." The rewards of public life go to those who are seen as "loyal" to the elected officials (especially the president) and to the institutions of the state (especially the military). As we have seen with McNamara, Wolfowitz, Tenet, and the others, loyalty to a president in a time of war is rewarded. The question of the correct moral action during conflicts is answered quickly—loyalty to the president above all other considerations! Despite well-publicized failures, these individuals in the government are primarily evaluated, often by friend and foe alike, to have served the president well. The value of "loyalty" rises above all other norms and becomes the most important principle to uphold.

For all of these (and other) reasons, it has historically been shown to be almost impossible for individuals in the government or military to speak out during a time of war. It remains extremely hard for those individuals who have moral qualms to show integrity and act on their ethical principles. We know, for example, that McNamara stayed in office, publicly promoting Vietnam War policies, even after he came to doubt whether the war could be won. And it wasn't just McNamara. It is alarming that no major figure in the Johnson or Nixon administrations quit in opposition to the Vietnam War.[10] Weisband and Franck note that this is a comment

> not solely on the ethical state of the men who occupy high-office, but also on the ethical climate of the nation. . . . We reject those who break faith with the system. . . . We prefer officials to be loyal to the President even if they are thereby disloyal to the Constitution and themselves. The men and women at the breaking point in the executive branch know this, and trim accordingly.[11]

Individuals in the government and military have not been elected and are bound to carry out the orders of others. Yet from an ethical perspective these individuals should not act contrary to their personal moral convictions. What should happen when the two come into conflict? From a perspective of democratic theory, policy is determined by the elected representatives, not civil servants or military personnel. A democratic government depends upon individuals in the civil service and military to enact these agreed-upon policies and not to attempt to impose their own views. This framework was agreed to when the individual joined the military or the civil service. Some argue, therefore, that since these individuals consented to this arrangement before signing up, they should not have joined if they could not accept this administrative structure for the determination of public policy. From this perspective, the moral obligations of civil servants and military personnel are fairly straightforward. One either obeys or resigns.

Yet is this view too simplistic? There are many avenues in the government and military to influence policy outcomes by working from within. Individual civil servants are called on all the time to exercise ethical judgment. All policy is not decided by either elected officials or the law but determined by individual civil servants. In addition, the best public servants are not those who simply "go along to get along." Rather, the outstanding civil servant will question decisions, probe contradictions in policy, and seek new directions forward. Individuals in the upper levels of government, with more freedom and ability to influence outcomes, have a particularly high duty to exercise moral reasoning in policy decisions. It would therefore be counterproductive to expect men and women with strong moral convictions to always resign. Furthermore, the loyalty of these public officials should be fundamentally to the American people and not to a particular elected official or bureaucracy. From this perspective, rather than resigning, this person should fight from within to represent the best interests of the broader public. Amy Gutmann and Dennis Thompson outline the "menu of moral options" available to public officials:

> Depending on how serious the moral violation is and the good that officials can do by opposing it, officials may be warranted in staying in office and expressing their opposition in other ways. They may, for example, organize internal opposition, issue public protests, refuse to carry out the policy personally, support outside opponents of the policy, or directly obstruct the implementation of a policy.[12]

Yet it is also the case that what can begin as an ethical justification for continuing to participate in the government or the military can end up as a rationalization to stay in a particular position. The easy path is to automatically assume that one can do more good by staying in rather than by getting out. The harder path is to take all the risks associated with resignation, including the loss of financial security for oneself and family. However, there is no one right path. Depending on the situation, the moral action may be to stay or it may be to go. The real issue is to accept that one is making an ethical (and not simply a policy) decision and to be able to defend the moral reasoning behind the particular action to fellow citizens.

STAYING IN

As already noted, in a democratic society the integrity of public officials is fundamentally linked to the obligations of the office or position held. Citizens expect their soldiers and civil servants to be honest and accountable and to uphold Constitutional values. Democratic decision-making, respect for due process, individual rights, and equality before the law are viewed as central. There is also an expectation that civil servants and military personnel accept the legitimacy of the political process and are committed to perform their jobs competently and efficiently.

If public officials do not adhere to these democratic principles, then few moral dilemmas will arise for them. As J. Patrick Dobel notes:

> If they ambitiously seek only self-aggrandizement, then no clear concerns for the rights of others or constitutional integrity will set boundaries to their deliberations. Likewise, if they possess consuming loyalty to a person or an ideology that admits no compromise, then they will acknowledge no limits set by democratic rules of the game, due process, or accountability since the leader's success or the dogma of the ideology override all other ethical considerations. For such people there will be no crises of conscience in politics, only narrow, self-interested calculations of power or clear-cut imperatives for action justified by infallible leaders or revealed ideologies. For such people there are no dilemmas, only tactics.[13]

Public officials dedicated to democratic values, however, understand the necessity and importance of compromise. While maintaining their moral standards, such officials understand that they will not win every battle and that, therefore, on issues that do not cross an absolute moral line, compromise is necessary. In our messy democratic system, public policy is produced only after taking into account the competing interests of diverse interest groups. Every group and every individual will not get everything they want. Respecting others' views, and participating in a process of dialogue, lobbying, persuasion, and coalition building, is central to a democratic political process. In the end, everyone involved in this process must compromise on some ideals and goals. As a result, there is a constant challenge to each individual's moral autonomy. The difficult issue is: when does "necessary compromise" become unacceptable degradation of one's personal integrity?

It is also the case that civil servants and military personnel must be ready to implement policies that they personally disagree with. One cannot be a purist about everything. The daily operation of the government and the military depends upon individual employees carrying out their jobs. If every policy were contingent upon the total agreement of all involved, nothing would get done. If a policy has gone through a good faith

process of debate, discussion, and resolution, the civil servant is expected
to be willing to implement that decision. But, again, the difficult issue
remains what to do if a final decision challenges one's basic ethics.

Dobel outlines four categories of behavior that

> strains or transgresses the bounds of acceptable ethical compromise in gov-
> ernment: (1) criminal conduct such as murder, theft, acceptance of bribes, or
> venality or negligence in procurement of equipment upon which security
> and lives will depend; (2) actions that undermine democratic accountability
> of the system of government such as illegal campaign contributions, electoral
> bribery or fakery, use of government agencies or paragovernmental groups
> to intimidate or hurt political opponents or suppression of information
> necessary to make informed choices about vital policy choices when the
> suppression has no plausible national security justification; (3) actions that
> violate the civil liberties of individual citizens or undermine the governmen-
> tal rules that make democratic decisions possible and accountable; and (4)
> actions that violate one's central moral convictions or standards of justice
> and that have no clear moral justification or excuse.[14]

It is this last category—actions that violate one's central moral convictions—that is the most difficult to sort out. Rather than confront the moral
issue head on, it is often easier to practice a degree of self-deception. In
the case of Iraq, none of us want to be thought of as "good Germans" and
not speaking out against or acting to oppose illegal (e.g., aggressive war)
and immoral (e.g., torture) policies. But rather than spelling out clearly
the ramifications of current war policies, it is easier to live in a fog and
not accept personal responsibility. And once one embarks on this morally
problematic course, it is very hard to later switch gears and accept this
responsibility. It is too easy to convince oneself that one is doing good
when, in reality, by staying in the government or military one is contributing to the wrong and immoral war policy.

One of the central arguments for "staying in" is the importance of le-
veraging access to power to be able to change and moderate offending
policies. Those who stay must determine that they can accomplish more
from the inside than from working outside. Yet after a person speaks out
against an established policy, he or she runs the risk of being sidelined,
losing access, and suffering a profound loss of influence on future decisions inside the government. This makes it difficult for the dissenter to
really accomplish much inside the government. This government employee may still be allowed to write his or her memos of protest, but the
impact will be negligible. Key decision-makers will, unfortunately, often
marginalize those who raise ethical objections to their decisions. As analyzed in chapter 4, this seems to have been the case with former Secretary
of State Colin Powell. It is clear that Powell's objections to war policies

were barely tolerated and certainly not followed. This marginalization effectively undermines one of the central arguments for "staying in." It often does not seem to be the case that by "staying in" one can necessarily have an impact on moderating dangerous policies. In fact, an internal dissenter can become insignificant and inconsequential by raising ethical disagreements during a time of war.[15]

To avoid this marginalization, there are great pressures to "choose one's battles wisely" and, in general, remain silent and not express disagreement to established policy. Many individuals in the government and the military remain silent to avoid marginalization and maintain access, thinking it better to "keep one's powder dry" in order to fight another day. James Thomson describes this as "the effectiveness trap": "The inclination to remain silent or to acquiesce in the presence of great men—to live to fight another day, to give on this issue so that you can be effective on later issues—is overwhelming."[16]

Dobel raises a further critical point regarding the dangers of staying in. "To hold strong moral convictions and act upon them, to resist the pressure to cave in, and to avoid self-deception are all morally necessary to justify staying in. But one more important condition must be met: a participant must not contribute more significant harm than possible good."[17] As head of intelligence for the State Department, Wayne White came to serious disagreements with the direction of the Bush administration's policies in Iraq and the Middle East. Yet, since he was able to raise his concerns directly to Powell and to Bush, he felt that he had an obligation to stay and fight on. In his view, his resignation would have only turned over one more office to those misleading our country. He concluded that the correct moral action was to stay in, fight on, and try from the inside to change policy. This issue, of course, gets much more complicated with Colin Powell, whose public role seemed to "contribute more significant harm than possible good."

Internal voices of dissent are needed. If everyone opposing a particular policy resigned, no honest policy discussions would take place. Resignations by those who disagree with established priorities would result in a narrower choice of policy options for the administration and the tendency for groupthink dynamics to prevail inside the government. The strongest argument for staying in is perhaps this negative outcome. Effective democratic governance depends upon the maintenance of a vibrant system of internal open dialogue and debate. To resign in protest is to give up one's voice in this process, which can result in the enhancement of the influence of those who are promoting the immoral policies that provoked the resignation to begin with.

GETTING OUT

A strategy of loyalty and "working from within" can often be more effective if there is an ongoing "exit" option. The "threat" of resignation alone can serve to enhance the voice of the dissenter inside the government. However, for this to occur, the "threat" needs to be considered serious, and resignation needs to be seen as an effective option. Unfortunately, in the United States there has not been a positive "ethic of principled resignation" in our culture that could help civil servants and military personnel sort out these difficult moral issues. Instead, the person who exits is often considered both disloyal and unwilling to engage with those who disagree over these ethical issues. "Rational" behavior is seen as remaining loyal to the organization despite moral disagreements.

There is another issue getting in the way of resignation. For a person to decide to resign, he or she must be convinced that the departure will not result in further damage to the organization and a worsening of the policy he or she vehemently opposes. In too many cases, a civil servant becomes convinced that he or she has to stay in government to prevent the worst from happening. It is well known that both Hubert Humphrey and Robert McNamara privately told their friends that they stayed in office to keep the escalation of the Vietnam War from getting worse. Former Secretary of State Colin Powell is reported to have told friends that he felt like the little poor Dutch boy with his finger in a hole in the dam. If Powell left office, the dam would burst. Yet by staying in office and not speaking publicly about their reservations, Humphrey, McNamara, and Powell contributed significantly to the selling of these wars to the American people and added to the harm caused by prolonging these ill-advised interventions. Resignations by these men would have significantly undermined the political support for these wars.

Albert Hirschman contextualizes this issue in relation to "public goods" and "public evils." Public goods are a well-known concept in economics, referring to those products that all can enjoy in common with each individual's consumption not detracting from the consumption or use by another. Examples of public goods include clean air, a public sidewalk, and national defense. All members of a given community are consumers of these public goods. According to Hirschman, public evils

> result not only from universally sensed inadequacies in the supply of public goods, but from the fact that what is a public good for some—say a plentiful supply of police dogs and atomic bombs—may well be judged a public evil by others in the community. It is also quite easy to conceive of a public good

turning into a public evil, for example if a country's foreign and military policies develop in such a way that their "output" changes from international
prestige into international disrepute.[18]

The majority of the public in America and the world in 2007 felt that the
Bush administration's war policies in the Middle East stood in international disrepute.[19] Some considered the occupation of Iraq to have become
a "public evil." Those personnel in the government and military who
agreed with this analysis were thus faced with a dilemma. On the one
side were those who argued that it would be wrongheaded and spineless
to resign to protest these policies. Those holding this view believed that
the consequence of leaving positions of responsibility in protest was that
alternative voices would subsequently not be voiced inside the government. Resignation would thus have the perverse result of enhancing the
power of those individuals pushing the misguided policies one was protesting against. In other words, it was better to stay and fight on.

The alternative is to exit, protest, and fight the misguided policies from
the outside. Or, as Hirschman puts it,

> the alternative is now not so much between voice and exit as between voice
> from within and voice from without (after exit). The exit decision then hinges
> on a totally new question: At what point is one more effective (besides being
> more at peace with oneself) fighting mistaken policies from without than
> continuing the attempt to change these policies from within?[20]

One of the key issues here is not to lose one's voice. We have too often
witnessed the "silent resignations" where an official will quit for "private
reasons," to "spend more time with his or her children," and so on. The
fundamental policy disagreement is kept under wraps. Loyalty again
raises its ugly head. Speaking out is seen as a violation of the trust that the
president or other elected official placed in the civil servant. Resignation
in silence is probably the least ethically defensible course, as it gives to the
public a false reassurance that nothing is really wrong.[21] Thompson has
argued that moral responsibility does not end with resignation and that the
former official has a responsibility to make some effort to at least bring the
negligence of their former colleagues to public attention: "There is a moral
life—and perhaps there should be a legal liability—after resignation."[22]

The other key issue here is effectiveness. As long as one can have an
impact on policy, it does seem wrong to resign. Why give up when it is
really possible to bring about change from within? However, as noted
above, speaking out against administration policy inside the government
can lead to marginalization and the loss of effectiveness. In this situation,
an individual with strong ethical and moral objections to war policies
should probably resign because continuing to carry out the job lends

credence to the immoral policy. In fact, if a person becomes wedded to a government job and will not resign under any circumstances, the individual risks violating his or her personal moral integrity and surrendering institutional effectiveness.[23]

There are many reasons why someone may feel the need to resign: inability because of age to fully perform the tasks of the job, failure to master the technical competencies required, and so on. These resignation issues are not of concern to this study. Rather, the issue here is resigning over principle—reaching the decision that the demands of the government are in conflict with an individual's basic moral beliefs. When one's ability to impact policy is gone, it is hard to accept staying in government and supporting a policy the individual believes is morally bankrupt.

There is a stronger tradition of resignation over principle in Britain than in the United States. For example, British Prime Minister Neville Chamberlain was faced with two resignations from his cabinet in protest of his appeasement policies toward Hitler's Germany. In February 1938, Foreign Secretary Anthony Eden resigned in protest. In his resignation letter, Eden wrote:

> I have become increasingly conscious . . . of the difference in outlook between us in respect to the international problems of the day and also as to the methods whereby we should seek to resolve them. It cannot be in the country's interest that those who are called upon to direct its affairs should work in uneasy partnership, fully conscious of differences in outlook yet hoping they will not recur.[24]

A few months later, the first lord of the Admiralty, Alfred Duff Cooper, resigned to protest against the "peace for our time" settlement that Chamberlain reached with Hitler in Munich. Striking "a discordant note" amid the general rejoicing, he wrote, "I profoundly distrust the foreign policy which this government is pursuing and seems likely to continue to pursue." Cooper concluded his speech to Parliament explaining his decision to leave by stating, "I have ruined, perhaps, my political career. But that is of little value—I can still walk in the world with my head erect."[25]

The war and occupation of Iraq raised troubling ethical issues of war, violence, and torture to the people interviewed for this book. These individuals in the military and the government no longer shared the vision of the Bush and Blair governments in Iraq, and some came to view the occupation as a "public evil." Many of these individuals tried, and failed, to change U.S. or British foreign policy. Principled resignation thus became an essential moral option for many of these brave souls, as they struggled to "walk in the world with [their] head[s] erect."

If America had a tradition of an "ethic of principled resignation," it is possible that President Bush's decisions on Iraq would have been challenged more potently inside and outside the government and potentially reversed. The Iraq war and occupation triggered profound ethical crises within thousands of Americans in the government and military, yet few were able to speak up and protect their moral autonomy. The strong expectation is that we will all quietly go along with the team and remain loyal to the administration. This fostering of conformity rather than conviction has been detrimental to our democracy and has meant there was no counter or break to some of the worst foreign policy decisions in America's history. The catastrophe of the Iraq occupation has painfully exposed the bankruptcy of an "ethics of loyalty" over an "ethics of personal conscience."

In the *Nicomachean Ethics*, Aristotle wrote:

> For the things we have to learn before we can do them, we learn by doing them, e.g.: men become builders by building and lyre-players by playing the lyre; so too we become just by just acts, temperate by doing temperate acts, brave by doing brave acts. This is confirmed by what happens in states; for legislators make the citizens good by forming habits in them. . . . It makes no small difference, then, whether we form habits of one kind or of another from our very youth; it makes a very great difference, or rather *all* the difference.[26]

Aristotle's focus on the importance of ingrained habits is crucial. Ingrained habits of conformity and loyalty undermine democracy and effective popular participation in governance. New habits based on moral autonomy would have a positive impact on the democratic process. An "ethic of principled resignation" can serve to support habits of personal integrity and moral autonomy. The first duty of all citizens, Foreign Service officers, and military personnel should be to individual conscience. Loyalty to one's country and administration would no longer be placed in opposition to one's moral role as a full, critical-thinking participant in the democratic process.

New habits of moral autonomy could mean that more unconscionable government policies would be exposed, issues of war and torture more fully debated, and objectionable policies reversed through legitimate public action. Aristotle is right—such a change in habits would make no small difference; rather, it would make *"all* the difference."

THE ETHICAL SOLDIER

As the war in Iraq continued into late 2007, surpassing by more than a year the entire U.S. military engagement in World War II, an explosion of self-reflection and criticism took place inside the U.S. military. Officers were divided over whether former Defense Secretary Donald H. Rumsfeld or the generals who submitted to him bore primary responsibility for the Iraq debacle. At the Army School for Officers at Fort Leavenworth, Kansas,[27] tensions over responsibility boiled over. Maj. Kareen P. Montague argued that responsibility did not lie with just Rumsfeld. He said that the Joint Chiefs of Staff and the top commanders were part of the decision to send in a small invasion force and not enough troops for the occupation. The one general who spoke up, Eric K. Shinseki, was sidelined after testifying that it would take several hundred thousand troops to achieve U.S. objectives in Iraq. "You didn't hear any of them [other top commanders] at the time, other than General Shinseki, screaming, saying that this was untenable," Major Montague said.[28]

Since the army traditionally has sought to show solidarity to the outside world during a time of ongoing conflict, this frank and open discussion on the responsibility for the Iraq war was unusual. The major criticisms within the military of both Rumsfeld and the Joint Chiefs were over sending in a small invasion force and failing to plan properly for the occupation. Even the former top commander in Iraq, Lt. Gen. Ricardo S. Sanchez, stepped forward to criticize the administration's handling of the war as "incompetent," "catastrophically flawed," and a "nightmare with no end in sight."[29] This internal army debate was partially touched off by a biting article by Lt. Col. Paul Yingling titled "A Failure in Generalship," published in the *Armed Forces Journal*. Yingling, an Iraq veteran who holds a master's degree in political science from the University of Chicago, wrote, "If the general remains silent while the statesman commits a nation to war with insufficient means, he shares culpability for the results."[30] The article is now required reading at Leavenworth.

Discussion among the young officers at Leavenworth focused on the "red line," the point at which they would defy a command from the president and defense secretary, who lead the military. According to Maj. Timothy Jacobsen,

> We have an obligation that if our civilian leaders give us an order, unless it is illegal, immoral or unethical, then we're supposed to execute it, and to not do so would be considered insubordinate. How do you define what is truly illegal, immoral or unethical? At what point do you cross that threshold where this is no longer right, I need to raise my hand or resign or go to the media?[31]

Col. Gregory Fontenot, on the other hand, questions whether Americans really want four-star generals to stand up and say no to the president in a nation where civilians control the armed forces. When asked if it would have stopped the war if enough four-star generals had done that, Fontenot responded, "Yeah, we'd call it a coup d'etat." He continued, "Do you want to have a coup d'etat? You kind of have to decide what you want. Do you like the Constitution, or are you so upset about the Iraq war that you're willing to dismiss the Constitution in just this one instance and hopefully things will be OK? I don't think so."[32]

Yet others felt differently, believing that it is an officer's duty to disagree with civilian authorities if he or she concludes that an egregious mistake has been made. If nothing changes after privately raising the ethical disagreement, that soldier's duty is to resign and publicly condemn the policy. Many believe that our generals' lack of courage to throw down their stars and condemn Rumsfeld's poor planning allowed hundreds of troops to die needlessly. This would not have been a coup d'etat, but an honest expression of loyalty to the American people to not accept "immoral and unethical" orders. Those who make this argument argue that the "red line" has been broached.

As with other citizens in a democracy, soldiers are also accountable for the government's decision to go to war. As previously noted, there are different degrees of moral accountability in our society for the war in Iraq. All of us who live in a democracy have some degree of moral responsibility for the government's decision to go to war in Iraq. On the one hand, citizens who oppose the war have avenues to express their opposition through voting and public protest. However, since there was no sustained antiwar movement comparable to that which rocked the White House during the Vietnam War, many of these individuals think that they should have done more to stop the violence and the killing and are thus burdened with a sense of moral failure. Yet it is hard to criticize those individuals who spoke out, signed petitions, lobbied Congress, and organized protests against the Iraq war, torture, and illegal detentions. These individuals, in fact, hold a very small degree of moral responsibility for the war.

On the other hand, as discussed previously, those who cooperated in planning, initiating, and waging the Iraq invasion and occupation are morally responsible for the outcome. The president, his cabinet, and those in positions of power in the government who initiated the invasion bear primary and fundamental responsibility for the occupation. In addition, those individuals who continued to support and vote for the administration, despite the widely publicized revelations of both the misleading case for the war and the torture and cruel treatment of prisoners, share moral responsibility for the occupation. All citizens in a democracy have a civic responsibility to morally assess the actions of the country in a time of war.

Michael Walzer, the preeminent scholar on the "just war" tradition, argues that soldiers should be placed into this context. Walzer writes that it is through their role as citizens, not soldiers, that individuals in the military can be held accountable. As individual citizens, soldiers have a duty to vote, speak out, and oppose immoral policies. Some soldiers will fight from within the military to change the direction of these policies. Other soldiers may ultimately refuse to fight in a war they consider immoral. According to Walzer, no matter what ultimate decision these soldier-citizens make, they should be respected and deserve our support. But these individuals take these actions as citizens and not as soldiers. Walzer explains:

> Why aren't they responsible as soldiers? If they are morally bound to vote against the war, why aren't they also bound to refuse to fight? The answer is that they vote as individuals, each one deciding for himself, but they fight as members of the political community, the collective decision having already been made. . . . They act very well if they refuse to fight, and we should honor those—they are likely to be few—who have the self-certainty and courage to stand against their fellows . . . democracies ought to respect such people and ought certainly to tolerate their refusals. . . . That doesn't mean, however, that the others can be called criminals. Patriotism may be the last refuge of scoundrels, but it is also the ordinary refuge of ordinary men and women, and it requires of us another sort of toleration.[33]

Ehren Watada, the first commissioned officer to publicly refuse deployment to Iraq due to his moral disagreements with the war, agrees with Walzer. While he encourages all Americans (including all soldiers) to oppose through nonviolent civil disobedience this war that he considers illegal and immoral, he does not consider those American soldiers fighting in Iraq war criminals: "I don't think I am calling anybody a war criminal. I am talking about everybody taking individual responsibility to evaluate what we are doing in Iraq." If these soldiers do this evaluation, Watada hopes that they would come to the same conclusion that he did and refuse to participate in an illegal war. A soldier can choose to stop fighting. And, according to Walzer, the ones who do this should be honored and respected (and certainly not prosecuted, as happened to Lieutenant Watada).[34]

The Moral Obligation to Refuse Illegal Orders

The U.S. military is expected to adhere to the international laws of war and international human rights law. The military trains soldiers in the laws of war and sends lawyers known as Judge Advocates General (JAGs) into not only the classroom but the fields of battle as well. And, according to Jack Goldsmith, the former head of the Office of Legal Counsel for Pres. George W. Bush, the targets and weapons used by the U.S. military are also vetted and cleared by lawyers in advance of their use.[35]

Jus in Bello—Justice in War

Under international and national law, U.S. soldiers are seen as responsible for their actions during a war. They will be prosecuted for war crimes and are to report those who commit acts of violence against civilians. Soldiers are to act to prevent and, if that fails, report acts of torture and other war crimes committed in a battle.

According to *The U.S. Army/Marine Corps Counterinsurgency Field Manual*,

> U.S. forces obey the law of war. The law of war is a body of international treaties and customs, recognized by the United States as binding. . . . The main law of war protections come from the Hague and Geneva Conventions. They apply at the tactical and operational levels and are summarized in ten rules:
>
> 1. Soldiers and Marines fight only enemy combatants.
> 2. Soldiers and Marines do not harm enemies who surrender. They disarm them and turn them over to their superiors.
> 3. Soldiers and Marines do not kill or torture enemy prisoners of war.
> 4. Soldiers and Marines collect and care for the wounded, whether friend or foe.
> 5. Soldiers and Marines do not attack medical personnel, facilities, or equipment.
> 6. Soldiers and Marines destroy no more than the mission requires.
> 7. Soldiers and Marines treat all civilians humanely.
> 8. Soldiers and Marines do not steal. They respect private property and possessions.
> 9. Soldiers and Marines do their best to prevent violations of the law of war.
> 10. Soldiers and Marines report all violations of the law of war to their superior.[36]

However, Lieutenant Watada notes that it's a "whole different story" being taught the laws of land warfare in class by a JAG lawyer compared to what actually happens in battle: "When you are fighting with your unit in a war, certain things often start to look differently. . . . [T]here is an understanding among fellow soldiers that 'Hey, we're all in this together, and we need to find a way to get out of here and survive.' Unfortunately, if that means committing war crimes then so be it."[37]

Watada's observations are sustained by the army itself. For example, an army summary of deaths and mistreatment of prisoners in American custody in Iraq and Afghanistan documented widespread abuse throughout 2003 and 2004. Army interrogators "forced into asphyxiation numerous detainees in an attempt to obtain information." A prisoner detained by navy commandos died in a suspected case of homicide blamed on "blunt force trauma to the torso and positional asphyxia." Army reserve military police were "involved in various times in assaulting and mistreating the detainee." By mid-2004, thirty-seven prisoners died in American custody in Iraq and Afghanistan. In many of these cases, the army did not conduct autopsies and says it cannot therefore determine the causes of death.[38] In 2007 researchers conducted detailed interviews with fifty combat veterans of the Iraq war. The common theme that emerged from these discussions was that fighting in densely populated urban areas led to the indiscriminate use of force, resulting in massive injuries and deaths to thousands of innocents by the occupying troops. The soldiers' testimony is both heartbreaking and disturbing, as these actions have been almost always unreported and unpunished.[39]

Furthermore, the Pentagon reported in 2007 that more than one-third of U.S. soldiers in Iraq surveyed by the army said they believed that torture should be allowed. Two-thirds of marines and one-half of army troops surveyed said they would not report a team member for mistreating a civilian or for destroying civilian property unnecessarily. The army report stated, "Less than half of Soldiers and Marines believed that non-combatants should be treated with dignity and respect." And about 10 percent of the 1,767 troops in this official survey reported that they had mistreated civilians in Iraq, such as kicking them or needlessly damaging their possessions. All of these thoughts and actions are against army rules and training which forbid the torture of enemy prisoners and states that civilians must be treated humanely.[40]

As a member of the U.S. Army Reserve in Iraq, Aidan Delgado witnessed the mistreatment of Iraqi prisoners and civilians. He found anti-Arab and anti-Muslim sentiment to be widespread. He describes drill sergeants motivating soldiers by reminding them of the attack on the World Trade Center and encouraging them to "kill us some towelheads." Before leaving for the Middle East, his commander told them to watch what they said: "Now, there's going to be media over there, so I don't want you to go telling them how you're going to go over there and kill some raghead and burn some turbans." Delgado saw this as "casual bigotry," and the soldiers got the message—Muslims and Arabs were the enemy. In Iraq, the anti-Arab, anti-Muslim epithet of choice became "hajji." A hajji is one who has gone on the Hajj, the pilgrimage to Mecca. But in Iraq it became a racist slur, like "gook" or "nigger," to refer to all Iraqis.[41]

Delgado saw this "dehumanization of the enemy" lead to gratuitous violence against Iraqis. He wrote: "I've come to see the Army in its worst form, a distortion of itself: violence, threats, dogma, and hatred. I see the way the soldiers bully each other for dominance, and then watch as those who are bullied turn and dominate the Iraqis. I feel my friends and comrades pulling apart from me, diverging from the ideals I believe in. They have changed; something in them has gone black."[42]

According to Watada, "a lot of soldiers and marines say when they go to a war zone anything goes." The law of war may say they are to treat civilians and prisoners with respect. But the other training these soldiers receive sends a different message. That message is to revenge 9/11, "kill us some towelheads," "kill some raghead," "burn some turbans." Delgado believes that it is this attitude and training from the top that created the conditions which led to the widely publicized abuse at Abu Ghraib.

Jus ad Bellum—The Justice of War

U.S. soldiers, however, are generally not held accountable for the decision to go to war or the overall justice of the war itself. Rather, it is the civilian politician who is held responsible for the morality and justice of the war. But can we really say that soldiers are not responsible to evaluate the justice of the wars they fight? Don't soldiers have a responsibility as citizens to assess whether the war in Iraq is just, legal, and moral? Or does the moral duty of citizenship end when they take the oath of service?

Many, if not most, just war theorists argue that if the decision to go to war is made by elected officials with the authority to make such decisions, then soldiers have a duty to go where they are ordered to go. A soldier is not in a position to determine if an intervention or a war is unjust and thus has little choice but to accept the government's decision. The soldier is not held accountable for the decision to go to war. As Walzer explains, "The reason has to do with the distinction of *jus ad bellum* and *jus in bello*. We draw a line between the war itself, for which soldiers are not responsible, and the conduct of the war, for which they are responsible, at least within their own sphere of activity."[43]

Paul Christopher agrees with Walzer and argues strongly that soldiers should not second-guess civilian authorities regarding the decision to go to war. He believes that the soldier's oath "constitutes an agreement to abide by political authority for all *jus ad bellum* decisions: that is, an agreement to fight in wars that are formally just, and also to fight them according to the Just War Tradition and warrior ethos that defines the professional military ethic." In other words, soldiers are not to act like responsible citizens who have a democratic duty to evaluate, assess, and question the direction of their country. Instead, according to Christopher, soldiers are simply to go into battle when called upon. To do otherwise, he believes, would be a profound breach of the country's trust and faith in the integrity of the armed forces: "A refusal to go when called upon constitutes an abandonment of the oath of office, the profession of arms, and the soldiers who depend on their officers for competent leadership—it is a betrayal of the national trust." [44]

Robert Nozick, on the other hand, insists that young soldiers should be accountable to the laws and morality surrounding wars of aggression. Nozick writes, "It is a soldier's responsibility to determine if his side's cause is just. . . ." He insists that "some bucks stop with each of us" and argues that young soldiers "are certainly not encouraged to think for themselves by the practice of absolving them of all responsibility for their actions within the rules of war." He believes that it is "morally elitist" to refuse to apply standards of responsibility equally across the board. [45]

The chief British prosecutor at Nuremberg took a similar position regarding the actions of German soldiers in World War II. The prosecutor stated, "The killing of combatants is justifiable . . . only where the war itself is legal. But where the war is illegal . . . there is nothing to justify the killing and these murders are not to be distinguished from those of any other lawless robber bands." [46]

Citizens of a democracy are called on to evaluate the justice surrounding a nation's decision to kill and invade another state. Citizens cannot claim "ignorance," nor can they just push off responsibility for war only to those at the highest levels of government. Many argue that one of the lessons from World War II was that there were too many "good Germans" who didn't speak up to oppose the genocide and Gestapo tactics occurring in front of their eyes. Applying this judgment to the Iraq war, the American and British people are also accountable to the morality of that war fought in their name. From this perspective, in a properly functioning democracy, the crimes of that nation are the crimes of the citizens collectively. [47]

J. Joseph Miller argues that we should apply the same logic to the soldier. Miller writes

> It is unclear why we should hold those who actively support the crimes of their nation to a lower standard. We would, I think, hold that a sheriff in Ohio during the Dred Scott era has some personal moral culpability for returning a runaway slave to his Southern owner, this despite the knowledge that the sheriff is subject to the coercive interests (e.g., legal obligations, the good of the nation) of the state. We would similarly condemn an executioner who performed his required task knowing the target of that action to be innocent. Why should the soldier who kills in support of an unjust war be held to a lower standard? [48]

In other words, the citizen's role trumps the soldier's role. The serious moral judgments all citizens in a democracy are called upon to make during a time of war apply as well to the soldier.

Miller, Watada, and many others contend that soldiers have a moral and legal obligation to refrain from participating in an immoral and illegal war. As outlined above in the *Counterinsurgency Field Manual*, soldiers and marines are not to follow orders from superiors which violate the Law of War. It would be morally wrong, and a violation of the military's codes of conduct, for a soldier to follow a formally legal order from a superior to rape civilians or torture prisoners. Many insist that it is also morally wrong, and a violation of the military's codes of conduct, for a soldier to follow a formally legal order to participate in a war of aggression. A soldier is only required to follow "just" orders. Accordingly, a soldier must refuse "immoral, illegal, or unethical" orders both in the taking of the country into war (*jus ad bellum*) and in the treatment of prisoners and civilians during the war (*jus in bello*).

Is this position correct? If a soldier concludes that the Iraq war is illegal and immoral, does he or she have an ethical duty to refuse to fight? Do soldiers have a moral duty to assess the morality of the wars they fight? There are a number of key issues at work here.

First, the diplomats and soldiers interviewed for this book present a compelling case that the United States lacked the legal authority to wage war in Iraq in 2003. The Charter of the United Nations is clear that a nation can only use force against another nation in self-defense or with the approval of the Security Council. Since the Charter of the United Nations has been ratified by the United States, and is thus part of the supreme law of the land, soldiers have no other choice but to refuse to fight. By their oath soldiers are to defend the Constitution. From this perspective, the invasion of Iraq is a violation of the laws affirmed by the U.S. Constitution and soldiers would thus uphold their oath by throwing down their arms.

Second, Walzer, Watada, and others make it clear that those soldiers who are fighting in Iraq are not war criminals. A young private, eighteen or nineteen years old and often recruited right out of high school, may not be aware of the legal case against U.S. actions in Iraq and thus has a limited amount of moral responsibility for the decision to engage in this war (*jus ad bellum*). The soldier is protected here by his or her ignorance. Yet degrees of moral responsibility rise up the chain of command. Lieutenant colonels, platoon leaders, battalion commanders, and generals do have the knowledge at their fingertips to access the legal and moral arguments for the intervention. Subsequently, their duty to speak out and oppose illegal acts is much higher.

Third, officers in the U.S. military are often very well educated and far better trained in Constitutional law than the average citizen, with all three military academies requiring a course in law. This training gives these officers the background necessary to determine the legality of orders. As Miller asserts,

> We have long held the not unreasonable expectation that officers use those resources to determine whether or not their orders are legal with respect to the principles of *jus in bello*. I can see no good reason for thinking that officers should not use those same resources to determine whether their orders are legal with respect to *jus ad bellum*. Given the training that military officers receive in constitutional law and given the extent to which the Oath is emphasized as a fundamental part of officership, it seems reasonable to hold military officers morally accountable when they wage illegal wars.[49]

If more members of the U.S. military had felt personal moral responsibility for the decision to go to war in Iraq, it would not be hard to envision a different outcome. Minimally, the planning for the war would have been more thorough and reflective of the reality on the ground. But, more importantly, such an open debate would have either galvanized the military behind this battle or caused these soldiers to fundamentally question the war. It is possible that such an open discussion would have helped the country consider all of the ethical dimensions to the violence and reconsider the path eventually chosen. The affirmation of an "ethic of principled resignation" within the U.S. military would facilitate such policy and ethical debates and enhance a soldier's understanding of personal moral responsibility in a time of war.

The importance of an "ethic of principled resignation" can be seen in the following three case studies. Secretaries of State William Jennings Bryan and Cyrus Vance both resigned from office over issues of principle and asserted their moral autonomy. Gen. Harold Johnson, on the other hand, after contemplating resignation during the Vietnam War, decided to remain in the army, a judgment he came to regret.

I. CASE STUDY
WILLIAM JENNINGS BRYAN, SECRETARY OF STATE
APPOINTED BY WOODROW WILSON
SERVED 1913–1915 (DEMOCRAT)

William Jennings Bryan resigned from office after a little more than two years over the proper U.S. response to German submarine warfare. Morality and ethics infused Bryan's approach to politics. He and Pres. Woodrow Wilson agreed that Christian principles ought to guide policy. "My father," Bryan recalled, ". . . saw no necessary conflict—and I have never been able to see any—between the principles of our government and the principles of Christian faith."[50] The broad ideal of Christian service bonded Bryan to Wilson. Bryan's brand of evangelical Protestantism stood up for the common man and preached moral uplift. This "Christian socialism" with its "Social Gospel" paved the way for the more secular Progressive Movement.[51]

Historian Nancy Mitchell notes that Wilson appointed Bryan to co-opt a powerful rival and appease influential supporters. Unfortunately, Bryan had little knowledge of foreign affairs. According to Lord James Bryce, the British ambassador in Washington, "Mr. Bryan, I incline to think culls his history from the morning papers, cursorily read over his coffee and rolls. . . . He is a rhetorician of a sentimental type, whose life has been spent on platforms and in addressing young men's Christian associations."[52] Diplomacy and foreign affairs were not among Bryan's many great strengths.

Bryan would accept the nomination for secretary of state only upon the condition that Wilson endorse his plan to outlaw war by submitting international disputes to an investigative tribunal. Wilson willingly agreed. Once in office, Bryan strove to keep the United States out of the war in Europe when it began in the summer of 1914. He hoped that America could be the peacemaker and discouraged any type of support for either side. Bryan stood alone in Wilson's cabinet with this position of strict neutrality. The key members of Wilson's inner group were fervent anglophiles striving to prevent a British defeat to imperial Germany. Furthermore, American financiers, who loaned billions to England, and American farmers and manufacturers supported the British war effort.[53]

As U.S. firms increased trade with the British and the French, Bryan feared the German reaction which quickly followed. Germany concluded that the trade had to be cut off to win the war. In 1915 Germany announced a "war zone" around Britain and declared that its submarines would attack Allied ships. Neutral ships were advised to avoid the area.[54]

Bryan and Wilson agreed to protest the German declaration and informed Berlin that the United States would hold Germany to "strict accountability" for harm to American ships or citizens. What this phrase exactly meant and how it was to be enforced is not clear. It was only when 128 Americans died with the German sinking of the British passenger liner *Lusitania* that Wilson made an unambiguous decision against Bryan's judgment. Bryan had contended that those who traveled in the war zone were guilty of "contributory negligence" and suggested to Wilson that Americans not travel on ships of warring nations. Bryan further argued that the United States should postpone demands for reparations until after the war. Wilson rejected this advice and instead sent a blunt note to Germany demanding the end of submarine warfare.[55]

It was this issue of war prevention that caused Bryan to resign. Bryan felt that Wilson's demand would drag the nation into war, and history proved him right. Bryan correctly saw that by demanding Germany cease submarine warfare, Wilson had surrendered to Berlin the decision as to whether and when the United States would enter the war. Wilson was willing to risk war to protect the rights of trade with the British. Bryan was willing to sacrifice some trade and postpone legal issues until after the war. On June 8, 1915, Bryan resigned in protest against the president's policies.[56]

William G. McAdoo, Wilson's son-in-law and the secretary of the treasury, warned Bryan that his career would end with this resignation. Bryan replied: "I think you are right. I think this will destroy me; but whether it does or not, I must do my duty according to my conscience, and if I am destroyed, it is, after all, merely the sacrifice that one must not hesitate to make to serve his God and his country."[57]

Bryan so strongly opposed the "drift to war" that he walked away from the highest government office he ever held. After resigning, he spoke out publicly and strongly against the war in Europe and for war prevention. In fact, every day for a week after his resignation, he produced a major article on current issues, primarily focusing on war prevention. And he held rallies and gave a series of speeches around the country, beginning in Carnegie Hall in New York City on June 20, 1915. Three days later Madison Square Garden was packed with an overflow crowd estimated to be more than 100,000 people from 23rd to 27th Streets. He spoke out against the violations of neutrality and the "gamble on war" the administration was pursuing. Throughout the summer of 1915, Bryan addressed numerous rallies for peace, including the Friends of Peace at the Medinah Temple in Chicago, the Panama Pacific Exposition in San Francisco, and the National League Baseball Park in Boston.[58]

The Eastern Establishment, including ex-President Roosevelt and ex-Secretaries of the Navy Truman H. Newberry and Charles J. Bonaparte, and the *New York Times* vehemently attacked Bryan. The *New York Times* accused him of "flagrant disloyalty," "dishonorable behavior," and "a befuddled mind."[59] Similar attacks were made by papers across the country, including the *Baltimore Sun, New York Tribune, Cleveland Plain Dealer, Louisville Courier-Journal, Chicago Herald, Seattle Post-Intelligencer,* and the *New York Press.* The substance of Bryan's cautious argument was ignored. These papers instead charged him with being either disloyal, launching another presidential campaign, or simply becoming a dangerous eccentric.[60]

Through all of this, Bryan remained a loyal Democrat and refrained from attacking Wilson. For example, he continued to support the party's policies for a minimum wage, an eight-hour workday, and the right of workers to organize and strike. Once war broke out, Bryan ended his antiwar agitating and urged the country to stand behind the president. He wired Wilson: "Please enroll me as a private whenever I am needed and assign me to any work that I can do."[61]

With America at war, Bryan couldn't imagine organizing opposition, and he came to defend the homeland. He thus did not speak out against the arrest of Debs and his followers for violating the Espionage Act or Sedition Act. He did not speak out against the government's establishment of a nationwide spy system to find allegedly subversive and dangerous antiwar organizations. He scolded antiwar protestors for "abusing free speech." He did not say a word when the Supreme Court ruled that opposition to the draft could be considered punishable as "a clear and present danger." The newspapers that earlier had denounced him as a traitor now praised his rallying to the nation's cause.[62]

Bryan's resignation meant that he lost the ability to influence U.S. policy. His resignation did not prevent the drift toward war. However, staying in office was not a viable option, either, as he was isolated in the administration and his views held little sway over Wilson.

History proved that Bryan's instincts were accurate and his resignation proper. As historian Michael Kazin writes:

> [I]n retrospect, he [Bryan] was quite correct to oppose American entry into the Great War. It was not a conflict that history has justified. The main consequence of turning Europe into a killing field was a great bitterness from which grew like poisonous plants, the trio of Fascism, Nazism, and Bolshevism. Bryan also foresaw that Wilson, by rejecting compromise, would lose the fight over the peace treaty and deprive the League of the one powerful nation that might have halted the drift toward a second world war. Disparaged as a pathetic utopian, Bryan proved himself a better prophet and realist than the erstwhile academic he did so much to place and keep in the White House.[63]

II. CASE STUDY
CYRUS VANCE, SECRETARY OF STATE
APPOINTED BY JIMMY CARTER
SERVED 1977–1980 (DEMOCRAT)

Cyrus Vance resigned as secretary of state in April of 1980 in protest of the Carter administration's "Operation Eagle Claw," the secret mission to rescue American hostages in Iran. During his tenure as secretary of state, Vance had pursued an agenda of negotiations and peaceful resolution of disputes on a wide variety of fronts, including arms limitations with the USSR, the return of the Canal Zone to Panama, and the Camp David Accords agreement between Israel and Egypt. Yet despite these successes, most observers believe that Vance's influence in the administration waned as that of the more hawkish National Security Advisor Zbigniew Brzezinski grew. These tensions came to a head when fifty-three Americans were taken hostage in Iran on November 4, 1979.

Soon after the hostages were seized, the president made it clear that all peaceful means would be utilized to secure their freedom before military force would be considered. Military planning, of course, went forward in case it was quickly needed to respond to abuse or harm to the hostages. However, as weeks turned into months, pressure for military action to free the hostages grew stronger inside the administration. Vance strongly opposed these proposals. At a meeting at Camp David on March 22, 1980, Vance spelled out his position:

> I expressed my opposition to the use of any military force, including a blockade or mining, as long as the hostages were unharmed and in no imminent danger. In addition to risking the lives of the hostages, I believed military action could jeopardize our interests in the Persian Gulf and perhaps lead Iran to turn to the Soviets. Even if Tehran did not seek support from Moscow, Khomeini and his followers, with a Shi'ite affinity for martyrdom, might welcome American military action as a way of uniting the Moslem world against the West.[64]

On April 10, Vance left for a long weekend with his family in Florida. In his absence, a meeting of the National Security Council (NSC) was hastily called on April 11 to consider a military rescue operation. Looking back now, it is hard not to conclude that those pushing for military action waited for Vance to leave town to convene this meeting. In Vance's absence, Warren Christopher attended the NSC meeting as acting secretary of state. Christopher, however, had not been fully briefed and declined to take a position on the rescue mission. Everyone else at the meeting supported the rescue attempt. President Carter made a tentative decision to launch the mission on April 24.[65]

When informed of this sequence of events upon his return to Washington on April 14, Vance was "stunned and angry that such a momentous decision had been made in . . . [his] . . . absence." As soon as possible, he met with the president to state his objections. Carter allowed Vance to present his views to the NSC. In preparing for his presentation to the NSC, Vance realized that if the president affirmed the decision to use military force, it called into question his ability to continue as secretary of state. Vance later wrote:

I had disagreed with policy decisions in the past, but accepting that men of forceful views would inevitably disagree from time to time, had acquiesced out of loyalty to the president knowing I could not win every battle. The decision to attempt to extract the hostages by force from the center of a city of over five million, more than six thousand miles from the United States, and which could be reached only by flying over difficult terrain, was different: I was convinced that the decision was wrong and that it carried great risks for the hostages and our national interests. It had to be faced squarely.[66]

No one on the NSC supported Vance's position, and the president affirmed his decision to go forward with the rescue mission. After much personal anguish, Vance decided on April 17 that he "could not honorably remain as secretary of state." He felt that the decision to use military force in this attempted rescue was wrong for the country and the hostages. He felt that substantial progress was being made through diplomacy and sanctions; that the hostages were in no physical danger; that, according to the Red Cross, the hostages were in satisfactory health; and that the raid, even if successful, would almost certainly lead to the deaths of some hostages and Iranians. He felt further that the whole region would be inflamed by the actions of the United States, which could severely damage U.S. national interests and potentially lead to an Islamic–Western war.[67]

On April 21, Vance delivered his formal resignation letter to President Carter. They agreed not to make the resignation public until after the rescue attempt. Vance would remain in his position until after the mission was completed. His decision to resign, however, was irrevocable, whether or not the mission was successful.

The rescue mission ended in failure. A low-level sandstorm, combined with equipment failure, caused the mission to be aborted. Tragically, eight U.S. servicemen were killed after a helicopter drifted into a C-130 while lifting off. This ill-conceived and unsuccessful hostage extraction had a profound effect on President Carter's reelection prospects.

III. CASE STUDY
GENERAL HAROLD JOHNSON
CHIEF OF STAFF OF THE UNITED STATES ARMY
1964–1968

In July 1965 General Westmoreland requested that an additional 100,000 U.S. troops be deployed immediately to Vietnam, to join with the 75,000 U.S. troops already stationed there. The secretary of defense, Robert S. McNamara, made clear in his report to President Johnson that Westmoreland regarded the 175,000 U.S. troops as enough only through 1965 and wrote, "it should be understood that more men (perhaps 100,000) may be necessary in early 1966, and that the deployment of additional forces thereafter is possible but will depend on developments." The military was requesting that up to 300,000 troops be sent to Vietnam by mid-1966.[68]

All of President Johnson's military advisers supported these positions and made clear in their meeting with the president that this troop increase to 300,000 was just the beginning. The military believed that many more troops would be needed to win the war in Vietnam, suggesting directly to the president that he should plan on sending between 500,000 and 600,000 U.S. troops over the next few years.[69]

Yet when he spoke to the American people later that month, President Johnson stated that, to meet General Westmoreland's needs, he was ordering 50,000 new troops to Vietnam, bringing the United States' total fighting strength to 125,000. The president implied that it was Westmoreland's conclusion that no more than 50,000 additional troops were needed. Johnson, however, was lying to the American people. He not only realized that Westmoreland and the Joint Chiefs had determined that they needed hundreds of thousands more troops, but he also intended to meet their request. In fact, President Johnson did meet Westmoreland's immediate request, and by the end of 1965 there were 184,314 U.S. troops in Vietnam. It was only the public who was to be kept in the dark. The president deliberately and with cold calculation misled the nation about his decision to escalate the U.S. commitment and lead our nation into a prolonged war.[70]

Gen. Harold Johnson, the army chief of staff, was appalled by Johnson's speech. The General felt it obligatory for the president to alert the public about the difficult and prolonged war that we now faced. Unfortunately, Lyndon Johnson's performance at this press conference demonstrated that he did not intend to pursue this honest direction. General Johnson felt it was unconstitutional and profoundly wrong to mislead the American people about such monumental decisions of war and death. Mark Perry describes General Johnson's reaction to the televised press conference from his office suite in the Pentagon:

> At the Pentagon, [Gen. Harold] Johnson was almost desperate. After the speech, he closed the door of his office and put on his best dress uniform. When he emerged, he ordered his driver to get his car; he was going to talk to the president, he told his staff. On the way into Washington, Johnson reached up and unpinned the stars from his shoulders, holding them lightly in his hands. When the car arrived at the White House gates, he ordered his driver to stop. He stared down at his stars, shook his head, and pinned them back on. Years later he reflected on the incident, regretting his own decision. "I should have gone to see the president," he reportedly told one colleague. "I should have taken off my stars. I should have resigned. It was the worst, the most immoral decision I've ever made."[71]

3

⟨⊗⟩

Ethical Theory and War

Ethics, also known as moral philosophy, attempts to distinguish between right and wrong behavior. Ethics have been applied to war and violence, with "just war" theories and human rights norms influencing policy-makers. A basic division in ethics is between consequentialist and deontological theories.

Consequentialist theories focus on the goodness of results; it is the ultimate outcome that is of overriding moral importance. For example, the reason it is wrong to torture is not because the act of torture is morally reprehensible but because a world in which people engage in torture is worse than a world in which they do not. Or, with preventive war, a consequentialist might reason that it is wrong to practice preventive war because a world in which all nations engaged in such actions is worse than a world in which they do not. Morality is determined by outcomes and not by means. Utilitarianism, the most influential consequentialist theory, is based on the premise that right action is that which produces the greatest happiness or utility. To a utilitarian, the moral worth of an action is thereby determined by its contribution to overall utility.[1]

An alternative ethical approach is that of deontology, from the Greek *deon* for "duty." A deontologist, rather than focusing on consequences, will examine the rightness of a particular action. The reason that it is wrong to torture is that it is inherently wrong to do so; it violates one's "duty" to central religious or secular moral principles. Or, with the example of preventive war, a deontologist might reason that it is wrong to practice preventive war because such action violates the "duty" not to kill innocent civilians.

41

This chapter examines the ethics of political realism, deontology and human rights, Peter Singer's utilitarianism, and the neoconservative values of the Bush administration. Do these ethical theories and approaches help us to better understand moral duty in a time of war?

POLITICAL REALISM

Political realism, the intellectual framework utilized by the overwhelming majority of the world's foreign policy decision-makers, on the surface appears as an "amoral" calculation of what action best serves the "national interest." The first-rate foreign policy expert will give absolute priority to the interests of his or her nation, which often means neglecting and opposing the material interests of those outside this partial community. Through this lens, policy options seem to pose few moral dilemmas, as these decisions are merely practical solutions to real-world problems. Some who call themselves political realists share such a view of the separation of ethics from politics.

To many political realists, history demonstrates that states must focus solely on power and wealth to survive in the international system. These realists argue that morality has a limited role to play in this anarchical, dangerous world. Since the time of Thucydides in ancient Greece, states have consistently chosen power over negotiated diplomatic agreements, with the "logic of fear and escalation" always pushing out the "logic of moderation and peaceful diplomacy." This overriding priority of "national security" means that ethics plays an extremely circumscribed role in the deliberations of states. Many realists thus argue that in international politics "only the weak resort to moral argument."[2]

Many powerful officials in the U.S. government have stated strongly that, in their view, moral considerations have no place in politics. For example, Dean Acheson, former secretary of state under Pres. Harry Truman, was asked by President Kennedy in 1962 to serve on the Executive Committee to advise the president on an appropriate response to the Cuban missile crisis. Acheson later wrote that during these discussions, when the lives of millions of people were in danger, "those involved . . . will remember the irrelevance of the supposed moral considerations brought out in the discussions . . . moral talk did not bear on the problem."[3] Realist counsel has often excluded morality from foreign policy and instead focused solely on the "national interest."

In fact, political realism does not embrace one single ethical perspective. At one extreme are those political realists who embrace a radical moral relativism and deny the importance of morality in politics altogether. At the other extreme are those who call themselves "ethical realists" and argue for a cosmopolitan approach based on central realist virtues.

American diplomat and historian George F. Kennan expresses the extreme moral relativist view clearly: "Our own national interest is all that we are really capable of knowing and understanding" . . . "The process of government . . . is a practical exercise and not a moral one" . . . "Let us not assume that our moral values . . . necessarily have validity for people everywhere."[4]

Kennan, in fact, goes even further to separate morality from politics. He argues that the nature of political office renders morality irrelevant: "When the individual's behavior passes through the machinery of political organization and merges with that of millions of other individuals to find its expression in the actions of a government, then it undergoes a general transmutation, and the same moral concepts are no longer relevant to it."[5]

Thus, Kennan strongly believed that policy recommendations should reflect the realistic assessment of American interests and not moral values. For example, Kennan opposed the American war in Vietnam for the simple reason that the engagement did not serve the national interest. In his testimony on Vietnam, Kennan stated, "I am trying to look at this whole problem not from the moral standpoint, but from the practical one." Kennan hated communism and the Viet Cong. But the point was not his (or his country's) moral stance toward communism but, rather, his assessment that the United States simply could not "shoulder the main burden of determining the political realities in any other country, and particularly not in one remote from our shores, from our culture, and from the experience of our people."[6]

"Ethical realists," on the other hand, argue that universal ethics do apply to statecraft. Key to this analysis is accepting a difference in the morals that apply to individuals versus those that apply to the state. An individual can base his or her conduct on such principles as honesty and nonviolence. The state, on the other hand, must protect its position of "power" in the international system. This means, on the one hand, that the state should not engage in ideological crusades for democracy and freedom which could dilute its power. But, on the other hand, there are key "realist" virtues that enhance the state's power position and should thus be embraced. These ethical norms are said to include prudence, humility, study, responsibility, and patriotism. Such an approach allows leaders to conduct a responsible and tough defense of the national interest but still show respect for others. The claim made for the cosmopolitan significance of this realist approach has been named "ethical realism." "Ethical realism," according to Anatol Lieven and John Hulsman, "is therefore of universal and eternal value for the conduct of international affairs, and especially useful as a guiding philosophy for the United States and its war on terror."[7]

As a representative of the community overall, the government official has a primary obligation to the national interest and, in particular, the security and integrity of the state. The ethics of "humility" and "prudence" can help protect the security of the state. However, most realists will argue that the necessities of national existence cannot be sorted out through an ethical lens of right and wrong conduct. Effective statecraft demands that officials act to protect the whole, even if individual and collective moral principles are sacrificed. The government official must protect the interests of the community above all else. As a result, according to international relations theorist Hans Morgenthau, there is a "difference in the moral principles that apply to the private citizen in his relations with other private citizens and to the public figure in dealing with other public figures."[8] As a result, many realists argue that the individual civil servant gives up his or her moral autonomy when he or she joins the government. In fact, many political realists embrace Machiavelli's division of morality between the public and private worlds.

MACHIAVELLI: TWO MORALITIES

Machiavelli's influence cannot be exaggerated, and his impact on leaders continues unabated into the twenty-first century. Machiavelli argued that since the welfare of the homeland represented the highest form of social existence attainable by humanity, it must be protected at all costs. He thus sought to refine the political methods necessary to protect the state, independent of personal morality. In fact, such methods may be morally detestable to one's personal code of ethics. A politician cannot afford the luxury of living a morally pure life, an option perhaps open for private citizens or isolated philosophers (like Socrates). However, if one makes himself or herself responsible for the welfare of others, Machiavelli believed that he or she has a moral duty to take actions that will provide them with protection. There are thus two moralities—one for the public world and the other for the private world. In this interpretation, he is not arguing against morality in public life but, rather, two alternative ethical frameworks, two conflicting systems of values, between the public and private realms.[9]

According to Machiavelli, any analogy between the state and an individual is false, and thus a different morality applies to each. Since it is the overall welfare of the community that makes a society great, as opposed to the welfare of an individual, Machiavelli's priority was the well-being of the state. His well-known, harsh, and terrifying methods are designed for a single purpose—a patriotic desire to protect and secure his nation. To protect the state, it is necessary for a leader to "have learned how to be other than good." A leader may employ terrorism or kindness as needed, keeping in mind that citizens prefer vengeance and security to liberty. It is "far safer to be feared than loved." But beware exciting hatred, for hatred will destroy you in the end.[10]

While Machiavelli did not believe that "might makes right," he did argue that the ends justify the means. Machiavelli makes this point unambiguously clear in the forty-first chapter of the third book of *The Discourses*:

> That advice deserves to be noted and observed by any citizen who finds himself counseling his fatherland, for where one deliberates entirely on the safety of his fatherland, there ought not to enter any consideration of either just or unjust, merciful or cruel, praiseworthy or ignominious; indeed every other concern put aside, one ought to follow entirely the policy that saves its life and maintains its liberty.[11]

The well-being of the state is much more important than the well-being of the individual. From this perspective, immoral actions (killing of innocents, terror, torture, and so on) are permitted in the pursuit of a society's basic interests. In exceptional circumstances such acts may be acceptable and necessary to protect the state. There is no moral conflict here.

Think of this as "Man of La Mancha" ethics: "to be willing to march into Hell for a heavenly cause." The "heavenly" cause is the security of the state. There is no higher ethic. Set personal morality aside and act with dispatch to protect the state. These are the necessities of politics. It is unfortunately "necessary" to have what modern philosophers call "dirty hands" in order to carry out the responsibilities of statecraft. To survive in our turbulent and anarchic world and protect our economic viability, political independence, and geographical borders, it is necessary to set aside traditional morality and, when needed, lie, cheat, spy, murder, torture, and commit other cruelties. The practice of politics seems to require the violation of key personal moral standards. Machiavelli believed, for example, that cruelty could be "well employed" and that "evil" acts were permissible if they were done for "the necessity of self-preservation."[12]

The clearest interpretation of Machiavelli, according to Isaiah Berlin, is that he is arguing only that it is sometimes necessary to override ethical standards.[13] However, this idea that it is "sometimes" necessary to set aside "ordinary" morality establishes a separate standard for the state as opposed to the individual. Politicians, community leaders, and activists, who deserve our moral scrutiny, are instead viewed as participating in a particular role where there is a need for "dirty hands."[14]

The phrase "dirty hands" comes from Jean-Paul Sartre's play *Les mains sales* (Dirty Hands). In the play, Hoederer explains the necessity of dirtying one's hands to Hugo, who resists acting immorally:

> HUGO: I never lie to my comrades. I—Why should you fight for the liberation of men, if you think no more of them than to stuff their heads with falsehoods?
>
> HOEDERER: I'll lie when I must, and I have contempt for no one. I wasn't the one who invented lying. . . . We shall not abolish lying by refusing to tell lies, but by using every means at hand. . . .
>
> HUGO: All means are not good.
>
> HOEDERER: All means are good when they're effective.
>
> . . .
>
> HOEDERER: . . . How you cling to your purity, young man! How afraid you are to soil your hands! All right, stay pure! What good will it do? Why did you join us? Purity is an idea for a yogi or a monk. You intellectuals . . . use it as a pretext for doing nothing. To do nothing, to remain motionless, arms at your sides, wearing kid gloves. Well, I have dirty hands. Right up to the elbows. I've plunged them in filth and blood. But what do you hope? Do you think you can govern innocently?[15]

For Hoederer and Machiavelli, the ends do justify the means; immoral behavior may be required to achieve moral ends. The key issue becomes one of pragmatism and efficiency; i.e., are the means effective or not? Public policy is seen as a tremendous responsibility, with a politician's actions potentially impacting on the lives of many. There are obligations and duties that flow from the acceptance of this role. One must be ruthless in the pursuit of the objectives of the state. To refuse to use all methods at one's disposal, including dishonesty and cunning, is to betray those who put their trust in that person to represent their interests. If there is a morality in politics, it is a consequentialist ethic with success measured by power, prestige, prosperity, and security for the individual state. Political realism can be understood to embrace this ethic of foremost concern for the welfare of the homeland.[16]

Through this pragmatic lens of national self-interest, good action is based on efficacy alone, and thus there is really no problem with dirty hands. "Guilt" in this situation is simply irrational. If one is acting in accordance with the dictates of one's official duty, there is no reason to feel degraded or "dirty." And the dictates of public position demand moral compromises. Machiavelli is quite clear on this point: "If all men were good, this would not be good advice, but since they are dishonest and do not keep faith with you, you, in return, need not keep faith with them."[17] Realists thus argue that survival in a wicked and corrupt world depends upon the willingness to use immoral means. And, clearly, the taking of innocent lives through the waging of aggressive war is perhaps the most momentous example of "dirty hands" in the real world. One systematic attempt to sort through the morality of war is "just war" theory. It attempts to put limits on the government's legitimate use of violence as an instrument of foreign policy. Yet all interpretations of just war theory recognize the injustice of war itself.

Such actions as preventive war and torture are thus not in themselves necessarily right or wrong but, rather, are evaluated on a case-by-case basis by their overall utility. Realists could approve of these actions if they protected the long-term interests of the nation. If preventive war and torture, however, were thought to create a more dangerous international system overall and thus threaten the security of the nation, most realists would oppose these policies.

DEONTOLOGY AND HUMAN RIGHTS

As noted, an alternative ethical approach is that of deontology, which, rather than focusing on consequences, examines the rightness of a particular action. Immanuel Kant is almost certainly the best-known philosopher who advocated a secular deontological ethic. Kant bases moral duty on the universal rightness or wrongness of actions that, he asserts, apply to all rational free agents. Kant's "Categorical Imperative" is based on the principle of universalizability, which is "never to act except in such a way *that I can also will that my maxim should become a universal law.*" Also central to Kant's perspective is his "principle of respect," which is to: "*Act in such a way that you always treat humanity, whether in your own person or in the person of any other, never simply as a means, but always at the same time as an end.*" These two maxims (or tenets) are treated equally by Kant, and he takes them as amounting to the same precept.[18]

Kant believed that the human race was united not just by biology but also by moral law. The categorical imperative is a component of who we are as human beings, as natural to our makeup as breathing and eating. It is part of the definition of what it means to be a human being. As rational, intelligent beings, we have the ability to apply these "maxims" and reach the right decisions in difficult circumstances. Although we come from different cultures and absorb diverse customs, the requirements of morality remain consistent everywhere. This feature of the human condition allows morality and notions of justice to move beyond the individual (or the family or the state) and become truly global and universal.[19] Unfortunately, our will to follow these natural dictates of morality is weak. Therefore, Kant believed that we need a legal, constitutional order that governs both our relations with fellow citizens and the relations of nation-states with one another. Kant further argues for "a constitution based on *cosmopolitan right* insofar as individuals and states, coexisting in an external relationship of mutual influences, may be regarded as citizens of a universal state of mankind (*ius cosmopoliticum*)."[20]

To a significant degree, the movement to establish international human rights after World War II attempted to establish a legal order based on cosmopolitan deontological maxims to govern the behavior of individuals and states. A right can be defined as a claim on others to a certain type of treatment. A "human" right is a claim that is made simply because one is a human being. Human rights are alleged to be universal and exist independently of the customs or legal systems of particular countries. Human rights establish the minimum standards of decency toward the treatment of the individual and imply duties for individuals, governments, and non-state actors (including international financial institutions and multinational corporations). International human rights carve out a realm of protection for individuals and groups. No actor can legitimately violate these norms.[21]

Does this human rights and international law framework provide a mechanism for an individual to be able to assert and protect his or her individual moral autonomy? Are these human rights claims helpful for individuals to be able to stand up for key ethical norms while working inside a government?

One problem, of course, is that rights frequently conflict. Developed countries in the North often prioritize civil and political liberties, claiming that these rights "trump" other claims. For example, rights to "freedom" and "democracy" are often privileged over economic and social human rights. Few actions are taken to meet the entire spectrum of rights articulated in the International Bill of Human Rights.[22] To make human rights the cornerstone of domestic and foreign policy means determining the often difficult trade-offs between rights that must be made to build a just society. There are conflicts between rights, and resolution of such conflicts might require the accommodation of different values. The metaphor of rights as trumps that override all competing considerations is thus only partially useful. Real life is more complex. International human rights law, for example, affirms both a right to security and a right to privacy. What if the government determines that to provide security it must violate citizens' privacy? Even the right to life can be abrogated in situations of self-defense.[23]

Kant dismissed such talk of trade-offs. He held that morally permissible behavior does not violate certain categorical imperatives. Torture, for example, would never be allowed; in fact, you would never treat a person as merely a means to an end. Even in a war on terror, Kant would demand that one never practice deceit, never lie, and act to uphold the dignity of all individuals. Yet, in the real world, is this consistent moral behavior possible? Is a lie, for example, never permitted? Is it always the case that one should tell the truth? The well-known illustration of a family hiding Jews during World War II starkly presents the dilemma. Shouldn't one lie to the Gestapo to protect the innocent Jews?

Michael J. Smith proposes a path out of this quandary by involving two stages of moral reasoning. "In the first stage, one follows Kant's categorical imperative procedure—choosing a maxim that can be followed by all rational beings, willing it to be a law in a presumed new social order, imagining the character of that new social order after the maxim has been adopted, asking himself whether he could consistently will and live in that order." This leads to an acceptance of a "common morality," for example, "one ought not to inflict evil or harm" or "the prima facie obligation of treating people equally." However, Smith believes that the application of these principles to states raises a new level of moral reasoning.[24]

This second stage of moral reasoning is concerned with "the translation of abstract maxims consecrated by the categorical imperative procedure into the real world," which requires an examination of consequences. Smith argues that while Kant excluded "hypothetical consequences in the *determination* of the right," this did not mean "he was indifferent to the consequences of the *application*" of that right (or moral maxim). And in the application of human rights/moral maxims, there are at least two significant problems. First, as we have seen, there are conflicts between rights and rules. In order to determine which rights shall prevail, we must examine the consequences of each choice and ask, for example, what are the consequences of privileging security over privacy or the right to life over preventive war. Second, moral principles on their own do not produce a strategy for justice. Strategies for justice are not simply "the mechanical application of abstract, if unassailable, moral principles, but also a skillful exercise of psychological, economic, social, and political judgment. Such judgment entails a shrewd assessment of the likely consequences of a given action."[25]

The ultimate goal of Smith's two stages of moral reasoning is not to loop back to a utilitarian focus on the maximization of "nonmoral" goods like utility or happiness. Rather, it is intended to develop a plan to the "moral" intentions of international human rights outlined above. To get there, Smith argues, we must start from the world as it is. And if the "possible and likely results of our action achieve these larger goals," then it is OK to compromise our moral maxims. Smith argues that we must "match our considered judgments against the rules derived deontologically": "I am simply suggesting that in undertaking rule-based actions, we consider the consequences of those actions for the larger goals we are seeking."[26]

Yet Smith leaves us with an opening for utilitarian calculations to move to the fore. It is easy to see how individual moral autonomy can be compromised through Smith's two stages. For in Smith's second stage, governments "need to protect either their nonmoral interests (like power and wealth) or their parochial, partial moral interests (like the maintenance of a separate community) that conflict with the interests of others." Smith suggests this is possible without "threaten[ing] the moral autonomy of others." Although I applaud Smith's attempt to overcome the dilemmas in a pure deontological approach, I fear the outcome. Once "power and wealth" are given priority, all else moves to the back of the line. In fact, one danger in this approach is that the human rights/deontological moral principles will merely serve as a façade for states to pursue the "national interest" traditionally defined. Do human rights, in the end, just give a moral justification for states to use force as they see fit? Does the language of "human rights" and "just war" perpetuate a charade?

WALZER AND GUILT

Michael Walzer, on the one hand, agrees with political realists that it may be impossible to govern innocently because political life is filled with real-world dilemmas that compromise moral clarity. On the other hand, he believes that a leader who makes such compromises should be filled with guilt and remorse. War may be necessary from a utilitarian point of view to protect the long-term interests of the nation. Yet a leader should always remember the innocents who are killed in war and, from a deontological perspective that privileges the right to life, experience feelings of shame and guilt. In the end, Walzer endorses, with qualifications, the conventional wisdom that no one succeeds in politics without getting his or her hands dirty.[27]

In fact, Walzer believes that it is only through the lens of "dirty hands" that we can identify a true "moral politician." He writes: "Here is the moral politician: it is by his dirty hands that we know him. If he were a moral man and nothing else, his hands would not be dirty; if he were a politician and nothing else, he would pretend that they were clean."[28] The moral politician feels guilty, and that is how he or she is identified. The leader knows he or she has done something wrong but also knows that the action was "the best thing to do on the whole in the circumstances." Walzer continues: "Indeed, if he did not feel guilty, 'he would not be such a good man.' It is by his feelings that we know him."[29]

Central to Walzer's thinking is the idea that politicians must feel some sense of shame, guilt, and pain. If they don't feel these emotions, they cannot be considered "moral politicians." This point of view stands in contrast to the politician who justifies his or her actions through the lens of political realism. The realist would argue that the political leader must overcome his or her moral inhibitions, or, as Machiavelli put it, learn "how not to be good" for the interests of the nation. A leader who authorizes the torture of a prisoner may, if the conditions are appropriate, then be described as good and "perhaps, to be honored for making the right decision when it was a hard decision to make."[30] This is the clear attitude of the Bush administration, which rewards those individuals from intelligence, justice, defense, and state who made the "hard decisions" that led to torture and preventive war. These individuals are proud of their actions and do not, publicly at least, show any sense of shame, guilt, or pain. Using Walzer's criteria, these powerful men and women cannot be described as "moral politicians" since they have no feelings of guilt.

Walzer calls on our leaders to be deeply reflective of some very high standards of decency before embarking on a "just war." For example, Walzer argues that a "politician with dirty hands needs to have a soul, and it is best for us all if he has some hope of personal salvation, however that is conceived." Walzer continues: "It is not the case that when he does bad in order to do good he surrenders himself forever to the demon of politics. He commits a determinate crime, and he must pay a determinate penalty. When he has done so, his hands will be clean again, or as clean as human hands can ever be."[31]

The analogy is to civil disobedience—one goes beyond the legal limit to do what is right and accepts the punishment for violating the law. Yet, as Walzer notes, "In most cases of dirty hands moral rules are broken for reasons of state, and no one provides the punishment." Therefore, it is up to us, through philosophical reflection and political activity, to "set the stakes and maintain the values." The moral stakes should be set "very high" so that they are never overridden "too quickly or too often." When politicians take moral risks and dirty their hands, a community's high ethical standard can evoke the sense of shame and guilt that will keep such immoral actions to a minimum.[32] Thus, on the one hand, Walzer attempts to set the bar high with clear deontological principles defining high moral and ethical standards for political leaders. On the other hand, he acknowledges the difficulties in politics of not committing a "moral wrong" and thus allows for "dirty hands." In the end, Walzer expects our leaders to adhere to moral principles regarding the use of force, with a "utilitarian escape hatch" allowing security to trump all other considerations and a deontological penalty of guilt.

Is Walzer's escape hatch too large? On the one hand, Walzer helps us to evaluate whether those in the Bush administration acted as "moral politicians." To many observers, the high standards written into just war theory were ignored in the rush to war in Iraq, and the leaders who made these decisions did not feel any sense of guilt or shame for their actions that resulted in tens of thousands of innocent deaths. Just war theory—*jus ad bellum* and *jus in bello*—gives us a language to morally evaluate and criticize the leaders who embarked on these perilous policies.

On the other hand, there is something deeply unsatisfying in Walzer's conclusions. In fact, doesn't his "utilitarian escape hatch" provide an opening for the Bush administration to ethically justify the war in Iraq? In the end, Walzer provides political leaders with an elaborate rationalization to set aside human rights norms and laws in the name of the interests of the community overall. While Walzer's personal sympathy for just war morality is clear, it is hard not to see his work used, or perhaps abused, by state leaders to justify utilitarian calculations. And, as we will see, it was precisely such utilitarian logic that was used to justify the actions of the Bush administration in Iraq.

Furthermore, does it all really just come down to "feelings" of guilt, shame, and pain? Is there nothing more that can be said? Is it really impossible to live and govern by moral principles and deontological norms? Does state security really depend on leaders succumbing to "dirty hands" and the sacrifice of basic moral principles? Does government service demand the sacrifices of personal moral autonomy?

It is clearly very difficult for an individual in the government to assert his or her moral autonomy. Government officials are often called upon to sacrifice personal morality in the name of the state. There are too few voices of dissent against groupthink; few individuals able to "stick to their guns" about what they feel, see, believe, and know; few individuals willing to assert that their individual ethical standards might be better in a particular situation.[33] The working hypothesis going into the Foreign Service is that one must be willing to set aside one's personal morality for the sake of the national interest. Thus, when a conflict arises, the response won't be to resign or act for moral principles. The expectation is that one will remain silent and accept that "dirty hands" are inevitable.

GOVERNMENT SERVICE AND MORAL AUTONOMY

Civil servants and military personnel are professionals with specific responsibilities for the welfare of the citizens of their country. Inevitable conflicts arise between how the world "is" and how it "ought" to be. In dealing with the world as it "is," a professional foreign policy expert must evaluate the propriety of the government's decisions in relation to his or her personal ethical framework. Furthermore, if one is aware of ethically dubious actions being carried out in other departments (black bag jobs, assassinations, illicit arms sales, and so on) doesn't the Foreign Service officer have a moral responsibility to oppose these actions? Is it possible in this situation for this professional to maintain his or her moral autonomy?

Moral compromises come not just from personally engaging in an action that one finds ethically problematic (murder, torture, lying, and so on). I think that "dirty hands" can also arise by not speaking up or acting to oppose such ethically dubious policies carried out by an individual's government. Foreign Service officers bear particular responsibility during a time of war. These officers may not be in a decision-making role or personally responsible for implementing the war policies. Yet their job is often to publicly defend the policies of the government. If an individual Foreign Service officer in this government comes to a decision that the war effort is ethically wrong, how does the individual protect his or her moral autonomy?

Giving up one's career through resignation is not the first thing that comes to mind for most people in this situation. In fact, most convince themselves that they are needed right where they are and that resignation would be a futile, wasted gesture. But, as Bernard Williams points out, this classic "working from within" argument "has kept many queasy people tied to many appalling ventures for remarkably long periods."[34] Yet the consequences of asserting one's moral autonomy could mean the termination of a career, which is an extremely thorny step.

Williams poses the dilemma as follows:

- Plato's question—how can the good rule?
- Machiavelli's question—how to rule the world as it is?
- Williams's question—how can the good rule the world as it is?[35]

Williams argues that different levels of moral compromise must be faced if the "good" are to "rule the world as it is." Democratic politics, in particular, involves bargaining between actors with conflicting interests and different priorities, and thus compromise is necessary. The government may align with a despicable regime in a temporary coalition, or break a promise, or mislead a friend. A Foreign Service officer may find these actions distasteful, shortsighted, and not in the long-term national interest of the United States. Yet this person would probably not resign in protest due to this recognition that ruling "the world as it is" involves moral compromise. Williams correctly points out that "democracy has a tendency to impose higher expectations with regard even to the means, since under democracy control of politicians is precisely supposed to be a function of the expectations of the electorate."[36]

In the end, Williams's argument is similar to that of Walzer and Smith. Williams believes that we need to hold on to the idea, "and to find some politicians who will hold on to the idea, that there are actions which remain morally disagreeable, even when politically justified. The point of this is not at all that it is edifying to have politicians who, while as ruthless in action as others, are unhappy about it. Sackcloth is not suitable dress for politicians, least of all successful ones. The point—and this is basic to my argument—is that only those who are reluctant or disinclined to do the morally disagreeable when it is really necessary have much chance of not doing it when it is not necessary."[37]

Again, the basic argument is that the moral ends of politics demand that an individual sacrifice his or her moral autonomy. The problem again, of course, is that this opens up a huge door for consequentialist reasoning at the expense of human rights. If, for example, the *expected* outcome of preemptive war is the liberation of twenty-five million people, the sacrifice of human rights (including the right to life) for thousands could be potentially "morally" justified. Unfortunately, history teaches us that victims often find their rights sacrificed for an outside chance of a successful intervention. Many experts, for example, predicted that the odds of success in Iraq were quite small. On the small chance that the action could succeed, the intervention and occupation went forward as a "just war" primarily with utilitarian justification.

THE NEOCONSERVATIVE FOREIGN POLICY OF THE BUSH ADMINISTRATION

The Bush administration has distinguished itself from traditional political realists through its forceful promotion of a "neoconservative" foreign policy agenda. These policies are based on the premise that national security is attained through democracy promotion abroad and, in general, a more muscular unilateralism in foreign affairs. In certain cases, neoconservative activists support unilateral U.S. military intervention to fight terrorists and support freedom. Neoconservative activists were critical of the presidencies of George H. W. Bush and Bill Clinton for lacking both moral clarity and the conviction to unilaterally act to pursue the American national interest. The "Bush Doctrine," adopted after September 11, 2001, embraced these central ideas of the neoconservative movement. The G. W. Bush administration endorsed the idea of unilateral preemptive military action against the threat of terrorism and declared that the United States "will be strong enough to dissuade potential adversaries from pursuing a military build-up in hopes of surpassing, or equaling, the power of the United States."[38] Neoconservatives applauded this policy change and urged America to embrace its new imperial role.

The invasion and occupation of Iraq was thus justified not only on grounds of political realism but also through the ethics of a neoconservative crusade. In fact, the realist fears of the dangers of overextension, and subsequent insolvency, through global campaigns for freedom and democracy were set aside. Instead, Iraq became the great "evil" with Hussein the new Hitler (or Stalin). Diplomacy and sanctions to contain Hussein were said to be not only ineffectual but also forms of appeasement. Harsh and brutal military force was thus seen as necessary to confront this evil and create an opening for a free and democratic Iraq and Middle East.

Since 2003, there has been wide discussion of the neoconservatives in the administration as protégés of the late University of Chicago philosopher Leo Strauss. A key component to Straussian political philosophy is the notion that lies are necessary to the smooth functioning of society and the triumph of one's own nation in war. This idea of the "noble lie," originated by Plato, emphasizes that due to the high levels of selfishness and individualism in open societies, it is essential for elites to create "myths" to hold those societies together. Leaders often find it useful, for example, to inflate the dangers of the "enemy" to unite the country behind foreign policy initiatives. Some observers, for example, felt that the exaggeration of the Soviet threat during the Cold War served this function. Overstating the danger of the threat coming from Saddam Hussein's weapons of mass destruction (WMD), and linking his regime to al-Qaeda, thus served a useful purpose to the neoconservatives. These actions (noble lies?) allowed the Bush administration to mobilize the country for war and pursue a global strategy of empire building and "democracy" promotion. The neoconservatives viewed such exaggerations (lies?) as virtuous as the country was engaged in a global fight involving a higher morality of good versus evil.[39]

The Bush administration considers its actions in Iraq to be moral because they are based on a (neoconservative) calculation of what is best for the long-term interests of the United States. The Bush administration justifies its actions in the "war on terrorism" through this utilitarian framework. For example, Amnesty International, the Red Cross, and many other human rights organizations have documented evidence of torture and widespread cruel, inhumane, and degrading treatment by the United States at the Guantanamo Bay detention camp. The administration's response has been to consistently attack the organizations and individuals who raise these issues. Vice Pres. Dick Cheney said that he was "offended" by those who criticize the United States and declared, "Just in this administration, we've liberated fifty million people from the Taliban in Afghanistan and from Saddam Hussein in Iraq, two terribly repressive regimes that slaughtered hundreds of thousands of their own people."[40] The United States has learned how "not to be good" in order to bring liberty and freedom to the world.

In this justification of U.S. policies in the war in Iraq, the Bush administration asserts this position of moral clarity to justify its harsh policies.

Walzer notes the difference between a "justification" (like Cheney's) and an "excuse." The latter is typically an admission of fault, whereas the former is not.[41] To the utilitarian who sees only the usefulness of his or her actions, feelings of guilt and fault will not apply. Laws and norms are set aside and annulled for a higher purpose. Why would an individual feel guilty "when he has no reason for believing that he *is* guilty?"[42] And this is exactly the public position of the Bush administration. Mistakes may have been made in the execution of the war policies in Iraq, but overall, according to the Bush administration, the cause is just and U.S. actions have moral integrity.

One does not get a sense that the members of the Bush foreign policy team are morally troubled by their decisions. Their almost religious certitude that these policies are correct is the opposite of the soul-searching politician Walzer promotes. Walzer calls on our leaders to be deeply reflective of some very high standards of decency before embarking on a "just war." As already noted, Walzer argues that a "politician with dirty hands needs to have a soul."[43]

However, the "soul-searching" done by the Bush administration led the president and others in the government to quickly declare the United States to be on the side of "good" and opposed to "evil." A clear component of the neoconservative agenda is ideological and normative: supporting freedom and democracy and opposing "evil."[44] All versions of the neoconservative project pit "evil" states (Iran, North Korea, Iraq, and so on) and non-state actors (terrorist groups) against the "good" political actors struggling to create a world of free markets and free elections. Many political realists oppose this visionary ideological agenda as misguided and dangerous and fear that the United States will exhaust itself in endless global wars for "freedom." These realists argue that the interventionist policies of the Bush administration are destabilizing to the global order and could potentially lead to ongoing conflict and violence between states.

Neoconservatives presented a utilitarian ethical justification for the war in Iraq. The ends justify the means; freedom for the Iraqi people was worth the costs of the destruction of war. "Regime change" in Iraq was linked to the long-term global fight against terrorism which served U.S. national interests. Human rights concerns (and deontological approaches) were discarded, and utilitarian calculation prevailed.

PETER SINGER'S UTILITARIANISM AND WAR

Yet the world's leading utilitarian philosopher, Peter Singer, came out against the war in Iraq. I decided to interview Professor Singer to see if he could help us with these difficult moral quandaries. Here's what he had to say:[45]

FELICE: Let's begin with Colin Powell (who has been both criticized and praised for his actions surrounding the Iraq war). Powell's internal memos expressed disagreement and ethical doubts with the decision to go to war in Iraq (and further disagreements with U.S. actions in Guantanamo and elsewhere). And yet he stayed the course and helped sell the war to the American people. Did he have a duty to resign?

SINGER: I think he did. Colin Powell is a tragic figure really because he was someone who could see exactly what was going wrong. I am struck by the remark in the Bob Woodward book where he said the Pottery Barn rule applied to Iraq: "You break it, you own it." And he was so right about that. And yet, despite saying that, despite having doubts about the evidence he was being fed about Iraq's weapons of mass destruction (WMD), he nevertheless became the spokesperson selling this evidence in that famous UN speech. Powell could have had a very significant impact if he had resigned and said he couldn't support this war. Maybe the nation would not have gone into the war; I don't know. But no one could have accused him of being someone who was soft on terrorism or afraid of military action or something like that; he could have had an enormous influence.

FELICE: What is the ethical line that was crossed?

SINGER: It was the decision to go to war. The president he served was making a decision to go to war that he thought was not justified. And this decision was going to lead to the loss of lives of American military personnel and Iraqi civilians. Powell must have known that, given the way the war was planned, there would be numbers of Iraqi civilians who would be killed. He was asked to sell, and to go along with selling and promoting the war, although he thought it was a bad idea that was likely to have terrible consequences for many people. He also had doubts about the evidentiary case that Saddam Hussein had WMD, so he had a responsibility to say: "No, I will not sell this to the American public, because it is wrong."

FELICE: The argument I've heard made is that Powell saw himself like the little Dutch boy with his finger in the dyke—that the others around (Wolfowitz, Rumsfeld, etc.) were so extreme that Powell had to stay to keep things from really going off track; he was holding back the more extreme forces.

SINGER: Well, it is hard to see how things would have gone worse. What can you say? They would have bombed more civilian areas? No, they wouldn't have done that—just from a public relations point of view, if for no other reason, that would have been inadvisable. Up to a point, it may have made sense for Powell to stay on to try to stop the decision to go to war. But once it was done, and once Bush made it clear to him that he had decided to go to war, then the situation was different. It became clear that he was being sidelined as a decision-maker. And the secretary of state should not just be someone who sells a product, whether or not he agrees with it. A secretary of state has a greater responsibility than that. If he were the media spokesperson, it would be a different matter. He was in a position of much more responsibility. You can't justify it in those terms. He has also said that he had a duty to serve the president. I don't think that's right. You don't have a duty to serve the president even when you think the president is wrong on something as major as going to war. McNamara said something similar about Vietnam.

FELICE: Yes, McNamara did, and, in fact, in the history of the United States only two secretaries of state have resigned for ethical/moral principles (William Jennings Bryan and Cyrus Vance). Why do you think that is? Why in America do personal ethical issues get submerged under loyalty to the president? Or the firm? The government? And so on . . . Why do individuals have such difficulty upholding principles of moral autonomy?

SINGER: Well, one difference between the American political system and that of a parliamentary democracy is that the secretary of state is completely the president's creature and is not there because of his or her political independence and political life and does not have a political career to go back to. So if a foreign minister resigns in a parliamentary system, and has a long career in this system, he can then maybe bring with him a faction of the party. Imagine a person in Powell's position as foreign minister in a parliamentary democracy, and he could say: "Well, I'll resign now and if things go as I expect they will, my conduct will be vindicated. And, after this political leader goes, I will still have a political career. In fact, my political standing will be enhanced as compared to what it would have been if I had stayed the course." But that doesn't happen in this system because, where do you go once you resign? The Brookings Institute or the American Enterprise Institute? . . . It's clearly not the same.

FELICE: Let's talk about a different level from the secretary of state. What about the Foreign Service officer (FSO)—who has twenty to thirty years of service to the country—who comes to the conclusion that the war in Iraq is morally wrong. Does this individual have an ethical duty and responsibility to resign?

SINGER: I think here it has more to do with what they're actually doing and what they are required to do. There are many FSOs whose work has nothing to do with the war in Iraq or the Middle East. An FSO for Africa, for example, doing useful work can get on with that useful work. If this individual is not involved with defending, promoting, or justifying the war, then there would be no point in resigning. There might be some point at which the nation was involved in such atrocities that you couldn't serve it, but not simply the decision of the country to go to war. On the other hand, if the person were continually called on to advance the cause of a war that he or she thought was wrong, for example, to bring more allies to the "coalition of the willing," that would be a different matter.

FELICE: So it hinges more on the individual's connection to the war actions or policies; there is a dissent channel in the State Department where they can express disagreement. But, if the person is not in a position of hierarchical responsibility, then you are saying that he or she is not morally responsible.

Let's shift a bit, in terms of public service. Walzer argues the "dirty hands" analogy and claims that it is almost impossible to be ethically pure in the Foreign Service. The demands of public office result in dirtying one's hands; real-world dilemmas mean that it is impossible to always have moral clarity, impossible to maintain moral autonomy. Do you agree?

SINGER: No, not when it is formulated in that way, because I hold a different ethic than Walzer—I hold a consequentialist ethic. In fact, I believe that you don't do anything morally wrong if, in order to produce better consequences in the end, you lie to other people to deceive them about the secret intent of your foreign policy (or whatever the example might be). So think about the dirty hands metaphor; it is the idea that whenever you touch some things, they dirty you—for example, telling a lie, or breaking an agreement, or more serious things like signing an order to have a terrorist assassinated. You can't just say these things are wrong and you get dirty hands from doing them, because, from my moral perspective you have to ask each time what are the circumstances and is this a justifiable thing to do. So it is not right to say that inevitably you will get dirty hands; it depends on how successful you are in sticking to doing what you see will have the best outcome.

FELICE: In the case of Iraq, some argued on utilitarian logic—freedom for twenty-five million Iraqis—was worth the price of the deaths of tens of thousands of civilians in Iraq.[46] Freedom for this country, ending the despotism of Hussein as an ultimate outcome, was worth the price. Utilitarian calculation. You are a utilitarian. What is wrong with this argument?

SINGER: One thing that was wrong with it at the time (never mind in hindsight) is the importance we give to civilian rights and the rule of law in international affairs. Had Bush gone to the UN Security Council and said, "Saddam is committing atrocities against his own people; we need humanitarian intervention, just as we should have had in Rwanda," and had the Security Council supported that, it would have been a very different situation. Now Bush couldn't do that because at the time Saddam was not committing atrocities against his own people. He had been some years earlier, but the United States was actually helping him during that period.

The point is that there could be a case for getting rid of a dictator on the basis of genocide and crimes against his people. But we have to have a system of international law that says when that can happen and the only one we have now is through the UN. So we ought to be very reluctant to justify humanitarian intervention against another sovereign country without UN sanction.

And the only exception I would make would be when, as in Rwanda, the killing is actually going on. If you can see ten thousand being murdered today, and another ten thousand will be murdered tomorrow, and another ten thousand every day for the next three months unless there is an intervention, that's clearly a different situation. And let's say that one of the permanent members of the Security Council is an ally of this government and vetoes the intervention. I think in cases like this, you would be justified to intervene. But this is *not* the type of circumstance that Iraq was in at the time of the invasion.

FELICE: With the conditions that you've laid out, utilizing utilitarian logic, you can justify violence and war.

SINGER: Oh, yes; I'm not a pacifist.

FELICE: What about torture and the utilitarian logic justifying torture?

SINGER: What I want to say about this is a little difficult to say publicly. The public stand should be that torture is never justified. Because when security forces believe that torture is justified, they seem always to misuse that power. And the costs of misusing it are extremely high. The costs of forgoing torture are completely unclear. Just now we've had this discussion, in the last couple of days, that it wasn't true that the torture carried out by the Bush administration was necessary. The FBI has said now that they were doing quite well with the "soft" treatment and that the CIA didn't find out any more by torturing prisoners.[47] So the benefits are very unclear. The risks of substantial, horrible abuse are very great. And for that reason, we should prohibit it.

Now, having said that, of course, you can always have the nuclear bomb in the Manhattan basement scenario, where if it were really true that there were no other way of getting the information on the location of the bomb without torture, then you should torture. But that is a purely hypothetical scenario, and I doubt that you will ever really be in that situation. And, therefore, since it is extremely unlikely that you will ever be in that situation, it is not the basis on which I would want to establish public policy on this issue.

FELICE: This discussion brings us again to the idea of "dirty hands" and Machiavelli's two moralities. Machiavelli argued that public officials had to do things that are "evil" in order to keep the security of the state and create "good." Unfortunately murder, torture—bad things—are often necessary for the state to undertake. But in one's personal life, an individual would never engage in these activities. Do you agree?

SINGER: I don't think it is two moralities, really. They are both the result of consequentialist thinking. The difference is that the prince's actions have larger consequences. So, if, in fact, you can foresee that this opponent of yours is likely to try to unseat you and the result will be a civil war which will ravage the country and millions will die . . . if you can really be confident in that, maybe you are justified in getting rid of this guy. This would not apply to a private individual, because getting rid of your enemies as a private individual will not have such far-reaching consequences. I don't think the outcome of morality is really different.

FELICE: So your lens is utilitarian in both cases.

SINGER: Yes, it is.

FELICE: And utilitarian ethics thus justify these different behaviors in the public versus the private realms.

SINGER: Yes, because circumstances and the consequences are different.

FELICE: Mark Danner wrote the piece "We Are All Torturers Now," published in the *New York Times*, implying that the reelection of Bush in 2004—and the public as a whole not responding with outrage about what is being carried out in our name—raises the whole issue of individual responsibility during a time of war. What are your thoughts on this?

SINGER: Obviously, there are a lot of possible things that you can do. You can vote against the Republicans, give money to MoveOn, turn out for a demonstration or something like that . . . it is difficult for me to say that you are a torturer if you did all that and, despite your attempts to oppose torture and put an end to it, Bush regrettably went forward with it.

It is a little like the question I'm asked regarding how much you have to give away to organizations/NGOs before you are not morally guilty of murder because millions of people die from poverty and hunger. And it is very hard to say exactly what that line is. Similarly, the question here is: how much do I have to do to oppose the government before I am not a torturer? Should I be protesting at his ranch whenever he is there or camp out outside the White House? Are you still a torturer because you happen to be an American? I don't really think so.

There is an argument about withholding taxes, of course, which was raised a lot during the Vietnam War but hasn't really been raised in relation to the Iraq war. It's interesting that it hasn't been raised. Because if you want to ask where is the complicity that you have as an individual American in the war (Singer clarifies that he's not an American) . . . you could say that the taxes paid go to support the war. So, should the individual withhold his or her tax payment? Perhaps a portion of the taxes? You could argue this. . . .

FELICE: Regarding the usefulness of ethical theory in a time of war, some look to Kant and his categorical imperative for help. Prof. Michael J. Smith argues that Kant does consider consequences in the application of his deontological principles. In the application of moral principles, one has to take consequences into account.

SINGER: We need to distinguish a few things, including which formulation of the categorical imperative is being talked about. The first formulation is perfectly compatible with utilitarianism, i.e., acting so that the maxim of your action can be a universal law. (It is definitely not anti-utilitarian.) There is something interesting about how specific rules can be, which relates to different levels of utilitarianism that people talk about—the public codes versus the private rule. You do have to give some weight to the idea of what is the standard or rule that you can expect the public to act upon that has the best ultimate consequences. This may be a different question from what actual action right now would have the best immediate consequences. So there are those issues surrounding the universalizing formulation of the categorical imperative.

The business of saying "use every person as an end and not merely as a means" is also something a utilitarian can really accept, if you stress well-being as an end. A utilitarian, for example, can never accept the enslavement of another race because it is disregarding the interests of the slaves for the benefit of others. Slaves (and mere animals) are ends in themselves; they are suffering, so it's not clear that Kant's categorical imperative is anti-utilitarian.

On the other hand, some of the actual applications that Kant talks about are anti-utilitarian. Some of them are quite embarrassing to Kantians, for example, the idea that you shouldn't lie to the murderer who comes to the door to kill the innocent person who is hiding in your house. Not many Kantians actually defend that position.

FELICE: One reason for asking these questions is: human rights are often viewed as deontological principles and often seen as "trumps" over other claims. But the reality is that there are often trade-offs between human rights, for example, the balance between rights of security and rights of freedom. One has to think of consequences to determine which right is correct to uphold.

SINGER: I agree . . . and this is similar to what Sidgwick wrote about in *The Methods of Ethics*—where he shows again and again that what people think of as deontological principles come into conflict with other principles and you appeal to utility to resolve the conflict. And that is why he felt that the deontological principles really operate as a subset of rules for public application toward a utilitarian framework. And I would say something similar about human rights. . . .

MORAL AUTONOMY IN A TIME OF WAR

Singer, Smith, Walzer, Williams, and other ethical theorists give us helpful avenues to deepen our moral reasoning. Yet most of us probably don't make our personal decisions on the basis of one ethical tradition but, rather, draw on a variety of moral frameworks. There are times when utilitarianism and consequences seem appropriate, for example, with the practice of triage to the wounded after a natural catastrophe on the level of the Katrina hurricane. Yet, at the same time, basic human rights and moral principles inform our conceptions of who we are in the world and our sense of personal autonomy and dignity. But no matter how we work out these moral dilemmas, too often during war many of us in and out of government sacrifice our moral autonomy and perfunctorily accept the decisions of our leaders. Why?

Part of this acquiescence stems from the merging of one's self-identity with the interests of the country. Plato called this a movement from Reason controlling the Body to Social Reason controlling the members of society. In a discussion of "higher nature" and "lower nature," Isaiah Berlin makes this point as follows:

> Presently the two selves may be represented as divided by an even larger gap: the real self may be conceived as something wider than the individual (as the term is normally understood), as a social "whole" of which the individual is an element or aspect: a tribe, a race, a church, a state, the great society of the living and the dead and the yet unborn. This entity is then identified as being the "true" self which, by imposing its collective, or "organic," single will upon its recalcitrant "members," achieves its own, and therefore their, "higher" freedom.[48]

In other words, an individual may feel that his or her personal identity is formed through the allegiance to the state. When asked to describe himself or herself, such an individual may begin by saying, "I am an American" (or French or British and so on). To then criticize "America" is to criticize one's sense of self, one's true identity. Morality is linked to the state. It is hard for an individual to break with these norms and go on a separate path. Society's beliefs and values impact all people's views of their individual lives. Unfortunately, moral autonomy is not such a strong societal norm. Instead, loyalty to one's friends, job, country, and president is a much stronger value.

Americans are not coerced into supporting the war in Iraq. Although the president's press spokesman, Ari Fleischer, threatened Americans to "watch what they say, watch what they do,"[49] it is still possible to feel relatively safe speaking out against the war in Iraq. There are the right-wing extremists who attempt to label all dissent as treason, and antiwar speakers have received death threats. But so far these individual extremists have not succeeded in changing the laws to curb through arrest the voices of protest.

There is, however, a psychological dimension to citizenship during a time of war. State authority during war tends to extract obedience as individuals set aside personal doubts and accept the decisions of the national leadership. In addition, strong societal pressures to conform are difficult, but not impossible, to resist in a time of war. Loyalty and the support of one's country are expected of all citizens, especially Foreign Service officers. Such pressures are strongest, of course, within the military and the government and can lead to individuals participating in acts which, on their own, they would detest. Yet even beyond those employed by the state, all citizens are confronted with the difficulty of breaking with societal expectations to "rally around the flag" and unify during a time of war.

In addition, it is difficult for many in the United States to prioritize the human rights of individuals in Iraq, halfway around the world on another continent. If one's moral universe is one's family and nation, what happens to the human rights of strangers is really a secondary issue. It is unfortunate that these individuals have to suffer, but the priority must be our family and country.

Finally, and perhaps most importantly, during warfare there is also a lack of a sense of individual responsibility. The responsibility for war is said to rest with the president, the cabinet, and the U.S. Congress. Other individuals in the government or the military didn't participate in these decisions and therefore feel little moral responsibility. In addition, the tasks of war are so fragmented that, again, it breeds a sense that no one has individual responsibility. Such fragmentation allows individuals to deny the importance of their own contribution—whether it was through voting, providing infrastructure, keeping the business of government running smoothly, and so on.

All of these explanations give us a rationale for turning inward and not even speaking out against acts we consider unjust carried out in our name. In this situation, citizens and government officials can lose an overall sense of moral responsibility and instead focus on individual and family needs. We gradually lose our moral autonomy. We suddenly lack the ability to judge the ethical behavior of our government and are unable to protect our moral integrity.

4

⟨∞⟩

Staying In

Colin Powell and Wayne White

Two individuals who "stayed in" the government and tried from within to moderate and change U.S. policy in Iraq were former Secretary of State Colin Powell and State Department intelligence expert Wayne White. Both Powell and White determined that, rather than resigning, they could be more effective inside the government opposing misguided policies and raising ethical concerns. As noted in chapter 2, outstanding civil servants will challenge groupthink, question decisions, raise moral dilemmas, and probe contradictions in policy. Key to the decision to "stay in" is one's expected effectiveness and the ability to leverage one's access to power in order to change unethical policies. The challenge for those who "stay in" is to maintain one's moral autonomy and integrity when asked to defend or implement policies felt to be either immoral or illegal. How Powell and White dealt with these issues while remaining in office is examined in this chapter.

One of the key arguments in favor of staying in the government is to be able to keep one's voice in policy formulation. It seems obvious that a cabinet member, Foreign Service officer, or intelligence expert with access to policy-makers could have a significant impact inside the government. Powell and White had such access. In their respective positions, each raised significant disagreements with both the rush to war in Iraq and the way in which the invasion and occupation were conducted. It is to their credit that they did speak up and raise their ethical concerns. Each achieved some success in moderating extreme policies. Powell was able to get the president to agree to not suspend the Geneva Convention with regard to Taliban fighters under U.S. control. After a long battle, White was able to get the intelligence services to accurately report on the real dangers of the Iraqi insurgency in 2003. These policy successes by Powell and White support the position of those who advocate a "working from within" strategy.

However, the differences between Powell and White are also revealing. White remained in his job as deputy director of the Office of Analysis for the Near East and South Asia in the State Department's Bureau of Intelligence and Research (INR) despite his serious misgivings about the Bush administration's war planning in Iraq. His formal February 2003 INR analysis, for example, warned of both military and political dangers for the United States even with a "successful" occupation of Iraq. White remained in his job in the State Department because he felt he was able to promote the truth about the conditions in Iraq within the highest levels of the administration. He could consistently voice his disagreements with the war policies. Health and family concerns finally forced White to retire from the State Department in March 2005.

Yet, in contrast to Powell, White had no public role. He was able to work behind the scenes and felt able to bring "reality" back into Middle East policy discussions. He never had to "sell" the misguided Iraq war policy to the American people. He was never called on to personally defend a policy that he felt was morally reprehensible. Therefore, he felt that no ethical lines were crossed for him by staying in the government. In fact, his position as an Iraqi expert meant that he could push with force to correct some of the erroneous conclusions of the radical right, such as the mythical democratic opening the Iraq war was supposed to bring to the region.

Powell, on the other hand, pursued a very public position in "selling" the war to the world. Most disturbing to Powell's critics is the very vocal role he took in pushing the flimsy case for war in Iraq. His many statements in support of the war were as extreme as any other member of the Bush administration. It is in this role, as a cheerleader for the administration, that many believe an ethical line was crossed.

Powell declined my request for an interview. However, his correspondence with me (reproduced below) is extremely revealing. Powell viewed the decision to go to war with Iraq as a "policy" and not an "ethical" choice. Since there was no moral dilemma for him, he never considered resigning, and instead he became the administration's chief salesman for the war. Powell's actions can be contrasted to those of Cyrus Vance. When an ethical line regarding the use of force was crossed for Vance, he resigned and maintained his moral autonomy.

If Powell's loyalty to the president had meant that he was able to strongly impact and mitigate war policies, then his "staying in" stand would perhaps be vindicated. Unfortunately, despite his loyalty, Powell was marginalized inside the administration and had little impact on the war and occupation. In fact, Powell's continued presence and active participation in the administration gave Bush vital and indispensable legitimacy to pursue questionable Iraq policies. If Powell did have strong objections to the war, it is hard not to conclude that he would have been more effective raising these views outside the government and publicly speaking out against the war. Instead, by continuing in office and loudly selling the war, his actions contributed more harm than good.

The actions of Colin Powell and Wayne White are analyzed here in relation to the issues surrounding "staying in" versus "getting out."

MY NON-INTERVIEW WITH COLIN POWELL

Former Secretary of State Colin Powell turned down my request for an interview in the summer of 2007. Here is our exchange of correspondence:

July 19, 2007

Dear General Powell,

I am working on a book manuscript titled "Individual Moral Responsibility in a Time of War."[1] Part of this project involves interviewing individuals in the U.S. and British Foreign Service who have struggled with personal ethical dilemmas while carrying out their official government responsibilities. In the interviews I have conducted thus far, I have been very impressed by the loyalty and affection that members of the State Department express toward you. These individuals convey strong admiration for your steadfast and effective leadership of the Department. Even those Foreign Service Officers who have fundamental disagreements with the decisions made by the Bush administration in Iraq stated unequivocally that they believed that you personally acted ethically. In their eyes, you were a voice of principle, working from within to try to prevent "worse stuff from happening."

I am writing now to request a one-hour interview with you to discuss the myriad of issues surrounding ethical autonomy in a time of war. How did you keep your "ethical balance" during the difficult debates in the administration surrounding the global war on terror? In the build-up to the war in Iraq, for example, you advocated patience and clarified the difficult path ahead. When the "Powell doctrine" was subsequently ignored in the war planning, how did you respond? Regarding the treatment of prisoners, you advocated maintaining adherence to the Geneva Conventions and told the president that a unilateral disregard of the conventions would put American soldiers at risk in Iraq and in future conflicts. What was your response when this advice was not taken? You have stated that you "never thought of resigning." Yet these issues seemed to cross a moral line for you, an ethical boundary. Is there a point at which you could see yourself saying "not in my name"? What other values, in your mind, supersede the virtue of "loyalty"?

Joel Rosenthal, the President of the Carnegie Council for Ethics in International Affairs, has kindly offered to host this interview at the Council's office in New York City. However, I am able to meet with you at any time and place of your convenience. I can come to DC or any other location of ease to you.

I know how much in demand you are and that "time" is a precious commodity. I believe that this project will prove to be a very good use of your time. I thank you for considering this interview request.

Sincerely,

William Felice
Professor

* * *

General Colin L. Powell, USA (Retired)

July 27, 2007

Dear Professor Felice:

Thank you for your recent letter requesting an interview. Due to an overwhelming volume of author interview requests and a desire to save something in case I write a book, I'll have to pass.

Also, I see things differently concerning what you call the "ethical balance." For example, the Powell Doctrine is not written in any Army manual and is not written doctrine. This was a policy dispute, not an ethical dispute. The President listened to my views and then followed the advice of his military commander, his Joint Chiefs and his Secretary of Defense. It was all argued out, which is the ethical way. And it looked like they were right when Baghdad fell.

The Geneva Convention debate is similar. I recommended a different course than that which he had decided upon. After a spirited debate, he compromised on our different points of view. His decision had the backing of his Attorney General, his intelligence and law enforcement officials and, I might add, the Congress and the American people. It was a policy dispute.

There were many instances where my colleagues lost the argument. If we all quit over policy disagreements, no one would be around.

Sincerely,
Colin L. Powell

Powell asserts that during his years as secretary of state for Pres. George W. Bush, there were no troubling ethical questions which led him to consider resignation. He maintains that he had no problem upholding his "ethical balance" during these years. He contends that he was able to keep his moral bearings during the administration's active policy discussions on war and torture. He claims that these issues of war were simply policy, not ethical issues. Since moral principles did not arise, resignation was not a consideration. His policy disagreements were fully discussed by the key decision-makers in the administration. Therefore, in his view, he did not sacrifice his moral autonomy because he was able to raise specific policy disagreements in the privacy of the White House. It was also no ethical dilemma for Powell to then actively, forcefully, and effectively lobby the nation and the world community to support the Bush administration's war policies. In many fundamental respects, Powell epitomizes both the hope and the tragedy of a strategy of "working from within."

THE LOGIC OF "STAYING IN": POWELL'S ARGUMENT

Powell's supporters often argue that things would have gotten much worse if he had resigned. The logic of "staying in" hinges on the individual's ability to influence policy and correct unethical and dangerous courses of action. If there were anyone in the administration during Bush's first term who could possibly counter the influence of Vice President Cheney and Defense Secretary Donald Rumsfeld, it had to be Powell. In fact, when Powell was first appointed, *New York Times* columnist Tom Friedman wrote half-seriously that Powell could wield too much power over Bush. Right after Powell's appointment to secretary of state was announced, Friedman wrote,

> I sure hope Colin Powell is always right in his advice to Mr. Bush because he so towered over the President elect . . . that it was impossible to imagine Mr. Bush ever challenging or overruling Mr. Powell on any issue. Mr. Powell is three things Mr. Bush is not—a war hero, worldly wise, and beloved by African-Americans. That combination gives him a great deal of leverage. It means he can never be fired. It means Mr. Bush can never allow him to resign in protest over anything.[2]

However, the neoconservative foreign policy team surrounding Cheney and Rumsfeld came prepared with a sweeping foreign policy agenda. For years before joining the administration, this group of right-wing radicals had published and spoken out on a range of foreign policy issues including Iraq, Russia, China, the Middle East, and the United Nations. While Powell represented continuity, multilateralism, and pragmatism, the neoconservatives pushed for a more muscular foreign policy based on American exceptionalism and unilateralism.

David Rothkopf describes this "core tension" within the Bush administration as a clash between "traditionalists" and "transformationalists."
According to Rothkopf, traditionalists, such as Powell, saw foreign policy
"as a way to manage our relations within a diverse global community,
moving in the direction of our ideas, but recognizing the limitations on us
and the need to balance the optimal with the practically possible." Transformationalists, on the other hand, Rothkopf wrote, "decry such views as
moral relativism or as implying a willingness to subjugate our national
interests to the wishes of the larger community of nations; in any event,
their view is that we need to make the world more like us." The transformationalists embraced the neoconservative agenda, described in chapter
3, which expanded the national interest beyond traditional conceptions
of geographical and economic security to include the global promotion of
democratic ideology.[3]

Well before the tragedy of September 11, 2001, Powell had a series of
conflicts with those pursuing the transformationalist agenda in the Bush
administration and lost ground fast. In his first year in office, Powell's
efforts to pursue a multilateralist, diplomatic approach toward global
warming, North Korea, Iraq sanctions, and the International Criminal
Court were torpedoed by the transformationalists surrounding Cheney
and Rumsfeld. Furthermore, the Bush administration seemed to go out
of its way to insult traditional allies. With no Allied consultation, Bush
announced that the United States was ready to move "beyond" the Anti-
Ballistic Missile (ABM) Treaty to deploy missile defenses. With no Allied
consultation, Rumsfeld announced that he intended a unilateral with-
drawal of American troops from NATO peacekeeping operations in Bosnia. Suddenly, the United States declared its opposition to internationally
drafted enforcement mechanisms for a biological weapons treaty and opposed a ban on nuclear testing as well. The U.S. Secretary of State seemed
to have little control over all of this new U.S. foreign policy. A growing
antipathy emerged "between Powell and the State Department, on one
side, and Cheney, Rumsfeld and their senior staffs, on the other."[4]

Powell responded to all of this by soldiering on. According Karen De-
Young, Powell believed that in the end his perspective would prevail:

> When his aides vented their frustration to Powell, he told them to keep their
> powder dry. He was playing for the long term, he would say; his way was
> not to seek confrontation but to prevail by working quietly and persistently
> over time. Powell thought Bush was being pulled in conflicting directions
> by different people on his team and differing instincts within himself—his
> Yale–Harvard education versus his Texas background. The president was
> throwing red meat to the conservatives on issues such as North Korea and
> the Middle East, but Powell was confident that circumstances and his experi-
> ence would eventually provide the perspective Bush needed.[5]

In his book *My American Journey*, Powell wrote: "Senior officials cannot fall on their swords every time they disagree with a President."[6] And in his correspondence with me, Powell stated: "If we all quit over policy disagreements, no one would be around." These principles underlining Powell's "working from within" strategy seem like common sense and clearly apply to the policy debates during his first year as secretary of state. No epic ethical line was crossed, for example, in the debates over the best mechanism to enforce the biological weapons treaty or to slow down global warming. There will be long-term ethical consequences for humanity if we as a global community do nothing to stop the human actions that are causing global warming. Similarly, there will be disastrous ethical consequences if we do not stop the spread of biological weapons. Yet to resign over the best policy to address these issues does seem totally counter-productive. It is better to stay and fight another day, better to keep trying to push policy in the right direction so that these central issues become top foreign policy priorities for the United States. Powell, as secretary of state, was in a position to keep up the battle, and it was wise for him to do so.

Powell applies the same "staying in" logic to the myriad of issues surrounding the "Global War on Terror" (GWOT) and the invasion and occupation of Iraq. He argues that these debates were on policy issues and he served the country well by staying in and raising his concerns. How well did Powell succeed with this "working from within" strategy? Was he able to protect his moral autonomy and integrity during this process?

Powell wants us to now know that in regard to some of the key ethical issues surrounding U.S. policy in the Middle East, he did speak up and tried to moderate policy on the Geneva Conventions and the invasion and occupation of Iraq.

The Geneva Conventions

Powell opposed the president's order that neither al-Qaeda nor the Taliban would be granted prisoner-of-war status and that the United States would not be bound by the Geneva Conventions in its treatment of them. The president made this decision while Powell was in Asia, and Rumsfeld issued written instructions to the military the next day. State Department Legal Adviser William Taft thought it was no accident that this had all transpired while the secretary of state was out of the country. After being informed that this decision had been made in hurried secrecy without his input, Powell called National Security Adviser Condoleezza Rice and said, "You'd better hold on. I think we're making some mistakes here." Powell asked to talk to the president in person.[7]

In an Oval Office meeting on January 21, 2002, Powell asked the president to reconsider this issue. Powell summarized the meeting to DeYoung:

He told the president that American soldiers depended on Geneva for their own safety and that a unilateral disregard of the conventions would put them at risk in this and future conflicts. "I said I wanted everybody covered, whether Taliban, al-Qaeda or whatever and I think the case was there for that." Powell was clear that he understood the urgent need for intelligence about future terrorist acts. Geneva did not prevent inter-rogations; it only meant that you couldn't try to get answers by treating prisoners in an inhumane or degrading way.[8]

Powell elaborated his argument in a memorandum to the legal counsel to the president, Alberto Gonzales. Powell's memo to Gonzales is forceful and clear. Powell notes that Gonzales's position that the Geneva Conven-tion does not apply to the Taliban and al-Qaeda would "reverse over a century of U.S. policy and practice in supporting the Geneva Conventions and undermine the protections of the law of war for our troops, both in this specific conflict and in general." He notes how this policy would create a high negative international reaction and undermine public sup-port of the United States among our allies. Powell further argues that the Geneva Convention provides a "defensible legal framework" and "preserves our flexibility under both domestic and international law." "It maintains POW status for U.S. forces, reinforces the importance of the Geneva Conventions, and generally supports the U.S. objective of ensur-ing its forces are accorded protection under the Convention."[9]

In response to Powell's intervention, Bush slightly modified his order. The president determined that none of the provisions of Geneva applied to al-Qaeda, but while the Constitution, he claimed, gave him the au-thority to suspend the conventions with regard to the Taliban fighters, Bush chose not to do so "at this time." Powell viewed this as a pointless distinction. And in practice the United States did not treat al-Qaeda and Taliban prisoners differently. Powell later stated, "I didn't agree with it. The President knows I didn't agree with it."[10]

The Invasion and Occupation of Iraq

Prior to 2002, Powell seemed to believe that Iraq was not a danger. In his Senate confirmation hearings, he said that Iraq was "fundamentally a broken, weak country." During his first tour of the Middle East as sec-retary of state in 2001, Powell said that containment and sanctions "had worked" and Saddam wasn't a threat: "He [Saddam] has not developed any significant capability with respect to weapons of mass destruction (WMD). He is unable to project conventional power against his neighbors. So, in effect, our policies have strengthened the security of the neighbors of Iraq, and these are the policies that we are going to keep in place."[11] Yet less than two years later, the Bush administration repudiated this position and suddenly presented Saddam as a frightening danger that had to be immediately disarmed.

In 2002 Powell was well aware that the United States had begun to mobilize for war and plan for regime change in Iraq. Yet Powell, for the most part, appears to have stayed on the sidelines during the initial Iraq war planning during this period. As the administration moved toward war, Powell stayed out of it. He said he did this out of respect for the chain of command. "I'm the secretary of state, not the defense secretary or the chairman of the Joint Chiefs or the national security adviser," he reportedly told aides who expressed concern over Iraq.[12] During this critical time, Powell did not utilize his position to argue forcefully against the invasion and occupation, nor did he present an alternative direction for resolving the situation in Iraq. As we will see in chapter 7, the revelations contained in the "Downing Street Memo" from Britain provide documentary proof that the United States decided to go to war in Iraq in early 2002. The issue by that summer was to see to it that "the intelligence and facts" would be "fixed around the policy." Tragically, Powell remained silent during this critical time, didn't challenge the clumsy and insufficient war planning of Rumsfeld or Wolfowitz, and didn't voice his concerns about the war to the president.

Finally, on August 5, 2002, Powell met with the president and articulated his anxiety about the planned invasion of Iraq. He wanted Bush to consider all the consequences, including the destabilization of the Middle East and the abrupt fluctuation in the price and supply of oil. The president, he felt, should also realize the ways in which war in Iraq would draw resources away from the larger war on terrorism and every other foreign policy priority. Powell warned that the war would dominate the Bush presidency. Furthermore, the United States needed to be clear on what it would do after ousting Saddam Hussein. Powell recalled telling the president, "When you hit this thing, it's like a crystal glass . . . it's going to shatter. There will be no government. There will be civil disorder. . . . I said to him, 'You break it, you own it. You're going to own it. You're not going to have a government, not a civil society. You'll have twenty-five million Iraqis standing around looking at each other.'"[13]

In a twelve-minute conversation on January 13, 2003, Bush told Powell, "I really think I'm going to have to take this guy [Saddam Hussein] out." Powell responded, "Okay, we'll continue to see if we can find a diplomatic way out of this. But you realize what you're getting into? You realize the consequences of this?" Bush replied, "Yes, I do." The president asked if he could count on Powell's support and Powell answered affirmatively. When later asked about this meeting, the president said, "I didn't need his permission."[14]

In the end, Powell did not try to talk Bush out of war. He did not advise against the Iraq invasion. Powell's concerns were on style over substance.

Chapter 4

He states that he warned Bush of the difficulties, counseled patience, and argued for a multilateral UN approach. However, in his meetings with the president, Powell did not make an argument against going to war with Iraq.[15] Powell ultimately viewed the decision to go to war as a policy decision that the president was authorized to make. He knew that Bush seemed determined to act against Saddam Hussein. Powell may have wished that the United States had pursued more diplomacy before war, but the decision was up to the president. In 2005, Barbara Walters of ABC News asked Powell, "When the president made the decision to go to war, you were for it?" Powell said, "Yes."[16]

In retirement, however, Powell has spun the August 5, 2002, meeting as an attempt by him to persuade the president not to invade Iraq. In July 2007, Powell stated at the Aspen Idea Festival in Colorado, "I tried to avoid this war. I took him [Bush] through the consequences of going into an Arab country and becoming the occupiers."[17] Yet other than "going to the UN," Powell has yet to explain if he had any other suggestions for the president. If Powell had ideas about what should have been done differently in Iraq in 2003, what were they? How did the president respond? Unfortunately, it appears that Powell presented few options. If Powell had presented a clear alternative to war with Iraq, it would have carried a lot of weight. Powell was a national hero, respected for his decency and integrity, with approval ratings 30 percent higher than Bush. In what ways did Powell really try to "avoid this war," and why did he lose this debate? The president clearly was not swayed either by Powell's standing with the American people or by Powell's arguments of caution regarding the invasion of Iraq.

If we accept Powell's current statements that in mid-2002 he fundamentally opposed the invasion and occupation of Iraq, the question of principled resignation immediately emerges. If Powell was genuinely opposed to going to war in Iraq, why hadn't he resigned after his advice was ignored? Powell states that "he never thought of resigning." His justification of this position is revealing. When Powell proposed trying diplomacy before resorting to war, the president agreed and took the case to the UN. When Bush later announced his decision to go to war, Powell supported him. Powell states, "I can't go on a long patrol and then say 'never mind.'"[18] So the issue for Powell was really not the moral and legal legitimacy of a preventive war strategy with Iraq. The only issue in Powell's mind seems to have been only one of timing. Powell thought that more time should be given for inspections and diplomacy. But it was the president's decision, not Powell's, as to whether the time for peaceful solutions had run out. When Bush decided on war, he had Powell's total support.

To justify his actions, Powell frequently talks to reporters about his hero George Marshall, the first career soldier to become secretary of state. Powell, in particular, is fond of one anecdote from Marshall's State Department tenure. In 1948, Truman and Marshall held different positions on the granting of early diplomatic recognition to the new State of Israel. Marshall held that such an action was premature since no recognized borders had been established and there was not yet an Israeli government. In his personal files, Marshall wrote that Truman's insistence was simply a "transparent dodge to win a few votes" from American Jews in a tight reelection year. Given his strong feelings on this issue, some of Marshall's aides suggested that he might consider resigning on principle. Marshall's response was "No, gentlemen, you don't take a post of this sort and then resign when the man who has the constitutional responsibility to make decisions makes one you don't like." To DeYoung, Powell paraphrased Marshall's response as "Nobody made me President. I serve." Marshall had "done his job. He had given the president his best advice. He had presented it strongly . . . [and] used every, every opportunity he had to press his case, and the ultimate responsibility lay with Harry S. Truman." DeYoung states that Powell found the story "a heck of a note of inspiration."[19] (Yet the most revealing aspect of this anecdote is one that Powell clearly chooses to ignore. While Marshall used "every, every opportunity to press his case," Powell did the opposite and never presented a forceful argument against the Iraq war. This anecdote thus serves to remind us of the dramatic differences between the bold and principled leadership of Secretary of State Marshall compared to that of Powell.)

A surprising defender of Colin Powell is Brady Kiesling, the first American diplomat to resign from his position in the State Department in opposition to U.S. policy in Iraq. While applying very high moral principles to himself, Kiesling gives Powell a lot of ethical latitude. According to Kiesling, Powell

genuinely believed that the U.S. [was] a force for good in the world and that getting rid of Saddam would be a good thing. So one can understand his feelings. For him the war was a judgment call. If he had been left to make the final decision on the war, his own judgment would have been against it. But the president, vice president, and his cabinet colleagues were firm in their decision, so he saw it as his goal to make it work. And the only way in his experience that the war would be cost effective for the U.S. was if the international community was on board with it. In a way it [Powell's UN speech] was one of the most self-sacrificial bits of patriotism you're ever going to see. He put all of his 35–40 years of professional prestige and integrity and credibility on the line in that speech.[20]

THE "TRAGEDY" OF "STAYING IN":
POWELL'S CRITICS (INCLUDING COLIN POWELL)

To his critics, Powell's claim that the myriad of issues surrounding the
Iraq war represented only "policy" and not "ethical" issues is both stunning and revealing. How is the decision to disregard the Geneva Conventions not an ethical issue? How is the decision to ignore the Powell Doctrine guidelines on the use of force not an ethical issue? In fact, it is hard to
imagine a decision with more ethical consequences than that of going to
war and taking responsibility for the deaths of the many innocents caught
in harm's way. Yet Powell claims that for him there was never a question
of maintaining his ethical balance or his personal moral autonomy. On the
surface, something here doesn't connect. If Powell strongly opposed the
decision to go to war in Iraq and the way the war was conducted, including the treatment of prisoners of war, how could he then serve as a leading cheerleader and international spokesperson defending these policies?
To many, Powell's comments on his actions are confusing, defensive, and
seem to demonstrate a man who did lose his moral bearings.

There are certain key moments when Powell not only could have more
forcefully objected to Iraq war policies but also, perhaps, could have
upped the ante by considering a principled resignation. It now seems
clear that Bush decided to invade and occupy Iraq before the summer
of 2002. As noted above, Powell remained silent during this time and
left war planning to the secretary of defense. It is hard to understand or
accept Powell's logic that he was simply trying to "respect the chain of
command." As secretary of state, he had a duty to fully voice any doubts
he had about the Iraq War to the president, yet he remained silent. War
preparations were certainly no secret and were widely reported in the
media. The White House staff and Powell were well aware that the
country was headed to war. Yet during this critical juncture, Powell not
only did not consider protesting the policy but excused himself from the
debate altogether.

Powell's August 5, 2002, meeting with Bush thus becomes extremely
significant, because it is reportedly the first time that Powell verbalized
his reservations directly to the president. Without Powell's support, it
would have been very difficult for Bush to proceed with the war. To his
credit, Powell raised his concerns about the preparations for war and
emphasized the degree of responsibility that the United States would
have for reconstruction and security following the war. Powell (and Tony
Blair) persuaded Bush to pursue a diplomatic UN endorsement of the
planned war with Iraq. Yet in this conversation, Powell didn't at all try to
talk the president out of war, nor did he apparently suggest an alternative course for the United States to pursue. At the key moment, when he

had the chance to prevent an unprovoked war, Powell remained silent. If he truly opposed the war, this moment reveals a profound lack of moral courage. (But if he supported the war, he should stop claiming otherwise. He can't have it both ways.)

Powell was uniquely positioned in August 2002 to profoundly impact the nation's debate on the morality of the upcoming invasion of Iraq. Had Powell become a voice of opposition, he would have provided political cover for moderate Republicans and Democrats who questioned the legality of aggressive war. Minimally, Powell's voice of opposition could have prevented the White House from being able to conduct the subsequent campaign of vilification of war opponents as weak, unmanly, unpatriotic, and disloyal to the troops. It is not an exaggeration to suggest that had Powell threatened a principled resignation, the rush to war could have been slowed to a crawl and possibly prevented altogether. Powell, of course, morally excused himself from this debate and decided to go along with whatever the president decided on the ethics of aggressive force.

When Bush asked for his support on January 13, 2003, Powell could have again expressed his reservations. But in that short meeting, Powell simply told the president that he could count on him. Perhaps by this date, it was impossible to stop the war (which was to occur in March). But if Powell really felt there were ethical problems with the aggressive preemptive war strategy, he had, at a minimum, a moral obligation to state them. Furthermore, here was a "Cyrus Vance moment." As discussed in chapter 2, Vance opposed President Carter's decision to attempt the rescue of hostages in Iran in 1980. However, he withheld the announcement of his resignation until the mission was completed (and failed). Again, if Powell really opposed the war, Vance represented an example of moral courage he could have followed.

However, it is what happens next which is most telling and morally problematic. After that January meeting, Powell became the leading public spokesperson for the war. Powell's February 2003 UN speech was critical to winning over a skeptical U.S. public on the necessity for war with Iraq. But the UN speech was far from the only time that Powell presented misleading and false information on Iraq. In fact, publicly Powell was as aggressive and militaristic toward Iraq as the vice president. A report by Rep. Henry Waxman (D-California) documents 125 different occasions between March 17, 2002, and January 22, 2004, when the five highest members of the Bush administration made a total of 237 misleading statements exaggerating and distorting the threat posed by Iraq. The breakdown was: Bush, 55 such statements; Rumsfeld, 52, Cheney, 51; Powell, 50; and Rice, 29.[21]

In January 2008, the Center for Public Integrity (CPI), a research group that focuses on ethics in government and public policy, posted a comprehensive database of top officials' statements before the invasion. The CPI data reveals that, in the run-up to the Iraq war, President Bush made 232 false statements about weapons of mass destruction in Iraq and 28 false statements about Iraq's links to al-Qaeda. Powell has the second-highest total in this two-year period, with 244 false statements about weapons of mass destruction and 10 about Iraq's links to al-Qaeda. Rumsfeld, Wolfowitz, Rice, and Cheney all made fewer false statements to the public than Powell. The Bush administration clearly cashed in on Powell's credibility to win public support for the war. Powell's actions dramatically demonstrate the danger of placing an "ethic of loyalty" above an "ethic of principled resignation."[22]

Powell now says that the 2003 speech to the UN, in which he gave a detailed description of the Iraqi weapons program, was "painful" for him personally and would be a permanent "blot" on his record.[23] Yet despite this semi-apology, he continues to justify and support the 2003 invasion and occupation of Iraq. Powell, in fact, seems unable to face the facts surrounding the occupation of Iraq.

For example, Powell continues to claim that the United States "tried to avoid" the Iraq war.[24] Yet the documentation on the early and unilateral decisions by the Bush administration to go to war in Iraq makes this Powell claim not credible. For example, when Powell gave his infamous UN speech on February 5, 2003, the decision for war had basically already been made. When Blair visited Bush in September 2002, he was told that the United States would bring the issue of Saddam's WMD to the UN one more time before going to war. But war would most likely still follow in the end.[25] Powell was set up to stage a UN melodrama, with a defiant Saddam standing firm against U.S. and British pressure. Yet Bush and Blair's plans were sabotaged by Iraq's cooperation. Saddam unconditionally accepted the UN's November 8 demand for intrusive new inspections, and the UN resumed inspections by the end of that month. Under the leadership of Hans Blix, UN inspectors searched hundreds of sites in Iraq and found nothing. Blix, to the fury of the White House, refused to declare Iraq in material breach of Resolution 1441 demanding that he disarm. Powell was sent to the UN in February 2003 to save this failing, staged diplomatic strategy.[26]

Powell, as we all know, rose to the occasion and delivered a bravo lecture, complete with PowerPoint and dramatic visual aids. But the problem, of course, was that the speech was based on specious assertions and not facts. The substance was all wrong. Iraq did not have WMD, did not have links to al-Qaeda, and did not pose a threat to the international community. The UN sanctions and inspections regime had worked; Iraq was disarmed. Powell, and others, now claim that everyone thought Iraq had WMD in 2002 and early 2003. But this is also not true. The UN weapons inspectors; the German, Canadian, and French intelligence services; and many Middle East experts thought that the United States exaggerated the Iraq threat and were appalled by the flimsy, misleading, and erroneous presentation made by Powell at the UN.

Most of the experts in U.S. intelligence agencies had also come to the conclusion that Iraq posed no imminent threat. Therefore, the 2002 National Intelligence Estimate used to justify the invasion must be read along with the other intelligence reports produced at the same time. Evaluated in their entirety, one reaches the conclusion that U.S. intelligence as a whole did not support a preemptive war against Iraq. These reports, for example, clearly warn of the substantial dangers of such an invasion. Paul Pillar, the CIA's national intelligence officer for the Near East and South Asia from 2000 to 2005, states that at the time of Powell's speech, "A view broadly held in the United States . . . was that deterrence of Iraq was working, that Saddam was being kept 'in his box,' and that the best way to deal with the weapons problem was through an aggressive inspections program to supplement the sanctions already in place."[27] Furthermore, the CIA produced two stark intelligence estimates in January 2003 about the dangers of a U.S. invasion. These reports are publicly available at the website of the Senate Intelligence Committee. The report on "Regional Consequences of Regime Change in Iraq" correctly warned that "A U.S.-led war against and occupation of Iraq would boost political Islam and increase popular sympathy for some terrorist objectives, at least in the short term." The report warns, "Increased popular Islamist sentiment would bolster both extremist groups and, in some countries, Islamic political parties that seek to gain power peacefully."[28] Furthermore, Powell's own intelligence unit in the State Department was arriving at similar conclusions and disputing exaggerated claims of Saddam's WMD capability. For example, the State Department submitted 60 pages of protest to the flawed 2002 National Intelligence Estimate objecting to the claim that "all intelligence experts agree" that a shipment of aluminum tubes bound for Iraq in 2001 were intended for a centrifuge enrichment program key to reinvigorate Saddam's nuclear weapons program. Powell had to be aware of this strong position of his own department's experts but went ahead and included the following false allegation in his speech: "Saddam Hussein is determined to get his hands on a nuclear bomb. He is so determined that he has made repeated covert attempts to acquire high-specification aluminum tubes from 11 different countries even after inspections resumed."

Greg Thielmann, the acting director of the Office of Strategic Proliferation and Military Affairs, which was responsible for analyzing the Iraqi weapons threat, had reported to Powell in 2002 that these tubes were not for a nuclear program. Yet a year later, Powell went along with using this false "evidence" to make the case for going to war. Why did Powell turn Thielmann's intelligence bureau's information on its head? "I can only assume that he was doing it to loyally support the president of the United States and build the strongest possible case for arguing that there was no alternative to the use of military force," replies Thielmann.[29]

There was a widely held, and erroneous, view among leading intelligence agencies that Iraq did possess some quantity of chemical and biological weapons. But there was never any evidence that after twelve years of sanctions and repeated bombing attacks in the no-fly zones that Iraq posed a threat beyond its borders. There was no indication that Iraq could not be contained. In fact, the UN was successfully disarming Iraq.

Examine, for example, the facts surrounding the UN weapons inspections in Iraq, which was information at Powell's fingertips. After the UN inspections resumed in November 2002, Blix followed every lead given to him by the American government. UN inspectors went to the Iraqi government ministries, seized computers, and looked for names and addresses on hard drives. All of this turned up no WMD. Blix thus writes: "I drew the conclusion that the U.S. did not itself know where things were."[30]

In fact, between late November and mid-March 2003, the UN inspectors made seven hundred separate visits to five hundred sites, many suggested by intelligence services, including the CIA. When no WMD were found, Blix stated, "Personally, I found it peculiar that those who wanted to take military action could—with 100 percent certainty—know that the weapons existed, and at the same time turn out to have zero percent knowledge of where they were."[31] At the same time, Mohammed ElBaradei, director general of the International Atomic Energy Agency, stated categorically that after three months of intrusive inspections, the IAEA had found no evidence or plausible indication of the revival of a nuclear weapons program in Iraq. ElBaradei presented irrefutable evidence that the much-publicized aluminum tubes were not related to the manufacture of centrifuges for the enrichment of uranium. He also showed that the "contract" between Iraq and Niger for the import of raw uranium—yellowcake—was not authentic. The claims made by the Bush administration, including those of the president of the United States, were shown to be false.[32] The conclusion of the official, bipartisan Senate Select Committee on Intelligence's review of the prewar handling of intelligence was: "Much of the information in Secretary Powell's speech was overstated, misleading, or incorrect."[33]

Within weeks after its delivery, Powell's speech to the UN was exposed to be full of misleading assertions and cherry-picked intelligence. The assertions about Iraq's WMD were flat wrong. If Powell really questioned the logic of the war, here was another opportunity to speak up inside the government to reevaluate the necessity for violence. For example, Powell could have forcefully urged the Bush administration to listen to other voices. The secretary general of the United Nations and the majority of the world's political and religious leaders, including the pope, were frantically searching for a way out of war. With the discrediting of the case for war made by Powell at the UN, the minimum moral obligation was for the United States to take a step back and rethink its war policy and consider other options. Powell, unfortunately, made absolutely no effort at this point to slow down the mad rush to war. Furthermore, not only did he refuse to reconsider his misleading presentation, but he also joined the Bush administration in condemning the antiwar forces. Powell was a very public part of the chorus chanting that we were "out of time" and that force was necessary. For example, in February 2003 Blix pleaded in a phone call to Powell for the opportunity to continue the inspections until April 15. Powell tragically said it was too late.[34] In sum, although Powell seems to have recognized the problematic nature of the WMD "evidence" for rationalizing the war in early 2003, he continued to overtly mislead the American public and the global community about the immediate need for the Iraq invasion.

Powell continues to mislead the public on the facts surrounding the invasion of Iraq. At the Aspen Ideas Festival in 2006, Powell said that Saddam "essentially made it impossible for the UN to continue to do its work . . . it was a case where we felt the danger was such, on a variety of levels that it could no longer be accepted or tolerated."[35] There is an "Alice-in-Wonderland" quality to this statement. In March 2003, it was the United States, not Iraq, that "made it impossible for the UN to continue to do its work." Kofi Annan and Hans Blix were pleading for a little more time to allow the inspections to continue. Yet this approach did not fit into U.S. war plans and was summarily rejected.

The tragedy is that the nation was taken to war on exaggerated threats and distorted intelligence. The alternative to war, rejected by Powell and Bush, was to continue the strategy of containment and weapons inspections. Despite the fact that this strategy was working, the Bush administration said "time is up" and proceeded to vilify and demean Annan, Blix, and the UN. In July 2003, Joseph Cirincione, director of the nonproliferation project at the Carnegie Endowment in Washington, wrote:

> In the light of the past three months of fruitless searches by U.S., British, and Australian experts, the UNMOVIC inspection process in Iraq now looks much better than critics at the time claimed. It appears that the inspection process was working, and if it had been given enough time and enough resources, could have continued to work and effectively stymied and prevented any new Iraqi efforts on weapons of mass destruction. Never have so few been criticized by so many with so little justification.[36]

POWELL VERSUS POWELL

It is revealing to compare how Powell framed issues of ethics and war in his earlier government service compared to his actions and statements as secretary of state. Examine his statements about Vietnam, the "Powell Doctrine," and resignation:

Vietnam

In 1995, in *My American Journey*, Powell writes emotionally about the lessons he drew from the Vietnam War: "I am proud of the way American soldiers answered the call in a war so poorly conceived, conducted, and explained by their country's leaders . . . you do not squander courage and lives without clear purpose, without the country's backing, and without full commitment."[37]

In 2003, Powell wholeheartedly supported going to war in Iraq without a clear purpose or a full commitment from the country.

In 1995, Powell writes: "I am so angry that so many of the sons of the powerful and well placed . . . managed to wangle slots in Reserve and National Guard units."[38]

In 2000, Powell supported for president the son of a powerful politician who managed to wangle a slot in the National Guard and avoided service in Vietnam.

In 1995, Powell wrote:

> In time, just as I came to reexamine my feelings about the war, the Army, as an institution, would do the same thing. We accepted that we had been sent to pursue a policy that had become bankrupt. Our political leaders had led us into a war for the one-size-fits-all rationale of anticommunism, which was only a partial fit in Vietnam, where the war had its own historical roots in nationalism, anticolonialism, and civil strife beyond the East–West conflict. Our senior officers knew the war was going badly. Yet they bowed to group-think pressure and kept up pretenses, the phony measure of body counts, the comforting illusion of secure hamlets, the inflated progress reports. As a corporate entity, the top leadership never went to the Secretary of Defense or the President and said, "This war is unwinnable the way we are fighting it." Many of my generation, the career captains, majors, and lieutenant colonels seasoned in that war, vowed that when our turn came to call the shots, we would not quietly acquiesce in halfhearted warfare for half-baked reasons that the American people could not understand or support. If we could make good on that promise to ourselves, to the civilian leadership, and to the country, then the sacrifices of Vietnam would not have been in vain.[39]

In 2003, Powell supported going to war in Iraq for reasons that remain to this day unclear to the American people. Many in the army today have come to feel that the current Iraq war policy has become bankrupt and for years have been arguing that the war is going badly. The historical roots of the sectarian violence in Iraq are not related to al-Qaeda and the broader war on terror (just as the "civil strife" in Vietnam went beyond the "East–West conflict"). While in office, Powell never fundamentally challenged the groupthink in the Bush administration's "logic" for war, never challenged the "comforting illusions" of progress, and never presented a clear alternative to war.

The Powell Doctrine

These "lessons" from Powell's experience in Vietnam led him to define a "Powell Doctrine" regarding America's use of the armed forces. Here is how Powell defines this doctrine in his own words: "Essentially it says: Avoid wars—and if that's not possible, and it's necessary to use arms to solve a political problem, then do it in a decisive way. You remove as much doubt as you can about the outcome. In addition, you need to have a clearly defined mission, and you must have some understanding of how it's going to end."[40]

The "Powell Doctrine" was drawn from both Powell's experience in Vietnam and his study of war. Powell writes:

> That wise Prussian Karl von Clausewitz was an awakening for me. His *On War*, written 106 years before I was born, was like a beam of light from the past, still illuminating present-day military quandaries. "No one starts a war, or rather no one in his senses should do so," Clausewitz wrote, "without first being clear in his mind what he intends to achieve by that war and how he intends to achieve it." Mistake number one in Vietnam. Which led to Clausewitz's rule number two. Political leaders must set a war's objectives, while armies achieve them. In Vietnam, one seemed to be looking to the other for the answers that never came. Finally, the people must support a war. Since they supply the treasure and the sons, and today the daughters too, they must be convinced that the sacrifice is justified. That essential pillar had crumbled as the Vietnam War ground on. Clausewitz's greatest lesson for my profession was that the soldier, for all his patriotism, valor, and skill, forms just one leg in a triad. Without all three legs engaged, the military, the government, and the people, the enterprise cannot stand.[41]

The U.S. invasion of Panama in 1989 confirmed Powell's thinking on the use of U.S. military force abroad. He writes:

> The lessons I absorbed from Panama confirmed all my convictions over the preceding twenty years, since the days of doubt over Vietnam. Have a clear political objective and stick to it. Use all the force necessary, and do not apologize for going in big if that is what it takes. Decisive force ends wars quickly

and in the long run saves lives. Whatever threats we faced in the future, I intended to make these rules the bedrock of my military counsel.[42]

Prior to his years as secretary of state, Powell had publicly articulated clear ethical guidelines on the use of force. Powell's forceful moral positions to lessen the suffering from warfare are clear: war as a last resort, overwhelming force to bring about a quick end to the suffering, and clear political and military objectives. If these guidelines are ignored by politicians, especially those who used their class positions to avoid military service, Powell said that he would speak up forcefully in opposition to flawed war plans.

When his time came, he "would not quietly acquiesce in halfhearted warfare for half-baked reasons that the American people could not understand or support." If he could make good on that promise, then "the sacrifices of Vietnam would not have been in vain." Powell is clearly describing the fact that there is no greater ethical decision than to go to war. His passion here betrays his later talk regarding the Iraq War as involving mere policy, and not ethical, decisions. No matter how "just" the cause, innocents die and the suffering is enormous. Powell thus articulates moral, ethical guidelines to carefully use force in order to limit the destruction of war.

It tragically appears that all of these guidelines on the use of force were ignored in the rushed invasion and occupation of Iraq. Powell squandered his legacy by staying in office and promoting such war policies that ran counter to his long-held moral principles.

Every component of the Powell Doctrine was violated in the 2003 invasion and occupation of Iraq. As documented above, war was not the last resort, as there were viable options to continue the successful regime of containment and sanctions that had disarmed Iraq. Most intelligence experts, including the CIA director, believed there was no imminent danger to our national security or that of our allies. After hundreds of searches, the UN arms inspectors could not find any WMD, and the intrusive containment of Saddam effectively limited his ability to rearm. Furthermore, the war was launched without the "overwhelming force to bring a quick end to the suffering" which is central to the Powell Doctrine. There was no satisfactory exit strategy and no plan to contain the upheaval unleashed in the post-invasion stage.

Powell is often described as "loyal." But loyalty to democracy would have required honesty to the American people. Loyalty to the U.S. soldiers, who have given their lives in Vietnam and elsewhere for "half-baked reasons," would have meant that Powell would not have acquiesced to the "halfhearted warfare" Rumsfeld planned for Iraq.

Powell, as we have seen, generally appears to believe that most subjects that arise in government service involve "policy" and not "ethical" issues. Policy debates and differences are the ongoing work of the government. It would have been foolish for him to consider resigning every time he didn't get his way in policy debates. However, this position becomes untenable when the policy under discussion becomes the intentional killing of human beings in warfare and the torture and degrading treatment of prisoners. If these actions run counter to one's individual moral beliefs, resignation is an ethical path to pursue.

The moral outrage Powell expresses in relation to the Vietnam War, and the ethical basis behind his "Powell Doctrine" on the use of force, indicates that he embraces the necessity for soldiers and statesmen to fight to protect their moral autonomy and moral integrity. In many respects, Powell wants it both ways. On the one hand, he wants to be the loyal soldier and cabinet member carrying out the policy decisions of the president and thus pushing all moral responsibility to the top. On the other hand, he speaks of individual moral responsibility and vows to never "quietly acquiesce" to a bankrupt war policy.

In fact, Powell himself has stated that under certain conditions, resignation is the appropriate action. He clarified his thoughts on resignation after Bill Clinton was elected president with the promise to integrate gays in the military. He told a group of navy midshipmen who had asked about gays in the military that when a decision "strikes at the heart of your moral beliefs," one had no choice but to resign. In this speech at the U.S. Naval Academy in Annapolis, Maryland, Powell said that if Clinton followed through on his promise, "We must conform to that policy. The debate will be over." Anyone who couldn't align the policy with his or her personal moral beliefs, he said, would "have to resign."[43]

It is interesting that Powell would draw such a strong line around this issue of basic rights for gay Americans. He seems to be saying that if your religion leads you to believe that homosexuality is immoral, you are on correct moral grounds to resign to protest the integration of gays in the military. It is striking that Powell doesn't apply this moral logic to issues of war. If a soldier, like Ehren Watada, determines that the war in Iraq "strikes at the heart" of his moral beliefs, doesn't he then also have a duty to resign and not participate in that war? Yet Powell refuses to support Watada or other soldiers who act on their moral principles and refuse the fight in Iraq. Furthermore, given the massive violations of all of the principles underlining the "Powell Doctrine" regarding the use of force, weren't these actions that struck "at the heart" of the Powell's moral principles? Yet he didn't resign. Instead, Powell's long-standing personal moral principles suddenly simply vanished.

Tragically, on the most important issue he would face as secretary of state, Powell was unable to rise above the infighting in the Bush administration and think clearly about the ethics of war. It is not good enough for him to say that his job was only to serve the man the people selected as president. It's not good enough to put one's loyalty to a political party and a man (Bush) above all other virtues. There was no vital national security issue at stake in Iraq. There were no WMD and no ties to al-Qaeda. There was no effective post-invasion strategy for protecting the innocent and rebuilding the country. The United States lost the respect of the world's people when it launched the war illegally without the authorization of the UN. The moral high ground was lost with the renditions, Guantanamo, Abu Ghraib, and the cruel and unusual punishment inflicted on prisoners. A loyal American and ethical leader would have resigned.

WAYNE WHITE
U.S. FOREIGN SERVICE, STATE DEPARTMENT INTELLIGENCE
1973–2005

Wayne White served as deputy director of the State Department's Bureau of Intelligence and Research Office of Analysis for the Near East and South Asia (INR/NESA) and senior regional analyst from 2002 to 2005. During this time he was also a principal Iraq analyst and head of INR/NESA's Iraq team. Over his twenty-six years with the INR, White became a leading U.S. intelligence expert on Iraq and the Middle East. White has received numerous awards, including being a five-time recipient of the State Department's Superior Honor Award, INR Analyst of the Year, National Intelligence Medal for Outstanding Achievement, and the Secretary's Career Achievement Award.

In 2002–2003, White did not believe that the United States had a legitimate case for going to war because Iraq posed no direct threat to the United States or its interests. White opposed this "war of choice" that he believed was "highly unethical." The United States had not been attacked and was not threatened with an imminent assault: "It wasn't like the U.S. going to war after being hit in Pearl Harbor on December 7, and then Germany following with a declaration of war on December 11, 1941." Furthermore, White states that the aim of the war was "not mainly to address the WMD issue." The WMD argument, he believed, was simply "a way of justifying a war." Instead, he said that the decision to go to war "was made under a false assumption that Iraq could turn into a model democracy in the Middle East and it could produce a domino effect around the region toppling other oppressive regimes." Some of these regimes, like Syria, are hostile to the United States' main ally in the region, Israel. The administration, therefore, made a pragmatic decision to attempt to bring these regimes down to further the interests of Israel and the United States in the region. Ethics were "dragged in to justify" the war, but it was mainly, according to White, a pragmatic decision based on a rather aggressive notion of the national interest.[44]

The pre-war decision-makers "often turned a blind eye to intelligence inconsistent with their Middle East agenda." In testimony delivered to an Ad Hoc Senate Hearing on Pre-War Iraq Intelligence, White stated,

> Equally disturbing is that the most senior officials involved—the President, the Vice-President, Defense Secretary Rumsfeld, and then NSC Director Rice—had relatively little past experience with the complex politics of the Middle East region, let alone Iraq—a major impediment to sound policymaking if one already does not have an open mind and one is agenda driven. . . . [I]t is my belief that some officials did intervene in the process of intelligence analysis in order to shape it to serve a regional agenda.[45]

White supports this claim of damaging political interference in the intelligence analysis on Iraq by pointing to the operations of the intelligence unit set up in the vice president's office and led by Doug Feith. This Cheney–Feith effort was simply, in White's eyes, an "effort to end-run established—and far more professional—intelligence channels." To this day, White believes that the public is unaware of the broad political interference in intelligence gathering that emanated from the vice president's office.[46]

Particularly disturbing to White were the many ways in which the professionals in diplomacy and intelligence gathering were either ignored or belittled. He points, for example, to INR rejection of the claim included in the fall 2002 National Intelligence Estimate (NIE) that Iraq had an active nuclear weapons program. INR rejection was supported by the Energy Department's technical experts, who, in their labs, "tested some of the [Iraqi bound] aluminum tubes associated with enrichment and declared them unfit for use in centrifuge." The INR view was thus "backed by the agency with the technical know-how to review" the information on Iraq's nuclear program and "found it very, very wanting." INR insisted that its dissent be included to counter the NIE report which falsely exaggerated Iraq's nuclear program and capabilities. It is unclear how seriously any senior official in the Bush administration (including Colin Powell) took this INR agency rebuke to one of the central justifications for the invasion of Iraq.

White's INR was thus right on the non-existence of an active nuclear weapons program in Iraq. INR was also right about the non-existence of an al-Qaeda—Saddam link. According to White, INR was always very clear that "Iraq had absolutely no meaningful links to al-Qaeda, let alone 9/11." On this point, "virtually the entire intelligence community agreed." Why did the president, vice president, Powell, and others then push these false conclusions? White states,

> The president decided just to go with what he wanted to go with. He decided to go with what Doug Feith was producing. In fact, the only document I ever saw pertaining to Doug Feith's office before the war was a listing of all the intelligence that "confirmed" that Iraq had a connection to al-Qaeda. The only reason I saw this two-page thing is because a terrorist analyst upstairs in our Terrorism Office brought it down to me as comic relief. It was so ludicrous. It was a mishmash of junky press articles and a few intelligence reports that had been debunked. It was trash.

White thinks very highly of Powell. However, concerning intelligence on Iraq, Powell clearly either ignored or didn't accept INR findings. Powell received "30 to 40 classified emails" documenting the flaws in the "intelligence" on Saddam's nuclear capability. Yet Powell went ahead at the UN and made false assertions against Iraq. White was mystified by Powell's actions and concluded the following:

> There is only one thing I can come to, because generally Powell is good. He must have been under incredible pressure, specifically on that point [nuclear weapons]. There is nothing that garners fear more than the mushroom cloud, a nuclear capability. He must have been pressured really hard and told that this was desperately needed to sell the case. "If this is not in your speech it will be viewed as a huge hole in the case for war." That's all I can think of . . . that in a weak moment he gambled.

White believes that Powell "had a conscience, a sense of honor, and probably felt that he had been ill-used."

In February 2003, White authored a formal INR analysis titled "Iraq, the Middle East and Change: No Dominoes." In this document he warned that "even a successful effort in Iraq, both militarily and politically, would not only fail to trigger a tsunami of democracy in the region, but potentially could endanger longstanding U.S. allies in the Middle East, like Jordan, not the region's anti-U.S. autocrats."

White notes that this conclusion was not extraordinary:

> Polling for a number of years and by a variety of polling sources had revealed clearly that the region's populations were (and are) predominantly more anti-American, anti-Israeli, and militantly Islamic than their existing governments. So, even if democracy had taken hold in various Middle East states, the result would have been governments more anti-American, anti-

Israeli and militantly Islamic than those previously in power, as with Hamas in the Palestinian context.[47]

White's 2003 INR analysis is still classified. However, in early March 2003, its contents were leaked to the *Los Angeles Times*, causing a public stir at the time of the invasion of Iraq. White's report debunked the idea that the United States could "democratize" the Middle East: "Knowing what I knew about the socioeconomic and political circumstances, [democratization] was just not going to happen. [I thought that] perhaps if I could put that forward it might stop the train or slow it down." The report publicly brought to light significant divisions within the Bush administration over the so-called democratic domino theory, one of the key arguments for invading Iraq. The report states categorically that daunting economic and social problems would likely undermine basic stability in the region for years and, thus, "liberal democracy would be difficult to achieve." Furthermore, "electoral democracy, were it to emerge, could well be subject to exploitation by anti-American elements." And, as noted, anti-United States sentiment is so pervasive that elections could lead to the rise of Islamic-controlled governments hostile to the United States.[48]

This INR report was dated February 26, 2003, the same day President Bush endorsed the democratic domino theory in a speech to the conservative American Enterprise Institute in Washington. "A new regime in Iraq would serve as a dramatic and inspiring example of freedom for other nations in the region," Bush said. This argument had been promoted most by the administration's neoconservatives, including Wolfowitz, the deputy defense secretary, and Richard Perle, chairman of the Defense Policy Board, an influential Pentagon advisory panel. For example, Wolfowitz stated that Iraq could be "the first Arab democracy" and that even modest democratic progress in Iraq would "cast a very large shadow, starting with Syria and Iran but across the whole Arab world." Perle joined the chorus, stating that a reformed Iraq "has the potential to transform the thinking of people around the world about the potential for democracy, even in Arab countries where people have been disparaging of their potential."[49] This democratic domino theory was used by the administration to counter critics, including the former chief of the U.S. Central Command, retired Marine General Anthony Zinni, who expressed concern that the invasion of Iraq would inflame the Muslim world and fuel terrorist activity against the United States.[50] Bush responded to these critics by assailing the "soft bigotry of low expectations."[51]

Such pressure from the president and his cabinet was partially intended to muzzle opponents of the administration's war policies inside the State Department's INR—and even beyond INR—as well as the many doubters throughout the intelligence community. The administration was on a very public campaign to minimize and downplay the costs and risks of war. The leaking of this INR document at such a critical moment (by persons unknown) was probably meant to give voice to widely held views in the intelligence community, certain policy circles in government, and a number of members on Capitol Hill that the removal of Saddam Hussein would not lead to a discernible movement toward the democratization of the Arab states.

There were many intelligence officers who supported White's position and were thrilled about the leaking of this INR report. White was at the CIA when word got around that a *Los Angeles Times* article on the report had been published. Some of his colleagues at INR were so delighted to see their views finally being part of the debate that they threw an impromptu party for him. "The whole office essentially knew that the main driver for war [the democratic domino theory] was foolish and delighted [with the leak] . . . since they had gotten the impression that the whole system was not listening and now this message was getting out more broadly." White, unfortunately, had to put a halt to the party and reminded his colleagues, "This is an intelligence office and we don't celebrate leaks. . . . So I had to shut down my own congratulations party, although I knew their hearts were in the right place."

White spoke out on two additional issues during this difficult time of war initiation in Iraq. In December 2002, he discovered that CENTCOM[52] was hoping to rely on non-governmental organizations (NGOs), like the Red Cross, for the treatment of Iraqi military and civilians wounded on the battlefield. White was appalled: "In two separate meetings, I reminded CENTCOM officers in no uncertain terms of their responsibilities under the second and fourth Geneva Conventions of 1949 regarding these duties and that NGOs almost never operate on active battlefields in any case." White could not bring himself "to believe that CENTCOM was thoroughly unaware of its responsibilities under international law." Instead, he saw this bizarre planning as a result of the administration's refusal to allocate adequate forces to the Iraq occupation. CENTCOM was probably "stretched so thin because of the limited U.S. military resources assigned to the Iraq campaign that officers were desperately casting about for ways in which to pass along to others certain basic duties."[53]

White was also one of the first to point to the dangers of the Iraqi insurgency in 2003. As is well known, high-level administration officials initially dismissed the insurgency as insignificant and composed of "foreign fighters," "common criminals," and "former regime elements." Rumsfeld would infamously describe the Iraqi resistance as "small elements" of ten to twenty people composed of "pockets of dead-enders." Wolfowitz claimed they were "the last remnants of a dying cause."[54] White knew better. He saw this analysis as "one-dimensional and badly flawed." In the first meeting to coordinate a National Intelligence Estimate on the Iraqi insurgency in July 2003, White found himself virtually alone in challenging these rosy conclusions:

> I argued that the insurgency had deep roots in generic opposition to foreign occupation among a very proud people, broad-based Sunni Arab anger over being disenfranchised, joblessness, lack of public services, and, what I termed "Pissed Off Iraqis," or POIs, for lack of a better term. POIs are people who lost relatives in the war, whose relatives were arrested and taken away to Abu Gharayb and other military holding areas, those imprisoned and released (many of whom were innocent), those whose property had been destroyed or damaged by Coalition action during the war or in the course of anti-insurgency operations, etc., etc. In other words, the insurgent recruiting pool was (and is) not only potentially vast, but renewable. I was pessimistic as early as late April 2003 about our chances for success in Iraq. As a matter of fact, I personally came to believe at that time that our chances for success in Iraq already might have been reduced to little more than 50/50.[55]

White continues,

> That conclusion was grounded on the tremendous impact of the devastation wrought by widespread looting that Coalition forces did virtually nothing to stop—something fairly consistently belittled at the time. The looting utterly devastated Iraq's power grid, government ministries, the educational system, state industries, etc. Simply getting the country back to where it was just before the war would even now in certain sectors, a mission impossible. As a result the supply of so-called "Pissed-Off Iraqis" would be that much more plentiful and continuous.[56]

White clearly struggled inside the government to voice his opposition to the ways in which intelligence was often painted in too rosy a light to support a flawed Iraq invasion and occupation. He decided to stay and "fight from within" to try to ameliorate the most harmful aspects to the defective Iraq strategy. He never considered resigning in protest. There was no question of sacrificing his moral autonomy or moral integrity. He was not in the public spotlight. He did not have to speak up (as did Powell, Kiesling, Brown, and Wright) and actively lobby foreign governments to back U.S. actions in the Middle East. Instead, he was able to voice his opposition to policies inside and push and push to try to correct the direction of U.S. foreign policy with the full support of his superiors in INR.

White notes that everyone in the Foreign Service or the intelligence community deals with "a certain amount of incremental compromise in their careers." Colleagues or bosses edit what is produced, often wanting to make a document "sexier," and so on. These pressures "pull us away from the truth, pure and simple, as we see it." It is therefore imperative for Foreign Service officers and civil servants to have "the courage to stand up ethically when they see a dramatic example of tampering with something or rejecting what they believe is the truth." This, unfortunately, is difficult because working in a bureaucracy conditions a person to expect interference and accept compromise. While White can accept "modifications on the edges," he feels, as an intelligence officer, that he must maintain "the highest possible standards" and not allow his briefings to be distorted. The government process often pushes people "over a line" and they begin to push back less, come close to not being able to deal with a situation in which they view something as immoral or wrong, and just shrug and think, "Well, that's the way things work."

According to White, INR provided an environment that encouraged moral autonomy and promoted free thinking and open questioning of established policy. White states, "INR was, and is, probably the one arm of the intelligence community with the most freedom in producing what we think is top-notch analysis and often breaking with groupthink and going outside the box." As an example of this freedom, White points to the 2003 NIE he helped prepare for CENTCOM on the sources of instability and violence in Iraq. As already noted, White stood virtually alone in the room in concluding that there was a burgeoning insurgency: "Initially, every single other agency of the intelligence community believed that there was no insurgency, that this was just residual, and that these were sort of Baathist dead-enders and Saddamist elements that would gradually diminish." Bitter, bruising arguments ensued. Four drafts later, with other agencies persuaded, White was able to get virtually every one of his changes into the NIE. But initially he was alone, as was often the case with INR analysts during this politicized time when the White House was eager to only recognize and highlight selected data that supported the Iraq war effort.

The White House and the Pentagon did not appreciate White's attempts to focus attention on the growing insurgency. With the glow of "success" in capturing Baghdad, the view of "mission accomplished" prevailed. White's prescient predictions were dismissed in the first few months after the invasion. The reactions to his analysis were telling. The response of one under secretary of state to one of White's memos warning of the rising insurgency was to belittle it. A deputy assistant secretary of state said, "Can somebody go and tell Wayne that we are winning the war?" The Pentagon and the White House thought that "everything was going according to plan." Analysts who disagreed and warned that something more dangerous was about to occur were "simply ignored." The initial hubris from the "shock and awe" of the invasion blinded the Bush administration from the reality of Iraq.

White and others in INR did try to resist these pressures and present the facts about the growing difficulties in Iraq. In fact, INR was called the "truth squad" by some other intelligence officers in recognition of this willingness to speak out. Colleagues recognized that within INR there was the ability to get beyond groupthink. White states, "One reason we have this kind of ability is that we have analysts on accounts for years. In other agencies you have two-year rotations. Up until recently in the CIA people were penalized careerwise for remaining too long in a position." White, for example, was an INR Iraq analyst for almost seven years. After his fourth year, his expertise was widely recognized in the government, and he often found himself "constantly correcting errors and . . . dealing with neophytes—new people in other agencies who had to be brought up to speed on the Iraq account."

White was in a position to reach top decision-makers and potentially mitigate the destructiveness of erroneous policy. Every formal INR assessment was widely distributed throughout the government through highly classified means to military commanders, cabinet secretaries, and their staffs (State, Defense, Treasury, Energy, and so on). In addition, INR reports were distributed to most embassies abroad that had the ability to receive highly classified intelligence. As White summarizes, "So when INR wrote an assessment, hundreds were in a position to read it all throughout the American Defense, Intelligence, and Foreign Policy apparatus. So, yes, staying in [my job] meant that I had the ability to make a difference. In fact, I felt almost an imperative to stay in the government." With the reputation of the "truth squad," INR staff could keep some pressure on the Bush administration. On the other hand, to quit in protest, White felt, would accomplish nothing. Here he could still not only be heard but, in the end, also influence policy.

Even Condoleezza Rice affirmed the independence and unique status of INR. After her appointment as secretary of state, she came to visit a State Department task force on which INR was represented. After White introduced himself, Rice responded, "Oh, I am so happy to be coming over here and taking over the best intelligence shop in the intelligence community."

White considered that his job was basically "finding the truth." He did not hold a public position but, rather, was located within the analytic/intelligence side of the Foreign Service. He provided the information to the policy-maker, who would then settle on the policy. White never had to then "sell" the final policy to the American people. White states, "I didn't do that. I was purely pounding away at the system with reality and trying to get changes in behavior related to that [reality]. If I left, maybe the person replacing me isn't going to be as determined to hammer away on those points." White recalls a former ambassador coming up to him and saying that he was retiring early. When White asked him why, the diplo-mat responded, "Wayne, I just can't sell this anymore."

If a person is on the side of the government where they have to "sell" the policy, the ethical issues rise up more often and with more force. White, on the other hand, didn't suffer a crisis of conscience, because he not only didn't have to take on this public role but could also keep raising how "reality" and "truth" needed to be brought back into the Iraq policy. He didn't feel that he was compromising anything by continuing to work for the government.

For example, in April 2004 White wrote a memo on the difficult situa-tion in al-Anbar province in Iraq and explained why some felt it was ir-retrievably lost. This was not information that the administration wanted to hear. Yet his analysis went directly to the secretary of state. Powell circulated it to Cheney, Tenet, Card, Rumsfeld, and National Security Agency Director Michael Hayden, with a cover note saying "interesting reading." According to White, Powell blasted this memo throughout the administration to show where he was personally coming from. "He [Pow-ell] was trying to get reality out."

Thus, White did have access and a sympathetic boss in Powell. Yet he often had to "yell and scream" to be heard. White was not immune from these pressures. The arguments over the capabilities of the Iraqi insur-gency were particularly vicious. All of this took its toll in terms of his health. While head of the Iraq team, White developed a rare stress-related illness that remains with him to this day. Others also experienced physi-cal reactions to the intense pushback and pressure coming from the Bush administration. For example, White notes,

> the nuclear analyst at INR, who put up a heroic effort against all the other in-telligence agencies (except for the Energy Department), had a severe stroke. There are various types of strokes, and this was definitely a stress-related stroke. One of our most outstanding senior African analysts had a heart at-tack while preparing at 5:30 in the morning for briefings . . . so there was a price to be paid for fighting back . . . sure we could fight back . . . sure we were not penalized inside the INR family . . . but it took a health toll . . . and some of us are still paying.

In addition, White notes that those in many agencies of the intelligence community who were willing to push back and challenge faulty analyses did not receive the highest promotions. "People who grant such promo-tions want people they know will look the other way on certain occasions. They don't want somebody who is the crusader as a senior ranking sub-ordinate."

Despite these pressures working against honest reporting, White feels that INR was able to consistently provide reality-based data to the administration on Iraq. He hopes the administration has learned from this experience. White concludes,

> I just hope this government has learned a lesson about wars of choice. Almost all wars of choice end badly, no matter who fights them, whether it's a well-meaning democracy or a ruthless dictatorship with ambitions of power and land. Wars of choice usually bring the worst possible disasters on the initiator themselves, let alone the other victims. In fact, such wars often result in the defeat of the initiator, and always produce scenarios never dreamed of by the initiator.

5

cᔇᔆᔄᔅᔆᔄᔈᔆᔂᔆ

Getting Out

John Brady Kiesling, John Brown, and Mary Ann Wright

When an individual joins the U.S. Foreign Service, he or she is required to take the following oath:

> I [full name], do solemnly swear that I will support and defend the Constitution of the United States against all enemies, foreign and domestic, that I will bear true faith and allegiance to the same, that I take this obligation freely, without any mental reservation or purpose of evasion, and I will well and faithfully discharge the duties of the office on which I am about to enter. So help me God.

In November 2007, Secretary of State Condoleezza Rice had to remind U.S. diplomats of their duty to serve their country amidst a reported revolt among some who were resisting forced assignments to Iraq. Rice made it clear that Foreign Service officers are obligated by their oath of office to accept assignments at any diplomatic mission worldwide, no matter what the risks or personal ethical disagreements about the administration's policies. While expressing an understanding of the safety and security concerns of those who might be ordered to go, Rice said they must uphold their commitments. Rice stated, "I would hope others would think about their obligation not just to the country but their obligation to those who have already served." The U.S. ambassador to Iraq, Ryan Crocker, spoke more forcefully, saying that diplomats have a responsibility to prioritize the nation's interest over their personal safety and that those who don't are "in the wrong line of business." Joining the Foreign Service, Ryan asserted, "does not mean you can choose the fight. It's not for us to decide if we like the policy or if the policy is rightly implemented. It's for us to go and serve, not to debate the policy, not to agree with it."[1]

Rice and Crocker were responding to a shortfall in State Department volunteers for service in Iraq. Despite offering generous incentives, including extra danger pay, leave time, and preference on next assignments, diplomats had not stepped forward for Iraq duty in sufficient numbers. As a result, the department announced that if not enough of the prime candidates agreed to go, some would be ordered to do so under threat of dismissal. This move represented the largest diplomatic call-up to an active war zone since Vietnam. At a town hall meeting of several hundred diplomats, many angrily complained about this new policy and applauded a colleague who likened it to a "potential death sentence."[2]

According to Rice and Crocker, diplomats are to defend and implement the foreign policy of the administration and willingly accept all foreign assignments, including war-zone postings. The responsible Foreign Service officer is not to debate the policy, but to carry it out. From this perspective, the morality of the state stands above that of the individual. Fulfilling the oath of office means that one should swallow his or her ethical qualms about war policies and agree to serve the higher good.

From this perspective, the Foreign Service oath itself limits the scope of individual moral autonomy. To be true to the oath, the diplomat must not be true to his or her individual moral convictions when those beliefs conflict with government policy.

Yet the view that the Foreign Service requires unconditional obedience (as described by Crocker) to implement and uphold the government's foreign policy is controversial. As already noted, many diplomats "work from within" to change policy. Others seek assignments out of ethically troublesome areas in order to fulfill the duties of the oath. In fact, by refusing to serve in Iraq, one could argue that State Department personnel "voted with their feet" and expressed sharp disapproval of U.S. policy in Iraq. Instead of resigning, these individuals simply tried to disassociate themselves and their actions from this morally problematic war. According to the results of a survey conducted by the American Foreign Service Association, the union that represents U.S. diplomats, 48 percent of the U.S. diplomats unwilling to volunteer to work in Iraq based their refusal on "disagreement" with the Bush administration's Iraq war policies.[3] A diplomatic posting to Santiago or Brussels poses fewer ethical dilemmas compared to Baghdad, and at these locations these diplomats felt they could fulfill their oath with good conscience.

For most of their public careers, Brady Kiesling, John Brown, and Ann Wright were able to "faithfully discharge the duties" of office without compromising their individual moral autonomy, despite moments of individual doubt. These three Foreign Service officers held postings in scores of countries around the world, including Afghanistan, Armenia, Greece, Grenada, India, Israel, Kyrgyzstan, Micronesia, Mongolia, Morocco, Nicaragua, Poland, Romania, Russia, Sierra Leone, Somalia, Uzbekistan, and the Federal Republic of Yugoslavia. For these three civil servants, representing the United States in these countries, even during difficult times, posed few moral dilemmas.

All this changed with the invasion and occupation of Iraq. After the president made the decision to go to war, in violation of the UN Charter and the will of most U.S. allies, it became impossible for any of them to remain in the government. All three diplomats were unable to publicly defend the policy of preemptive war. And all three determined that continuing to serve the government would lend credence and validation to policies that they had come to conclude were both illegal and immoral. By asserting an "ethic of principled resignation," these three diplomats regained their individual moral bearings and recovered their public political voices.

After exploring the individual journey of each of these former Foreign Service officers to principled resignation, this chapter then analyzes some of the common issues and themes raised by all three, including: a rejection of the arguments for war based on humanitarian grounds, links between Iraq and al-Qaeda, and weapons of mass destruction (WMD); the difficult personal process culminating in a decision to resign; respect of and disappointment in Colin Powell; and the wearing personal toll and individual sacrifice each endured.

JOHN BRADY KIESLING
CAREER STATE DEPARTMENT DIPLOMAT
RESIGNATION: FEBRUARY 27, 2003

In February 2003, John Brady Kiesling[4] resigned from the U.S. Foreign Service to protest the U.S. decision to invade and occupy Iraq. With his letter to Secretary of State Colin Powell, Kiesling became the first American diplomat to leave his or her job in opposition to U.S. policy on Iraq. In his letter of resignation, Kiesling argues:

> The policies we are now asked to advance are incompatible not only with American values but also with American interests. Our fervent pursuit of war with Iraq is driving us to squander the international legitimacy that has been America's most potent weapon of both offense and defense since the days of Woodrow Wilson. We have begun to dismantle the largest and most effective web of international relationships the world has ever known. Our current course will bring instability and danger, not security.[5]

As a career State Department diplomat, Kiesling served for twenty years in embassies around the world. He joined the U.S. Foreign Service in 1983 during the Reagan administration and held diplomatic postings in Israel, Morocco, Greece, Romania, India, and Armenia. In 1994 he was honored by his peers for his constructive dissent on Bosnia while serving as the Romanian desk officer in Washington.

Initially, Kiesling's resignation letter attracted only minor attention, receiving just one hundred words in the *Washington Post* and four hundred words in the *New York Times*. But the letter was picked up on the Internet and struck a chord among many who were frustrated with the Bush administration's aggressive war plans. On the Senate floor, Senator Patrick Leahy (D-Vermont) mentioned Kiesling's "eloquent and heartfelt explanation" for resigning and wondered aloud how many others in the State Department felt the same way.[6]

Kiesling views the devastating failures of the Bush administration's foreign policy as a result of misguided "idealism" which he now rejects, and instead embraces "realism." He writes: "'Realism' is used as a dirty word in U.S. foreign policy, a synonym for selfishness and indifference to human suffering. The White House and the Pentagon are full of proud idealists with the moral courage to torture and kill in the name of freedom. When I joined the Foreign Service, I too thought I was an idealist. The United States was a moral superpower, and we diplomats had a moral duty to use our country's wealth and power to make the world peaceful, prosperous, and democratic. Now, with the benefit of twenty years' experience, I am a State Department realist."[7]

Once he confronted his internal moral conflicts with U.S. foreign policy, Brady Kiesling quickly came to the conclusion that he could not defend the foreign policy of the U.S. government and had to resign. As he stated: "Everything came together in that one instant. Really, it took just a couple of minutes for me to be sure that this was the right thing to do. It was the anger that triggered it. I had become more and more miserable as my nation rushed toward an unjust war. I wasn't dysfunctional—I was doing everything that needed to be done. But I wasn't getting any pleasure out of it and, in fact, I was getting sick." He describes this moment as "liberating" and pushing him to the first "moment of moral clarity" he ever had in his life. Standing up for principle allowed him to "operate on a much higher level."

Despite his resignation from the government, Kiesling remains strikingly loyal and patriotic to America. He continues to view the world through a lens of the U.S. national interest. He sees the country's current path as a tragic result of the messianic idealism of the neoconservatives. But he believes that the country can self-correct and return to the internationalist, multilateral foreign policy that he feels served the United States well from the 1940s through the 1990s.

This realist political stand means that it is very hard for Kiesling to criticize Colin Powell. On the one hand, Kiesling hoped Powell's UN speech could get other countries to move in "our direction." On the other hand, Kiesling recognizes that it would have been "better for the world" had Powell resigned and spoken out against the war. His political realism also meant that he saw no contradiction between, on the one hand, his decision to resign from the Foreign Service because of his opposition to the war, and, on the other hand, at the same time pleading with the chief of staff of the Archbishop of Athens not to oppose the U.S. invasion of Iraq. In this meeting, as a good diplomat, he could set aside his personal moral reservations and promote current U.S. policy in the hope that in the long run his actions would help to stabilize relations between the two countries. Kiesling's support of Powell and lobbying of the Archbishop of Athens demonstrate how hard it is for an individual to break from his or her training.

Brady Kiesling gave up a lot when he resigned—his career, financial security, and his base of professional support in the State Department. Yet he gained much more than he lost. He regained not only his health but also, of equal importance, his sense of honor, moral autonomy, and purpose.

A career of twenty years in the Foreign Service gave Kiesling a degree of moral capital that he could wield. Kiesling recognized this clearly: "Any number of people could have written exactly the same letter I wrote and no one in the world would have read it. But since I had just sacrificed a twenty-year career, people did read it." As the first Foreign Service officer to resign, he inspired others, in and out of government, to speak out and oppose the occupation of Iraq. There is no question about it: Kiesling's actions had a remarkable impact on thousands of Americans deeply troubled by the violent direction of U.S. foreign policy.

JOHN H. BROWN
U.S. PUBLIC DIPLOMACY FOREIGN SERVICE OFFICER
RESIGNATION: MARCH 10, 2003

As a member of the U.S. Foreign Service from 1981 to 2003, John Brown[8] served in London, Prague, Krakow, Kiev, Belgrade, and Moscow. Brown's area of expertise was public diplomacy—which includes press and cultural affairs—that made him extremely valuable to the State Department during the Reagan years. Brown feels particularly privileged to have been in contact with dissidents in Eastern Europe during the height of the Cold War.

Brady Kiesling's letter of resignation on February 27, 2003, made a powerful impression on John Brown. Brown had never met Kiesling but felt that his letter eloquently expressed the grave problems with the United States' fervent pursuit of war with Iraq. Brown writes that Brady's "words were among the most articulate refutations of pre-emptive unilateralism that I had seen."[9]

Following the administration's failure to win the support of the United Nations for war, President Bush addressed the American people on March 6, 2003. Bush's scripted performance was "the straw that broke the camel's back" in making Brown decide to resign. In Brown's eyes, the president's speech was "a disastrous effort to explain why the United States should attack Iraq at this time." Brown writes: "After that debacle, I could not see myself continuing to work for the State Department, knowing that I had done nothing against a war that I now believed was totally unjustified." On March 10, 2003, John Brown submitted his letter of resignation and "immediately felt an enormous sense of relief."[10]

Brown's public resignation, ending his distinguished career in the Foreign Service, also helped to stimulate others to oppose the Iraq war and occupation. Since resigning, Brown has continued to try to correct the path of U.S. foreign policy with his work on public diplomacy. As a senior fellow at the University of Southern California Center on Public Diplomacy, Brown for several years after leaving the State Department aggregated current public diplomacy-related news into an online publication titled "John Brown's Public Diplomacy Press & Blog Review."[11] This public diplomacy review provided valuable resources for policy-makers, scholars, and the general public attempting to understand U.S. foreign policy initiatives. Brown plans to continue as a private citizen to use his expertise to impact U.S. foreign policy.

What is the connection between the ethics of war and public diplomacy? Listening to Brown, one is struck by his relentless desire for the United States to break out of its "parochialism." His examples of how domestic concerns distort foreign policy are compelling. The United States often seems to simply have no desire to move off its perch and, thus, neither empathizes with others nor recognizes the limitations of its power. These traits were perhaps most clearly seen in the buildup to the invasion of Iraq. When the entire world—through the UN, massive demonstrations, and global public opinion polls—pleaded with the United States not to invade Iraq, the country went ahead with the war as planned. This act was too much for John Brown, a betrayal of the principles of public diplomacy, and he resigned.

As Brown argues, public diplomacy should be "intelligent persuasion," not propaganda. Diplomacy involves a give-and-take; listening to others; empathy and compromise; and above all, negotiations, not ultimatums. There is most likely something wrong with a country's policy if the whole world is lined up against it. It quickly became apparent to Brown that the Bush administration was failing in the realm of diplomacy. Instead, the selling of the Iraq war became "a base propaganda campaign." And Brown reveals this effort to be "propaganda at its worst": the demonization of the opponent, the simplification of the issues, the constant repetition of slogans, and a near-total disregard for truth.

Unfortunately, we will live with the consequences of this misleading propaganda campaign for decades. Brown speaks optimistically of America's ability to reinvent itself, as the country did after the Vietnam War debacle. One must hope that he is right, and that the country is up for this challenge. The alternative consequence, which Brown also identifies, is that the twenty-first century becomes the "anti-American century" as hostility toward American foreign policy in the Middle East turns into hatred of America. Perhaps the lessons of public diplomacy that Brown articulates so clearly can help the United States avoid this catastrophic course.

MARY ANN WRIGHT
COLONEL U.S. ARMY, DEPUTY CHIEF OF MISSION, U.S. FOREIGN SERVICE RESIGNATION: MARCH 19, 2003

Mary Ann Wright[12] was the third, and final, U.S. diplomat to resign from the federal government in 2003 to express opposition to the war in Iraq. Prior to her resignation, Ann had served the United States for more than thirty-five years. During her sixteen years in the diplomatic corps, she rose to deputy chief of mission in U.S. embassies in Sierra Leone, Micronesia, Afghanistan, and Mongolia; she was also chosen to be a member of the small team that reopened the U.S. Embassy in Kabul, Afghanistan, in December 2001. Ann's earlier diplomatic assignments included Somalia, Uzbekistan, Kyrgyzstan, Grenada, and Nicaragua. Prior to this diplomatic service, Ann spent twenty-nine years in the U.S. Army/Army Reserves and participated in civil reconstruction projects after military operations in Grenada, Panama, and Somalia, retiring with the rank of colonel.

Ann Wright had dedicated her life to protecting and defending the national interest of the United States. Such loyalty had not always been easy; during her years as a civil servant, she had privately objected to specific policies of various administrations. In those cases, she had been able to set aside her ethical disagreements with U.S. policies and publicly support her country. The Bush administration's preventive war in Iraq, however, crossed basic ethical boundaries for Ann. To protect her honor and moral integrity, she felt that she could no longer stay in the government. She had to resign.

To discuss this difficult journey with Ann, I caught up with her in Crawford, Texas, during the summer of 2005, where she had joined with Cindy Sheehan to create "Camp Casey"[13] to protest the U.S. war in Iraq. In many respects, Ann Wright was the "Mayor of Camp Casey" in August 2005. She applied her remarkable organizational and diplomatic skills to keeping the demonstration focused, structured, and effective. Her military and diplomatic expertise meant that she could establish a field operation for peace that involved (while I was there) some eighty cars, forty tents, and some three to four hundred people. These individuals arrived in Crawford from all over the country to stand with Cindy Sheehan and proclaim that the Iraq war was not a noble cause.

In Sierra Leone, Ann had managed the evacuation of the U.S. Embassy personnel and other Americans when a coup d'etat took place in 1997. As the acting ambassador, she had to suddenly mobilize resources to get people out of harm's way. The evacuation took three days and ended up being the largest evacuation since the mass departure from Saigon. The rebels were out of control, with looting, raping, and pillaging occurring. There was no way to protect people. Ann got nine hundred people out the first day, three hundred the second, and more than thirteen hundred on the third and last day. For this effort, Ann was awarded the State Department's Award for Heroism.

The leadership abilities that allowed her to save lives in Sierra Leone were on display in Crawford. She was indispensable to the operation of Camp Casey and earned the respect not only of the protestors but of the Texas police as well.

Wright was clearly able to use her resignation to reassert her moral autonomy and regain her political courage. She is now a prominent figure in the antiwar movement. In addition to her work at Camp Casey, she has participated in the "Bring Them Home Now" bus tour. She testified at an Article 32 hearing on behalf of Lt. Ehren Watada, who, on June 22, 2006, refused to deploy to Iraq, asserting that the war violated the U.S. Constitution and international law.

In 2007, Wright was awarded the first annual Truthout Freedom and Democracy Award. The Truthout citation in part reads:

> Ann Wright has shown immense bravery and resolve in her quest for peace and her efforts to restore the reputation of the United States around the world. She has worked continuously to resist the war in Iraq. She has fought

against the destruction of constitutionally guaranteed human rights under the Bush Administration and has been a steadfast supporter of other activists. For her energy and commitment to peace, justice, and strengthening democratic principles, Ann Wright has earned the first annual Truthout Freedom and Democracy award.[14]

Before leaving Crawford, I asked Ann about other Foreign Service officers who had similar misgivings about the war in Iraq but didn't resign. I wondered how they were doing. Were these individuals at peace with themselves and able to protect their honor and assert their moral autonomy within the administration?

Ann said that she had received countless messages from colleagues agreeing with her critique of U.S. foreign policy. Yet most of these critics said that they would stay in their jobs and try to moderate these policies by working from within the government. Ann's response to this argument revealed the personal toll this takes on an individual's mental and physical health:

> It just doesn't work in this administration. I know there are some who are trying hard, but this administration will not broach any dissent. They know what they are going to do. And I feel really badly for these people. I don't know how they sleep at night. I was having so much trouble dealing with this moral dilemma while serving the country. It created such stress for me that I became a very unhealthy person, including symptoms of a heart attack. I had chest pains, pains in my arms, and so on. The medical officer said that "we can't mess around with this," and I was medically evacuated to Singapore (from Mongolia).

Fortunately, Ann's health problems were treatable.

But if Ann Wright had not resigned, the stress and pressure of defending a policy she found to be profoundly immoral would have continued to damage her health and her soul. What is remarkable is that her resignation has allowed her to flourish and grow and be at peace with herself in such a profound (and Buddhist) way. There is clearly a lesson here for all of us. The personal costs of sacrificing one's moral integrity can indeed be devastating.

REJECTING THE HUMANITARIAN ARGUMENT FOR WAR

Brown, Kiesling, and Wright reject the "humanitarian intervention" rationale for the Iraq war. As already noted, supporters of the invasion often justify the war with an "ends justify the means" consequentialist argument. In this perspective, the violence and horror of the war are the unfortunate price that must be paid to end a brutal dictatorship and give the Iraqis the chance to build a free society. Those who hold this position understand the terrible suffering caused by this war, including the deaths of potentially hundreds of thousands of innocent civilians and the creation of millions of refugees. Their argument, however, is that the long-term freedom of twenty-five million Iraqis eliminates the perceived greater harm being done by Saddam and, thus, the war can be viewed as a humanitarian intervention.

Had the United States intervened at one of the times when Saddam was actively killing massive numbers of his own population, Kiesling would most likely have supported the military intervention. For Kiesling, "the idea of saving life is central. If you can argue that you're keeping alive more people than you are killing, then it's worth it." He continues:

> When the world sees that innocent people are dying, the moral imperative to intervene to save them is real enough to justify some fairly brutal measures from the international community or from us. One of the key problems with Iraq was that Saddam wasn't behaving particularly badly at this point [2003] and there were a lot of times when U.S. intervention would have been far more justifiable than it was now.

Wright observes that none of Saddam's earlier horrific acts against his own citizens had triggered any U.S. intervention. She notes, for example, that the massacre of the Kurds happened before the first Gulf War. In contrast, by 2002–2003, "Certainly there was a lot of political repression/torture going on, but that is not a reason to invade a country; you approach/pressure them on the diplomatic front. You try to use economic sanctions to get them to stop. But to invade, occupy, and destroy a country is an illegal act of aggression."

For Brown,

> the bottom line is he [Saddam] wasn't a threat that required the military actions we undertook. If we wanted to help the people of Iraq, I think it would have been much easier if we just let them handle Saddam Hussein themselves. I think we should have just let time run its course on Mr. Saddam Hussein. Nobody is eternal, and eventually he would have been out and we wouldn't be occupying the country. We would be much more popular without being there. You don't go and free people or prevent their suffering by invading and occupying their country, even if you don't like their ruler or if you happen to think their ruler is a monster.

Kiesling points to an even bigger problem with the United States raising a humanitarian argument for the Iraq invasion. The United States itself is implicated in many of the worst actions of Saddam Hussein:

First of all, we [the United States] made no real effort to stop the Iran/Iraq war, which was one of the most murderous wars in human history. In fact, we propped up Iraq to make sure it wouldn't be defeated, but not with the aim of reducing the bloodshed, simply making sure the bloodshed was equal on both sides. Then the Kurdish and Shiite uprisings: we had directly or indirectly encouraged them, or at least the CIA, when it was using Kurds and Shiites for narrow tactical purposes in the Gulf War, misled them that the United States would intervene on their behalf. That tactical use of the local population led to tens or hundreds of thousands of deaths. We committed an immoral act by using the civilian population or quasi-civilian population as a military tool and then abandoning them.

The most notorious example of the United States "propping up Iraq" took place in the 1980s, when America continued to support and protect Saddam Hussein even after he gassed his own people. In 1982, after Iran gained an upper hand in the war with Iraq, the United States accelerated a covert operation to arm and aid Saddam. NSDD (National Security Decision Directive) 114 of November 26, 1983, declared that the United States would do "whatever was necessary and legal" to prevent Iraq from losing the war. The Reagan administration clandestinely supplied Saddam with satellite intelligence on Iran's deployments and, discarding legal scruples, channeled $5.5 billion in fraudulent loans to help Iraq buy arms. According to Chalmers Johnson, weapons were sent directly to Saddam via CIA fronts in Chile and Saudi Arabia. Johnson reports that "between 1986 and 1989, some seventy-three transactions took place that included bacterial cultures to make weapons-grade anthrax, advanced computers, and equipment to repair jet engines and rockets."[15]

To convince Saddam of U.S. support in his war with Iran, the Reagan administration in 1983 (and again in 1984) dispatched the president's special envoy, Donald Rumsfeld, to Baghdad, bearing a gift for Saddam from Reagan: a pair of golden spurs. Despite U.S. knowledge that Iraq had introduced chemical weapons into the war in 1983, Rumsfeld barely mentioned WMD to Saddam and instead focused on normalizing relations and limiting Iran's regional influence. The clear message from Rumsfeld to Saddam was that the United States would close its eyes to Iraq's chemical weapons use.[16] In fact, in November 1984, the United States restored full diplomatic relations with Saddam and stepped up sales of munitions and helicopters, subsequently used in gas attacks. With this green light, Saddam proceeded to plan Operation Anfal, a genocidal campaign against the Kurds that occurred between 1986 and 1989. During this campaign, on March 16, 1988, the Iraqi air force dropped mustard and nerve gas bombs on Halabja, a Kurdish town of about 70,000 people located on Iraq's northeast frontier with Iran. In the name of fighting Kurdish separatists, Saddam committed mass murder. The lethal vapors pursued victims into their cellars and along the roads as they fled in panic. As national security adviser to President Reagan from 1987 to 1989, Colin Powell played a key role in preventing an early, strong, and unequivocal international condemnation of Iraq for this use of chemical weapons. Instead, U.S. diplomats moved quickly to protect Saddam Hussein and promote the lie that the Halabjans had died from Iranian chemical weapons. The United States made sure that the UN Security Council resolution contained no specific condemnation of Iraq but, rather, urged both sides to refrain from the use of chemical weapons. Furthermore, between 1983 and 1988, the United States supplied Iraq with more than $500 million per year in credits so it could purchase American farm products. The United States did not even complain when Iraq acquired between 2,000 and 4,000 tons of deadly chemical agents and used them approximately 195 times against Iranians. According to Joost Hiltermann, these actions signaled to Iraq that the regime could continue, and even escalate, chemical weapons use during the Anfal campaign, leading to the deaths of 200,000 Kurds. Samantha Power notes, "At no point during the eighteen-month Iraqi campaign of destruction [against the Kurds] did Reagan administration officials condemn it, and they did all they could to kill the Senate sanctions package [designed to punish Saddam]." Hiltermann writes, "[T]he Reagan administration's wartime collusion with Iraq and its virtual silence over Halabja amounted to a green light that culminated in genocide in Iraqi Kurdistan."[17]

George W. Bush would later cynically deploy Halabja as a justification for the 2003 war against Iraq when he accused Saddam Hussein of being a man who had gassed his own people. As secretary of state, Colin Powell on September 15, 2003, visited Halabja to inaugurate a new museum to commemorate the 5,000 victims. Powell spoke movingly of the "choking mothers [who] died holding their choking babies to their chests" and the "suffering of those who were poisoned but nevertheless lived."[18] After the ceremony, Powell told the press corps, "If you want evidence of the existence and use of weapons of mass destruction, come here now to Halabja, look today and see it."[19] Yet the Kurds and the world also know of the critical role that the United States played to encourage, support, and protect the tyrant during his acts of genocide. To those in the global human rights community who had fought for years to expose Hussein's crimes over the objections of the United States, the brazen insincerity of Bush and Powell using the dead Halabjans as a justification for war was breathtaking in its deceit.

According to Kiesling, this U.S. complicity with the bloody track record of Saddam Hussein led many officials from the first Bush administration, and also from the Clinton administration, to labor "under a substantial moral burden precisely because they recognized that U.S. actions had caused a lot of innocent Iraqis, especially Kurds and Shiites, to die." As a result, Kiesling believes "that there was a substantial group of people, especially in the CIA (because the CIA was most implicated in this) who felt this moral burden. These CIA case officers who worked with the Iraqis in 1990 and 1991 had made personal commitments to Iraqis—you work with us and we will take care of you—commitments that were then violated not by themselves personally, but by their government." According to Kiesling, the desire to expiate that moral failing played a significant role in the 2003 U.S. intervention in Iraq.

Since there was no humanitarian emergency in Iraq and the country posed no imminent threat to the security of its neighbors or the United States, these three diplomats could not support this war. According to Wright, since the end of the first Gulf War in 1992,

> the Iraqis had not committed any acts of aggression against anyone, although the Clinton administration had said that there was an attempt on George Bush Sr.'s life—and they attributed it to somebody—but was it Saddam, al-Qaeda, who was it? The fact that we had had two no-fly zones over that country for over twelve years, that we were able to keep an eye on anything that we wanted to at any time. And now we know through the Downing Street memo that the chief of staff of the air force, in their summation, proudly gave the numbers of air sorties over Iraq over ten years (reportedly over four hundred thousand). Maybe not all of them dropped bombs, but a hell of a lot of them did, or had missiles taking out whatever they wanted. We controlled the skies, we controlled the ground, we were taking out any infrastructure that we wanted, we could take out whatever installation—communications, radar—whatever we wanted we were taking it out.

In Wright's analysis, international law is central to a global framework to maintain the peace. She argues that we must hold ourselves to the same legal norms to which we hold other states accountable:

> If you are going to adhere to, and say that other countries must adhere to, certain laws regarding the use of force and military operations, then you have to abide by them yourself. And we hold everyone else to follow these norms and not invade one another. If another country invades a sovereign state to take out another leader (or for territory), we are the first ones to scream bloody murder about that. The legality of what we do is very important. The purpose of what we do is very important. The purpose has to imply a legal rationale. Taking out a dictator because we don't like him is not legal. Otherwise, there are lots of them around here we don't like. Until the Bush administration came in, there was a pretty reasonable system for working this out, although you can look back in time and we have attempted to do similar unilateral things in the past. For example, Nicaragua in the 1980s,

Guatemala in the 1950s, Iran, and so on; there is an historical pattern. But one would hope that over the years we would be *evolving* more and adhering more to international law.

REJECTING THE WEAPONS OF MASS DESTRUCTION AND AL-QAEDA ARGUMENTS FOR WAR

The bottom line for Brown was when he read the statement in September 2002 by White House Chief of Staff Andrew Card that the reason the Bush administration hadn't spoken about the invasion in the summer, even though the decision had been made, was that you don't roll out a new product in the summer.[20] "To reduce a war to a 'product' was an outrage to me, and that's when I started really questioning whether I could stay in the government. And my break came just a couple months later." It is within this context of deceit that Brown places the issues of Iraqi WMD and supposed connections to al-Qaeda. Brown viewed all of this as part of the public relations campaign to sell the war to the American people: "The Bush administration obviously did not think it through. Many thought it was going to be a cake walk.[21] Furthermore, had they truly believed that there were weapons of mass destruction (WMD), it is hard to believe they would have sent American troops there: it would have been horrible domestic PR if WMD had killed our troops." Brown had been stationed in Eastern Europe and personally experienced the Russian occupation. This posting caused him to more deeply understand the difficulties confronting an occupying nation. He sees similarities between the Soviet brutality and naiveté about occupying Eastern Europe and the naïve U.S. occupation in Iraq: "As an outside power, you are a resented occupier."

The Bush administration's idealistic naiveté (or perhaps "mindless brutality"), according to Brown, led it to make the decision for going to war and then searched for the winning rationale to take to the public. In fact, Paul Wolfowitz seemed to confirm this in a widely read interview in *Vanity Fair*, when he admitted that the administration chose the WMD rationale for "bureaucratic reasons," as it was "the one reason everyone could agree on."[22] Brown claims that "the decision is made to take out Saddam (regime change). After that decision, officials then try to figure out the best-selling rationale. Somebody says, 'WMD.' 'Yes, yes, what about WMD?' 'Oh, yeah, we could all agree on that, yeah, yeah.' And then they try to gather the 'intelligence' to reinforce this 'reason' for going to war."

As a political counselor to the U.S. mission in Greece, Kiesling was privy to key intelligence reports on WMD in Iraq. He did not find these reports persuasive and begged for more intelligence to persuade the Greeks. It was politically critical to persuade our allies, so Kiesling felt certain that any evidence the United States had would be shared. It was clear at that point that the United States was losing the public relations battle with its allies:

> If we didn't give them the best material we had, we would be screwing our-selves. So when I finally saw what we had to share, I discovered that it was crap. It was mealy-mouthed stuff written in language that made clear we didn't have something specific to offer. I concluded from that that our case was lousy. I read everything I could on the subject. I went back to the old UN reports and realized that our quotations from them were selective and highly misleading. We were desperate for any evidence, and the fact that we couldn't come up with anything better led me to the conclusion that we were—I wouldn't say that we were lying, but making a leap of faith. That's certainly what Powell did; he made a leap of faith.

The weakness of the U.S. case against Iraq was exposed through the work of Hans Blix and the UN inspection teams. Every time the United States gave its "intelligence" on WMD in Iraq, the inspectors would in-vestigate these leads, search the suspected locations, and come back and say there was nothing there. Through these inspections, the international community learned how flimsy the "intelligence" really was. These revelations further confirmed to Kiesling that the U.S. information on WMD in Iraq wasn't any good. Yet instead of facing up to this reality, the United States engaged in a smear campaign against Blix, which infuriated Kiesling: "It was clear to me that Blix was a very careful, non-ideologi-cal diplomat attempting to keep an alliance together. He was part of the reality-based community. And it became our duty to hate him! It didn't seem to me that he was doing anything that justified the contempt we were pouring on him."

Brown, Kiesling, and Wright all dismiss the attempts by Bush, Cheney, and Powell to tie Saddam Hussein to al-Qaeda. As Kiesling succinctly states,

> The al-Qaeda/Iraq link was ludicrous on the face of it. Saddam was a secu-lar dictator whose greatest threat was the Islamic movement, since that was the only organized movement in the country that internally threatened him. Why would he cut a deal with al-Qaeda? To what end? His goal was regime survival. He probably wouldn't mind punishing the United States, but it's a luxury that he couldn't afford, and he did not get where he was by being a crazy man. Al-Qaeda thought he was corrupt and evil and wanted to de-stroy him. Anybody who knew anything about the Middle East thought our argument was ludicrous. And, since we were making it with no evidence, we were further discrediting ourselves.

Wright points to the many times that Cheney, Rice, and the others "lied, lied, lied" about how Iraq was somehow connected to 9/11. Unfortunately, this deceit was tragically believed by the majority of the American people in their initial support of the invasion of Iraq in 2003.

THE DECISION TO RESIGN

Neither Brown, Kiesling, nor Wright had direct hierarchical responsibility for the decision to invade Iraq or direct obligations in the Middle East to implement the war policies. Yet all three came to feel an ethical duty to speak out against these policies and to resign from the government. All of these individuals came to the conclusion that they could not compromise their honor and moral autonomy by publicly supporting U.S. war policies. The only moral choice open for each of them individually was resignation. Wright's decision came from a position of Buddhist morality, Kiesling's from that of a political realist, and Brown's from his grounding in public diplomacy.

As noted, Wright was serving as deputy chief of mission for the U.S. Embassy in Mongolia during the Iraq debates in 2002–2003. When the United States decided to go ahead and invade Iraq without the approval of the UN Security Council, Wright considered this action to be illegal and immoral and felt that she had to resign. Wright explains,

> I didn't want it on my karma. One of the interesting things that evolved down my path was the assignment to Mongolia. Mongolia was under the thumb of the Soviets for seventy years. Prior to that it was one of the strongest Buddhist countries in the world; it rivaled Tibet. The term "Dalai Lama" is actually a Mongolian term. And after the Soviets left in the late '80s, Buddhism is really coming back, a part of their daily lives. I had always been interested in Buddhism but had never served in a country where that was their religion (or attempted religion). Starting in November 2002, I started to get really concerned about what was going on in the world—talking to people in Washington—how can this be happening? What is going on?—and unfortunately got no responses (nobody wanted to raise criticisms in their state emails about policies in D.C.). Anyway, at the same time, I was e-mailing friends in D.C.; every morning I got up at 4 or 4:30 and did my readings in Buddhism. And it seemed like every day the readings were directly related to what was going on in Iraq.

The Dalai Lama had spoken out strongly against the war in Iraq and violence. He warned that if "you destroy your enemy, you destroy yourself." Nonviolent strategies for change draw from Gandhi's principles of Satyagraha, affirming the absolute link between means and ends, similar to a seed and a tree. For Wright, this implies that the means you use to combat terrorism will affect the ends you create:

> The means that we have used to go after Saddam have come back to haunt us. And you knew it was going to happen. Even though I wasn't a Middle East expert, having been involved in international relations for a period of time, I knew that for the United States to go into an oil-rich Arab country to invade and occupy—I mean, it was like putting a bulls eye on the head of every American in the country, because the Muslim/Arab world was not going to stand for it, and they would take us on—take on the strongest military in the world. It was predictable and predicted and it happened. The Bush administration turned a blind eye; they purposefully negated the voices of opposition. There were a lot of people who were telling them this was stupid. Even Colin Powell behind the scenes said this is crazy. Talk about bad karma . . . that guy is going to come back as an ant (nothing against ants). His resignation was the one thing that possibly could have derailed this.

Kiesling's decision to resign, on the other hand, was not based on a deeply held ethical tradition (like Buddhism) but, rather, on his belief that the Bush administration's actions were a danger to the national interest of the United States. His opposition to the war in Iraq was grounded in a traditional realist framework of international relations. He saw the Iraq policy as merely a symptom of a deeper problem in U.S. foreign policy:

> I was trying to argue that a model that worked for the United States, as a leader in the international community, was the utilization of the UN and international law. It worked effectively, it kept us secure, and it had prospects of making us even more secure. Furthermore, there were several other key points. First, the Iraq occupation wasn't going to work. And second, unilateralism in Iraq was a direct repudiation of the model on which the U.S. had been a useful and effective superpower, because we were trampling on the UN, we were violating international law, we were convincing our allies that our values and interests were antithetical to theirs. A lot of what had driven me over the edge was just how, in the process of pushing Iraq, we had directly insulted our allies, NATO, and the European Union. As a result, the pursuit of the Iraq war was detrimental to the system of international relations that had served us so well, and we were making the world a much more dangerous place.

Even though Clinton also violated international law with the NATO intervention in Kosovo, Kiesling did not feel that these actions threatened the framework of international diplomacy established after World War II:

> In the case of Kosovo, we could not use the UN because of the Russian veto. There was a grudging acceptance, especially in Europe, that Kosovo could

not be allowed to go the way of Bosnia. You could make the argument that genocide in Kosovo was possible and thus humanitarian intervention necessary. . . . Since it was done under the NATO flag, there was no harm to our European alliance. And because we were intervening on behalf of Muslims against Christians, there was no harm done to us in the Middle East. It was at least international and it was humanitarian, even if it was not done in the legal framework that I wanted.

Brown joined the Foreign Service in 1981 with a certain amount of trepidation. His fluency in several languages and experience living abroad (as the son of a Foreign Service officer whom he much admired) made him an ideal candidate to excel in the world of diplomacy. However, when asked to sign a statement saying that he would always support U.S. foreign policy, Brown flinched: "I was close to not signing. It was something of a moral compromise for me. I wanted to be a diplomat, but this was signing almost a loyalty oath. So I joined with a sense of moral compromise and uneasiness."

Brown was thus aware from the beginning of his government service of the potential conflicts that might come up between his individual moral values and the policies of the government. Brown stated,

I'm not a cheerleader. As I look back on it, having the sense of moral uneasiness about being part of the bureaucratic machine during the Reagan administration allowed me to keep a certain moral independence, because I never completely committed myself to the system. I always felt uneasy about being in the system. Now, having said all that, once you've kind of jumped in the pool, so to speak, you forget very quickly about the morality of what you're doing because there is so much to do abroad. You actually can do so much good that the initial uneasiness, which remains, nevertheless is not a daily concern.

Brown had wondered throughout his entire Foreign Service career about issues of honesty, integrity, and loyalty. Although he "always had doubts about some policies up to a certain point," he states that he always felt that he could make the U.S. case: "But the Iraq occupation was different to me; it is unacceptable. This is an aggressive war. And that's when I said I can't do it, I can't support it, no way."

As war preparations heated up in 2002–2003, Brown was stationed back in Washington and had the time to closely study the State Department materials on Iraq. He was appalled at what he read and immediately thought "what is going on here? this is madness." Brown's background in public diplomacy gave him a unique perspective on the actions of the Bush administration. For Brown, public diplomacy should be "gentle persuasion, or, at its best, intelligent persuasion." Brown concluded that not only was the Bush administration failing in this public diplomacy task, but it was also engaged in a "base propaganda campaign." Having been stationed in Eastern Europe under Soviet domination, Brown knew something about propaganda.

COLIN POWELL

All three of these ex-diplomats speak highly of Colin Powell's tenure as secretary of state. Powell gained a reputation in the State Department as a leader who, as Kiesling states, "was loyal to his troops." Kiesling argues that historically few "people in the leadership of the State Department have really fought for their staff." As a result, Powell won the respect and allegiance of many of the professionals in the U.S. Foreign Service. This also meant that it was difficult for these experts to criticize or attack Powell's decisions and actions.

As noted in chapter 4, Kiesling defends Powell's actions regarding Iraq. Kiesling claims:

> Powell did not knowingly lie. Powell made a classic mathematical mistake that if you add zero plus zero plus zero enough times you will get something. Each individual piece of evidence he looked at, if he looked at it in detail, evaporated. But there were so many pieces of evidence that somehow he assumed that somewhere along the line there were people who knew what they were talking about. He made a hard-nosed effort to look at the material, and threw out an enormous amount, and just used the stuff that seemed pretty solid. But I think because he had thrown out so much stuff, he felt he had done his intellectual duty of due diligence. All of us have faith that somebody somewhere actually knows what he or she is doing. It's a crucial human belief that the system works somewhere, even if everything in your own life reflects confusion and incompetence. Powell didn't have a lot of respect for the CIA, but he didn't think they would get it so far wrong. The CIA, I think, had lost track of how much of their evidence was out of date or spurious or wishful thinking. The bureaucratic process gives everyone such a small piece of the operation and such limited responsibility for what happens that a series of tiny self-serving misjudgments cascaded into a massively false picture. For example, you have a defector's report saying Saddam has a tunnel in a mountain full of nuclear weapons. As an analyst, you would conclude that the source of this report is a defector who can't be trusted. He must have fabricated the part about nuclear weapons because we know that Saddam hasn't gotten quite that far. But there is another guy who has a similar story, so you don't discard it completely. You keep the tunnels. But if he has tunnels, he must be hiding something. Only long afterwards do you learn that the tunnels were a fabrication as well. People thought they were being hardnosed analysts simply because they were reducing these spurious accounts to some common denominator that was plausible.

Kiesling continues,

> It would have been better for the world if he [Powell] had resigned. But I can
> understand intellectually and even emotionally why the choice he was faced
> with didn't seem so stark to him. There were a huge number of reasons for
> staying in the administration which he would seize on, and many of them
> were compelling. First of all, he felt he was the only real, competent adult in
> the administration, with the others (the ideologues) all a little bit crazy. His
> sense of personal responsibility meant that he saw himself as the guide on
> a ship being thrown about by an ideological hurricane, and he had to stay
> onboard. Second, Powell had a genuine belief that Saddam was a very evil
> person who probably had WMD. . . . He knew the evidence was not very
> good, but his conservative instincts were that no country that ever has such
> weapons ever really gives them up. Look how hard it has been for the U.S.
> to get rid of its own WMD. The military is indoctrinated with the idea that
> you must assume the worst about your enemy's capabilities.

Wright, on the other hand, is much less sympathetic to Powell's actions
of support for the war in Iraq. She sees Powell as "more loyal to the Bush
family than to the country," which caused him to lose his ethical bearings:

> The Bush family had appointed him through the Reagan administration
> (Bush Sr. was vice president); that is when he got his real start at the high
> level—national security adviser, head of NATO forces, chairman of the Joint
> Chiefs. For the entire time when Bush Sr. was president, Powell was either
> chairman of the Joint Chiefs or in senior-most positions in the U.S. military.
> Another reason he should have resigned was because he was telling Rums-
> feld and crew, "You're crazy as a loon if you think your operational plans are
> going to succeed because you've shortchanged yourself by several hundred
> thousand people" (just as Army Chief of Staff Eric Shinseki publicly stated in
> Congress and then got shit for it[23]), and then Secretary of the Army White got
> fired for speaking up.[24] Colin Powell, behind the scenes, was telling them the
> same thing. But it was his own doctrine (the Powell Doctrine of overwhelm-
> ing force) that he refused to stand up for (and it fell off the table). If you think
> about the number of forces it took, that he required to go into Kuwait, to get
> Saddam's troops out . . . small geographical area compared to Iraq . . . yet,
> we had more than 500,000 troops. You have Iraq and we put in at the peak
> maybe 300,000, but it's been more [consistently] around 220,000 [or less].
> The result was that there were enough troops to succeed in the invasion but
> not the occupation. Knowing the volatility of the region and the probability
> of foreign fighters coming in . . . we knew what was going to happen. And
> then the lack of planning for post-conflict (which was my specialty), going
> in with civil affairs units that were to redo things—for example, first make
> sure not to bomb critical infrastructure because you know that it will be your
> responsibility as an occupying power to get things running. We created post-

conflict plans back in the early '80s with the rapid development forces. We had on the shelf plans for invasion of Iraq. These plans are still there. The number of U.S. military we planned on for Iraq was around 500,000 . . . So Powell should have stood up and publicly said that these operation plans suck and that if you're going to do it, do it right. But, instead, there was no planning for post-invasion Iraq. There was no plan to protect the museums, ammo sites, WMD (nuclear) facilities, nothing. And, of course, a lot of that stuff consequently went missing.

Wright continues,

At the time it was unbelievable. As a military person watching these things happen, I was incensed. I was incensed about the looting of the national museum—ransacking of the museum—that was our responsibility. In our plans from the 1980s, you take the UNESCO list of cultural properties of every nation, plot them on the map—those are circled big time and you don't bomb them and you protect them.

Brown agrees with Wright and argues forcefully that Powell should have resigned. "If he had resigned, we might not have had this war. He didn't resign because he's a soldier. Yes, sir. He's loyal to the Chief." Brown believes that Powell's loyalty led him to not ask the hard, important questions about the superficial analysis and data circulating on Iraq. Unfortunately, he was unable (or unwilling) to bring reasonableness to the Bush foreign policy from the inside. Therefore,

the situation was such that he could only have made a difference by going outside his circle and raising hell outside. He needed to say—look, these guys in the administration (and their neocon propagandists) are crazy; they're getting us into a stupid war which will cost us billions; innocent civilians will die; we will be hated throughout the world. If he felt this way, then he should have said, the hell with you, Mr. Commander in Chief. But his loyalties as a soldier prevented him from doing this. He's a very good briefer. But he is not good at asking and struggling with the tough questions.

While Kiesling does not agree with Brown or Wright that Powell should have resigned to protest the Iraq war, he does raise a different incident when he thought Powell's position was so compromised he should have walked out:

I did, however, think that he should have resigned in the run-up to the 2004 elections, when Sharon made his visit and got the president of the United States to symbolically appear to authorize the permanent acquisition of the West Bank. At that point, I would have made the argument to Colin Powell that there was no American foreign policy anymore. Decisions are purely a matter of U.S. domestic electoral politics. Therefore, we do not need a good foreign policy secretary of state. If he stayed on, there is nothing useful he can do in policy terms, whereas if he were to resign before the election, he could have potentially made a bad foreign policy so politically expensive that it wouldn't be repeated.

THE ISSUE OF LOYALTY

As noted in chapter 2, in the entire history of the United States, only two secretaries of state have resigned over ethical issues. The United States does not have a tradition of either career civil servants or political appointees breaking their loyalty to their president. In fact, in the hierarchy of normative principles at work in the U.S. government, loyalty to the commander in chief stands above all other norms, including individual moral autonomy. Many believe that this tradition of absolute loyalty to the president does not serve America well and is detrimental to democracy and the American system of government. Weisband and Franck, for example, argue that loyalty is not just a problem in the government but also throughout American society. Americans are brought up to be loyal to their communities, to their nation, to their employers (universities, law firms, corporations, and so on). Loyalty then takes priority over other ethical issues and moral considerations. In terms of the government, it means that the people in the State Department and the White House are not loyal to the people but, rather, to the president. This elevation of loyalty has been identified as a weakness of democracy because the American people don't hear dissent or alternative viewpoints. There is not a full public debate of the issues. The people only hear the party line or whatever comes out of the White House, and that stifles the free and open discussion critical to a functioning democracy.[25]

Wright disagrees with this analysis. She believes that loyalty "is not a problem of democracy, because there are plenty of 'leakers' all the time. Throughout the history of our country, individuals who have been in government service, when they feel that the current administration is jeopardizing the nation, they've taken steps to alert the public about what is going on."

Wright believes, however, that the political appointees, who are selected because they are "loyal," are the least accountable to the American people. This places an additional moral duty on the career civil servants to challenge troublesome policies, which is often very difficult:

> Very seldom do you have an administration brave enough to put someone in who would hold them accountable. You don't have Republicans appointing Democrats (or vice versa). So it really does rest on the apolitical career bureaucrats to try to balance out the loyalists of every administration. In ev-

ery administration there are programs that I may personally have disagreed with. But you were hired to implement the policies of whomever the American people elect. So there may be policies that you don't like, but you may have to hold your nose and go ahead and do it. Or, what most often happens, people will not work on programs that they disagree with. They ask for a transfer or a change so that they don't have to work on it. So you find some niche where you can be productive and morally justify your continuation in the government, in particular, if you have kids and family obligations and so on. It is really hard to give up your whole career.

Kiesling notes that cabinet officers in the United States are appointed by the president and serve at the pleasure of the president:

This creates a very powerful instinct of loyalty which is even stronger among conservatives. I believe that one of the key elements of conservative calculation is loyalty to the president as the highest virtue. I think that is a fatal flaw of conservatism because there are values more important than loyalty. In this administration we have seen repeatedly that someone who is loyal but incompetent will not be punished. In fact, I think we have a president who basically cannot judge people's competence or incompetence but can judge their loyalty. Powell was a product of this environment. For me, the essence of the liberal tradition is that you are an autonomous moral agent using your intellect to understand the world and to make personal moral decisions, and loyalty is a subsidiary part of that process. Obviously, your loyalty is an instrumental virtue in the sense that if you are not perceived as loyal, you will not be allowed into a position where you can do good things.

Brown argues that the problem runs deeper than simply blind loyalty. He believes that an additional corrosive impact of working in a large bureaucracy is the stifling of imagination:

When you're in the system (government, corporation, etc.) you lose the capacity of imagining a world beyond the system. In the State Department, that certainly is true. A lot of Foreign Service officers become total State Department creatures. What happens is they are there safely for ten years and they can't quit anymore or leave without financial disruptions, and what they really worry about now is getting promoted . . . get[ting] to the top of the pyramid . . . and they know that the way essentially to get promoted is loyalty—not brilliance, not being idiosyncratic or iconoclastic. Rather, you are promoted by becoming "a company man." You're reliable and you're loyal and bottom line is you'll do what you're told. The bottom line in the State Department is loyalty. . . . When push comes to shove, you get an instruction and you do it. In a sense it is just like the military. I have no illusions about that. . . . You become a creature of the organization. There are some remarkable people in the Foreign Service, brilliant people, and I don't want to demean them. However, one must stay on one's toes and not become a total creature of the organization, because then you are basically useless. You might as well be a fax machine or an e-mail system. People in the USIA [United States Information Agency] were more individualistic, a little crazier. But even in the USIA there was this almost blind allegiance to the organization.

PERSONAL TOLL/INDIVIDUAL SACRIFICE

As U.S. Foreign Service officers, Brown, Kiesling, and Wright were expected to publicly defend the Bush administration's rush to war in Iraq. As we have seen, this expectation ultimately led each of these diplomats to resign. Yet this path to resignation was not smooth sailing. It is difficult and scary to "burn bridges" and jeopardize one's financial security. Some viewed these acts of resignation during a time of war as close to treasonous. However, in the end, all three of these individuals felt liberated and at peace with their decisions to resign and publicly oppose U.S. foreign policy in Iraq.

For Kiesling, the war in Iraq basically drove him into a depression:

It became clear that we were going to invade Iraq in any case. U.S. diplomacy didn't matter. There was nothing that we could tell our allies that would convince them. There was nothing our allies could tell us that Washington was willing to hear. I concluded that this was the model of this administration, that it had no need for diplomacy. Everything was being done in Washington and by Washington for Washington, for domestic political and bureaucratic reasons, so the profession of diplomacy had become meaningless. My response to that was not anger, but depression. I was going through the motions, feeling miserable. My immune system collapsed and I got bronchitis.

With his resignation, Kiesling felt liberated and was able to pull out of this depression:

I think it was the first moment of moral clarity that I have ever had in my life. Once I made the decision to resign, personal stuff did not matter anymore. I was back doing what I was supposed to be doing, taking personal responsibility for achieving something good in the world. So, yeah, a really liberating moment, and after I made the decision I started operating on a much higher level.

Yet this road to resignation was not without its risks. Kiesling, in particular, suffered significant financial hardships as a result of his decision, and future monetary stability remains unclear:

Every once in a while, I wake up in the middle of the night thinking that I'm going to be starving in the street at some point, which probably won't happen, but I am living off capital right now and I have to find a job very quickly. I can't count on the book [*Diplomacy Lessons*] making me rich. I am hoping it will at least pay my alimony for a year. Being cut off from an all-embracing society (the State Department) can be costly. I lost a couple of friends, but only one close friend, and that friendship had been eroding in any case.

After President Bush's press conference on March 6, 2003, Brown could not honestly see himself "going to the office with a newspaper under my arm as if everything was going fine and dandy. I just couldn't see myself doing that. I just had a sense that there was something about the Iraq policy that just was totally wrong. I don't think my actions were particularly brave. I simply could not defend the policy and had to get out."

Brown reports that he received support via e-mail from a considerable number of his colleagues in the State Department for taking this dramatic action. Yet no others followed his lead. After these three quit, there were no further resignations over Iraq:

I was amazed by the number of e-mails I received from Foreign Service people (and the general public) supporting my decision to leave the Foreign Service. Given this high degree of opposition to the war in the State Department, I was frankly surprised that more professionals didn't quit. I guess a lot of these people have debts, mortgages, family responsibilities, and so on. The reality is that if you're a smart guy quitting from the State Department and you're thirty or thirty-five, you can get another job and get paid a lot more. Yet there is a fear of the unknown. The economy is not doing that well, and the future is unknown. But frankly, given the level of dissatisfaction in the department, I'm surprised there weren't more people who said, "I quit."

As with Kiesling, Brown also feels liberated by his decision. "I'm glad I quit because the one other thing that is also worthy of note is self-censorship. I realized after I left the Foreign Service that I could write whatever I wanted. It's a wonderful feeling that I'm free at last after more than twenty years of self-censorship. That's the price you pay of being in an organization."

As already noted above, the stress of defending the Bush administration's policies had led to severe physical health problems for Ann Wright. Fortunately, with her resignation, Ann's physical health improved and she was free to act from her moral, Buddhist framework. She regained her voice and her moral integrity and felt whole again.

Yet Wright does not criticize others who chose to remain in their jobs in the State Department. She believes there is no "one path" correct for all individuals. She notes that in her past

there were many other times that people used the dissent channel over ethical issues and resigned, and I didn't. So I'm not about to say that the path that I took is the path that others ought to take, because there are variations in everybody's path. For me, I think this is the way that federal bureaucrats have to lead their lives; we rationalize how you can be effective and still work for an administration when you have a real beef with the policy. Sometimes you can get right in the middle of the discussion and try to change the policy from within (battle the system).

Kiesling agrees and notes, "You have to have people willing to resign to keep the system honest, but you also need people in the system to benefit from that process. Resignation is a strategy that makes sense if some people do it, but not very many. The more of us who resign, the less room there is for others to do so." Kiesling believes that the nature of the State Department limits the possibility of effective mass resignations. He found himself, for example, unable to share his misgivings about the war with very many colleagues:

We're trapped in a sense by our version of morality and also by a certain loyalty. We retreated into ourselves, into personal misery. I did not feel that I could talk about politics with my junior officers because it was putting them in a professional quandary (since I was their superior). Something about professional ethics told me it was wrong for me to share my dissents with them. It was alright to share dissent with colleagues of my own level that I trusted, my peers, but not with my subordinates.

After Kiesling resigned, a senior diplomat approached him for advice. This Foreign Service officer, fed up with the war and opposed to the unilateral approach of U.S. foreign policy, was considering resigning. Kiesling advised him not to resign. To Kiesling, this individual was an effective, conscientious diplomat in a position where he was senior enough to work at a policy level. Kiesling felt that such people should not leave the government: "We need people on the inside." In fact, one of the saddest things for Kiesling is watching so many of the people he has respected for years retiring from government early. They were also fed up.

ETHICS AND FOREIGN POLICY

Bush administration officials often frame U.S. foreign policy with a verbal commitment to the norms of freedom and democracy. But to many in other countries, these noble words ring hollow and are seen as merely rhetorical justifications for power politics and unilateral action. These critics see empire-building, not democracy, as the main normative framework undergirding U.S. foreign policy. The views, interests, and priorities of people in countries outside the borders of the United States don't seem to be factored into a definition of how the United States defines its "national interest."

However, there is a variety of new security threats to America that unite the "national interest" with the "human interest" of everyone. Unfortunately, the U.S. government has not made this new agenda a priority for action. Concerning global warming, for example, some believe that fifty years from now people are going to look back at us and say, "What were they thinking? They destroyed the planet!" From a moral point of view, the United States and the other great powers, working through the UN, should be acting forcefully on environmental preservation. The lack of progress not only on these environmental concerns, but also on other central critical issues confronting all nations, including population stabilization, poverty alleviation, and the control of infectious diseases, can lead one to despair. It is as if we are living in a delusion. Neither the president nor Congress has risen to the challenge and pushed the government to adopt the many workable policy proposals experts have developed to address this tough agenda. As a result, these enormous long-term security threats to our country and the world are ignored.[26]

Brown sees this dangerous pattern occurring in the government due to parochialism:

> We simply refuse to accept the fact that we are only a small part of humanity. We are living in this American biosphere. It always strikes me when I come back to this wonderful country, after having lived abroad for many years, how completely self-immersed we are. We are in a bubble. The Bush regime has made this bubble even thicker. Issues outside the U.S. are not what concern Americans. There may be some talk about global warming; there may be some about the "war on terrorism." Yet the American people don't get up in the morning and worry about the war on terror, global poverty and income distribution, Africa, genocide, and so on. Most people here don't consider these things. There is something peculiarly American about isolation despite our absolutely remarkable access to information. We have become enveloped by a very distinctive American lifestyle.

Kiesling believes that a thriving foreign policy will take account of ordinary people's basic moral instincts:

> Successful foreign policy is based on understanding the moral instincts of foreigners, which are actually almost identical to our own, except refracted through a different prism of nationalism. We should only attempt those things that can be put in moral terms that are intelligible to the foreigners whom we are working with or on. What America needs to accomplish in the world, looked at with a long-term perspective, doesn't conflict with the fundamental interests or instincts of foreigners. When our policy is sensible, we can find a way to express it in morally intelligible terms. We often don't

bother, but it's possible to do it. A policy that we cannot express in [morally] intelligible terms is one that we should not do at all.

Kiesling continues:

The contradiction between morality and realism in foreign policy is spurious. If it's immoral, it's unrealistic. The real contradiction in foreign policy is between realism and fantasy. Too often our foreign policy is an incidental afterthought of domestic bureaucratic competition in the United States and everywhere. Domestic politics rewards short-term opportunistic fantasies about the world and can blind us to the fact that what we think of as moral arguments generally have no effective impact on foreigners. Bush, for example, thinks that when he talks about liberty and democracy, he is communicating successfully with foreigners who share those aspirations. And indeed they do share those aspirations, but he does not have standing to talk about those issues given the preconceptions with which foreigners view our policy. It is possible to talk persuasively to foreigners about those issues but in very different terms and in a very different setting, using relationships of trust and confidence built up over time through diplomacy. But the good news is that doing the moral thing *is* doing the correct thing in foreign policy. The bad news is that very, very few of us can stand back and remove the nationalist filters that help us convince ourselves that in pursuing short-term and selfish interests we are serving a higher good. It is a permanent intellectual battle. You need to broaden the dialogue and make sure that you are regularly correcting your view of the world through regular contact with foreigners and integrating their moral perspective into your own.

When he was stationed in Russia, Brown gave lectures on "Re-inventing Oneself in America." He would tell the Russian audience that in America one didn't have to have the same job or continue in the same profession all his or her life. "In fact, you don't have to be the same person all your life. Think of Benjamin Franklin, the Great Gatsby, and yes, Madonna. Think of Las Vegas, the icon of American reinvention, now becoming, among all its many incarnations, a center of high culture." This American ability to recover, reinvent, and move forward gives Brown hope for the future. "[T]his constant reinvention . . . means we can remake ourselves and move on."

6

⌒∞⌒

The Ethical Soldier
Ehren Watada and Aidan Delgado

The oath of enlistment for U.S. soldiers states:

> I do solemnly swear (or affirm) that I will support and defend the Constitution of the United States against all enemies, foreign and domestic; that I will bear true faith and allegiance to the same; and that I will obey the orders of the President of the United States and orders of the officers appointed over me, according to regulations and the Uniform Code of Military Justice. So help me God.[1]

Army officers are required to take a more detailed oath of commissioning, which states:

> I [full name], having been appointed an officer in the Army of the United States, as indicated above in the grade of [rank] do solemnly swear (or affirm) that I will support and defend the Constitution of the United States against all enemies, foreign and domestic, that I will bear true faith and allegiance to the same; that I take this obligation freely, without any mental reservation or purpose of evasion; and that I will well and faithfully discharge the duties of the office upon which I am about to enter; So help me God.[2]

An individual's status changes from civilian to soldier when he or she takes the enlistment or commissioning oath. The soldier now has a legal and moral obligation to defend the U.S. Constitution and the rules of the U.S. military. The soldier is now individually accountable to the military profession and the American people.

The enlistment and commissioning oaths clearly require all soldiers to accept both the duty to obey orders and the duty to obey the Constitution.

But what if a legal order violates the Constitution and is immoral? In this "catch-22" situation, soldiers must determine for themselves if the orders are just. If an order or law is immoral or illegal, it is not to be followed. An order to murder innocent civilians, for example, should not be followed. Similarly, a law authorizing torture, genocide, or rape should also not be followed.

As previously discussed in chapter 2, to be true to their oath, soldiers have an individual moral responsibility to determine if orders are moral and legal. They are not to simply "follow orders." From this perspective, soldiers who believed that the rushed and inadequate planning for the Iraq occupation was immoral because it would lead to senseless deaths of American soldiers had a duty to speak up. If their voices were silenced, they should have then resigned and publicly voiced their concerns. Officers, in particular, who are able to identify the weaknesses in war preparations have a duty to oppose such dangerous policies.

U.S. Army 1st Lt. Ehren Watada and U.S. Army Reservist Aidan Delgado struggled with these issues of a soldier's personal moral responsibility during a time of war. Both Watada and Delgado concluded that they could not fight in Iraq. Watada's decision was based on his determination that the war in Iraq was both illegal and immoral. Delgado's experiences in Iraq, particularly at the prison Abu Ghraib, pushed him in a pacifist direction and he eventually declared himself to be a conscientious objector.

My separate discussions with Watada and Delgado focused on what it meant to be an "ethical soldier." We explored the moral obligation to refuse illegal orders and the soldier's duty to oppose wars of aggression (*Jus ad bellum*) and uphold the laws of war (*Jus in bello*). As their views developed, both men experienced profound rejection from fellow soldiers and superiors. Each of them took great risks to speak out and act on their moral principles. After brief summaries of the individual journeys of Watada and Delgado, this chapter analyzes the reflections of these soldiers on individual moral autonomy in a time of war.

EHREN K. WATADA
U.S. ARMY FIRST LIEUTENANT
MILITARY SERVICE: 2003–

At 2:00 A.M. on June 22, 2006, U.S. Army 1st Lt. Ehren K. Watada[3] reported for duty in Fort Lewis, Washington. After refusing orders to move to the adjacent McChord Air Force Base to prepare to fly to Iraq, Lieutenant Watada became the first commissioned officer to publicly repudiate deployment to the war. Watada had come to believe that the war and continued occupation of Iraq were immoral and illegal and that under the doctrine of command responsibility his participation in the war would also be illegal.

Watada joined the U.S. Army in 2003 out of a desire, he stated, to "protect our country" and "help people." At the time he believed that the army stood for noble ideals. He attended the army's Officer Candidate School in Fort Benning, Georgia, and was commissioned as a second lieutenant of field artillery. Watada then served one year in South Korea before being reassigned in 2005 to Fort Lewis.

Soon after reporting to Fort Lewis, Watada learned that his unit was going to be deployed to Iraq. To prepare to be an effective officer, he began an intensive period of study on the history and culture of Iraq and spoke to veterans returning from the war front. He deepened his knowledge of international law and investigated the administration's justifications for the U.S. invasion and occupation of the country. Many revelations from this period of study shocked Watada. Most disturbing to him was the documentation of the many instances that the government intentionally misled, misdirected, and ultimately lied to the soldiers it sent into harm's way. It was as if someone had punched him in the stomach. Watada explained his emotional reaction:

> You join the military; you put on the uniform, and this is supposed to be a really noble and honorable profession. . . . You realize that you may be sacrificing your life. You are putting your life in the hands of these people and you say, "Use my life in the defense of our country, but please just don't lie to me. Allow me to trust you. Don't exploit me. Don't throw my life away." And to come to the realization that all of that has been for naught, I mean, that's mind blowing, to say the least. I just felt a deep sense of betrayal and disillusionment.

Watada's moral conscience could not allow him to serve as an officer in Iraq. By January 2006, he no longer believed in the legality or morality of the war and attempted to resign his commission. To Watada, the Iraq war violated fundamental American and international laws which had served our country so well since World War II. He concluded that since the UN Charter, the Geneva Convention, and the Nuremberg Principles all ban wars of aggression, the Iraq war was illegal under international law. Since the United States has ratified these treaties, the war is in violation of U.S. law as well. Watada also argued that the laws governing land warfare found in the Army Field Manual 27-10 were not being upheld by the U.S. military in Iraq, violating its own legal rules of conduct for occupying a country. He further determined that the war was based on misleading and false premises regarding weapons of mass destruction (WMD) and links between Saddam Hussein and al-Qaeda. Watada stated, "I am wholeheartedly opposed to the continued war in Iraq, the deception used to wage this war, and the lawlessness that has pervaded every aspect of our civilian leadership."[4]

Watada's conclusion that the war in Iraq is an illegal "war of aggression" left him with few options. He felt he had to resign. If he assumed command responsibility, he would become personally responsible and liable for legal challenges for violating international law. Yet the army denied his resignation request and made it clear that it believed he had a legal obligation to fulfill his eight-year commitment to the armed services. Serving in Iraq, however, was no longer an option for Watada. In fact, he believed that he had a right and a duty to refuse to follow illegal orders. Lieutenant Watada said,

> Although I have tried to resign out of protest, I am forced to participate in a war that is manifestly illegal. As the order to take part in an illegal act is ultimately unlawful as well, I must as an officer of honor and integrity refuse that order. It is my duty not to follow unlawful orders and not to participate in things I find morally reprehensible.[5]

Watada made it clear that he was not a conscientious objector. He was not opposed to all wars. In fact, he offered to serve in Afghanistan, which he saw as an "unambiguous war linked to the September 11th attacks." This was denied and instead the U.S. Army decided to prosecute Watada for violations of the Uniform Code of Military Justice (UCMJ).

The U.S. military is prosecuting Lieutenant Watada under the UCMJ for deliberately missing the order to deploy (Article 88) and, by making public antiwar statements, for conduct unbecoming an officer and a gentleman (Article 133). Attempts by Watada to present evidence and testimony supporting his belief that the war was illegal were not allowed in his court-martial proceedings. There was also no consideration given in these proceedings to his claim that speaking in public against the war was within his rights to free speech as an American citizen. International law professor Richard Falk points out that these penal charges present Lieutenant Watada, and all military personnel, with an ethical and moral dilemma. On the one hand, an aggressive war is defined as a "crime against peace" in the Army Field Manual 27-10 (Article 498), and members of the armed forces are "bound only to obey lawful orders" (Article 509(b), with reference to Article 92). On the other hand, a soldier who refuses to be deployed to fight in an illegal and aggressive war can be punished for disobedience. Lieutenant Watada is thus "deep in Catch-22 territory."[6]

Despite the initial court-martial hearing ending in a mistrial on February 7, 2007, the U.S. military is continuing its efforts to prosecute Watada. On October 6, 2007, a U.S. district court judge put Watada's court-martial on hold pending a decision regarding whether the second trial should proceed or be quashed as a violation of the officer's constitutional rights that protect against double jeopardy (being tried twice for the same crime). The army immediately announced its intent to file briefs in the U.S. district court to try to prevent the injunction from becoming permanent. With a successful prosecution, Watada could still be sentenced to two to six years in prison.[7]

AIDAN DELGADO
U.S. ARMY RESERVES
MILITARY SERVICE: 2001–2004

On September 11, 2001, Aidan Delgado,[8] a disenchanted college student, enlisted in the U.S. Army Reserves just as the planes hit the World Trade Center in New York. As he finished his enlistment paperwork, Delgado was unaware of the attacks on America. When he later saw a television broadcast of the events in New York City, District of Columbia, and Pennsylvania, he realized that he might get called to more serious action than one weekend a month of low-key service. Delgado felt

> a swirl of emotion: confusion, fear, excitement, adrenaline. We're under attack. We're under attack. America. The country is under attack and I'm in the army, sort of. This is the reason we have an army, and I joined *before* it happened. . . . I'm proud of myself. Everyone who told me not to join the army will see now; they'll see why what I did was right.

Nineteen-year-old Delgado was inducted one week later.[9]

At the same time that he joined the army, Delgado had also embarked on an exploration of Buddhism. While he was going through basic training and advanced training in the army, he got deeper and deeper into his study of Buddhism. After a year of reflection, Delgado became a vegetarian and began to define himself as a Buddhist. He found the essence of Buddhism to be to "do no evil, do as much good as possible, and purify your own mind."[10]

Delgado believes that both the philosophical and the practical components to Buddhism are essential. The philosophical truth "is essentially that all evil and suffering comes from a fundamental misunderstanding of what reality is. The world is centered on a misconception that I am a person separate from everything else. That self-conception poisons everything and renders all other negative actions possible, like greed and hatred." Flowing from this understanding, the practical component calls on individuals "to meditate to help weaken the centrality of 'self,' to be kind, to understand that others have the same problems, and to show compassion, all of which descends from the philosophical truth."

Delgado's military training soon came into conflict with his newfound Buddhist principles of compassion and nonviolence. Delgado views the Buddhist doctrine of nonviolence as taking many forms. He states, "When you practice nonviolence, you can't steal because stealing is a kind of violence; you can't lie because lying is a kind of intellectual violence against someone else; you can't abuse your sexuality, because that would be sexual violence against another being. Nonviolence is basically the central teaching [of Buddhism]. Compassion is nonviolence."

Delgado began a yearlong tour of Iraq in April 2003. As the only member of his unit who spoke Arabic, Delgado was able to interact with Iraqi civilians. During this time, Delgado came to see the warrior mentality of the U.S. Army as counter to Buddhist principles of compassion, love, peace, and respect. He came to openly question whether he could remain in the military and, specifically, whether he could continue to participate in the war in Iraq. While this internal struggle was going on, Delgado witnessed what he described as American racism, arrogance, and abuse of unarmed Iraqis. The conflict within him exploded:

> I feel intensely hypocritical, believing in compassion, meditation, and nonviolence while simultaneously carrying a machine gun and serving in an occupation force. The conflict seems irreconcilable. Every day that I stay in the military I feel more a traitor to my beliefs. The Army that I imagined, the mythological Army that captured my imagination as a boy, has proved illusory. I've come to see the Army in its worst form, a distortion of itself: violence, threats, dogma, and hatred. I see the way the soldiers bully each other for dominance and then watch as those who are bullied turn and dominate the Iraqis. I feel my friends and comrades pulling apart from me, diverging from the ideals I believe in. They have changed; something in them has gone black. I have changed, too; the man I am now and the boy I was in Sarasota have grown vastly apart. Between me and the other privates, those who hate "ragheads" and long to kill the enemy, there is an unfathomable gulf. Seeing the prisoners, seeing the Iraqi civilians, fills me with profound sadness and loss. I have no bloodlust in me. I do not wish to fight.[11]

Delgado decided to file for conscientious objector (CO) status and continued to serve in Iraq while the request was being processed. After he turned in his weapon, he was ostracized by his fellow soldiers and punished by his officers. Delgado's unit, the 320th Military Police Company, spent six months in the city of Nasiriyah and another six months helping to administer the notorious Abu Ghraib prison outside Baghdad.

After being honorably discharged as a CO, Delgado began to speak out and write about what he had witnessed in Iraq. He describes shocking and disgraceful cases of American soldiers' perpetrating abuse against Iraqi civilians and prisoners. Delgado explains,

It starts very subtly with people testing the boundaries. If they get away with a little thing, then they do a little bit more. First, it is using the term "hajji"[12] or "raghead" or "sand nigger"—testing the water to see if the command is going to respond. When there is no response, the soldier feels justified in shoving the Iraqis. Then I see guys in my unit pointing their rifles in people's faces, which I consider a huge breach, threatening innocent civilians for no reason. Then I see a lot of physical contact like punching and kicking. I saw a master sergeant striking children with a Humvee antenna and a marine kicking a kid in the chest. They did this and nothing happens. It passes without comment, so the violence escalates further. At Abu Ghraib there was even less oversight and even more motivation to hurt people. Then there were the instances of shooting prisoners, shooting them behind the legs and dragging them out. I want to emphasize that it was not like one moment they were totally pure and the next moment they were devils. It was a series of reinforcements. The violating soldiers didn't get any repercussions and so they pushed a little further; nothing happened and they kept going to see where the line was.

He says that prisoners were beaten to within an inch of their lives and some killed for throwing stones.

Many in the United States did not want to hear or believe these charges against American soldiers. After *New York Times* columnist Bob Herbert published an interview with him, Delgado received death threats and public denunciations. He was called a fabricator, a liar, and a traitor. Distressed by this violent reaction to his accurate reporting, Delgado called Herbert to seek his support and advice. Herbert responded by telling him, "Son, take it as a marker that you are doing good."

JUS AD BELLUM—THE JUSTICE OF WAR

As noted in chapter 2, U.S. soldiers are generally not held accountable for the decision to wage war in Iraq. Instead, the civilian leadership (Bush, Cheney, Powell, and the others) who made the decisions to use force are said to be morally and legally responsible for these acts. However, just as citizens in a democracy cannot claim "ignorance" and push off all responsibility for war to their leaders, soldiers also have a degree of moral responsibility to evaluate the decision to wage war in their name. Some argue further that, in addition, soldiers have a duty to put down their rifles and refuse to fight in a war of aggression.

Spanish theologian and philosopher Francisco de Vitoria's *On the Law of War*, written in the early sixteenth century, had a formative influence on the idea of a "just war" and the development of our modern conception of the legitimate use of force by sovereign states. In this work, Vitoria is clear:

> [I]f the war seems patently unjust to the subject, he must not fight, even if he is ordered to do so by the prince. This is obvious, since one may not lawfully kill an innocent man on any authority. . . . Therefore it is unlawful to kill him. In this case, the prince commits a sin in declaring the war. . . . So even soldiers . . . are not excused. Furthermore, one may not kill innocent members of the commonwealth at the prince's behest, and therefore one may not kill foreigners either.

Later, Vitoria argues that "ignorance" cannot be used as an excuse for following immoral orders to engage in aggressive war: "[T]here may nevertheless be arguments and proofs of the injustice of war so powerful, that even citizens and subjects of the lower class may not use ignorance as an excuse for serving as soldiers."[13]

In the seventeenth century, Dutch Protestant Hugo Grotius systematized the theory of the "just war" in a major work titled *On the Law of War and Peace*. Grotius's aim was to summarize the earlier tradition of the just war and provide a complete account of all relevant issues pertinent to war. In this work, Grotius agrees with Vitoria in outlining the duty of soldiers not to fight aggressive and unjust wars. Grotius writes, "If those under the command of another are ordered to take the field, as often occurs, they should altogether refrain from so doing if it is clear to them that the cause of the war is unjust."[14]

In the twentieth century, the decisions at Nuremberg after World War II to hold Nazi soldiers accountable for unjustifiable killing in a war of aggression further support the view of individual moral responsibility of those fighting a war. The *Principles of International Law Recognized in the Charter of the Nuremberg Tribunal and Judgment of the Tribunal* were adopted unanimously by the General Assembly of the United Nations. Principle I states, "Any person who commits an act which constitutes a crime under international law is responsible therefore and liable to punishment." Principle IV states, "The fact that a person acted pursuant to order of his Government or of a superior does not relieve him from responsibility under international law, provided a moral choice was in fact possible to him." And Principle VI (a) states, "Crimes against peace: (i) Planning, preparation, initiation or waging of a war of aggression or a war in violation of international treaties, agreements or assurances."[15]

Watada clarifies,

> People often say that the Nuremberg Principles only apply to high-ranking military or high-ranking civilian officers. This is wrong. Nuremberg applies to everyone in the military and in society. It deals with everybody—every-

one's individual moral responsibility. We all have a responsibility from the lowest-ranking private to the highest-ranking general, from the ordinary civilian to the CEO of a corporation and administration officials; everyone has an individual responsibility to not be part of a criminal act, whether it's international law or domestic law. And the Nuremberg Principles actually state that international law will supersede domestic law.[16]

Watada points to the power individual citizens and soldiers have to affect a country's foreign policy:

A nation can't invade another country unless all those soldiers who are going to be taking part in that invasion are with you. On the other hand, if all those soldiers in the army or the military, and the people who are paying the taxes to fund the military, say no, then the leader is really powerless and can't do anything. A leader then may want to invade but can't because the military won't follow the order and the people won't pay the taxes to fund the invasion. A leader is powerless without the support of the people. Leaders need the people to follow, and they get this obedience in various ways, including through fear, propaganda, and persuasion. You, therefore, can't just say that only those who are at the highest levels, those who are issuing the orders, are the only ones who are guilty. All of us have a moral responsibility to act during a time of war. For example, when the Nazis were committing the Holocaust and killing Jews in Poland, Germany, and throughout Europe, they needed first to have the soldiers to guard the Jewish prisoners. They needed civilians to set up the fences, to build the shacks, and to build the roads to go to those prison camps. The Nazis needed civilians to do all these things. One person or one leader (like Hitler) or a handful of leaders can't do all of this. Therefore, you have a prison camp, you have gas chambers, and you have the German soldiers leading the Jews into the prison camps. But these German soldiers have to be fed, they have to be clothed, they need bullets for their weapons, they need weapons to be built for them. Once a person has the knowledge that the end result involves massive human suffering, then the person who is making that bullet, the person who is making the food for the German soldiers, once they know that the end result of what they are doing is the extermination of the Jews, then yes, they are a part of it and bear moral responsibility for their actions. They were an intricate part of that process where the end result was to commit a crime against humanity, and it's the same moral equation in a war of aggression and an invasion of another country.

Watada continues,

The general or the civilian official ordering an illegal and precipitous invasion is, of course, morally culpable and legally guilty. But one single person can't carry out a war of aggression by himself or herself. They can't do it without the cooks, the mechanics, the medics, the logistics guys, the supply guys, and so on. When the end result is a crime, everybody who takes part in the process to get to the end result is morally responsible for what happened. I remember hearing about a German man who was employed by the Nazis at a train-switching station in Poland where they were putting Jews on the trains to ship them to the concentration camps. This man operated the train switches and wasn't involved with the Nazi party. When the Third Reich fell, he escaped to South America and hid out for a long time. The Israelis found him, sent out an extraction team, arrested him, and brought him back to Israel to be tried. In his defense, he told the court that in Nazi Germany to re-fuse Hitler would mean death. If you didn't do what you were told—which in his case was switching the train car—he would either be taken out in the back and shot or taken to a prison camp where he would likely have died. The Israelis didn't care. They executed him. What they were saying is that it doesn't matter. It doesn't matter whether you are the lowliest guy; if you take part in it, you are responsible.

Yet it can be argued that this position goes too far in placing moral blame on the shoulders of the soldiers. These enlisted men and women did not make the decision to go to war in Iraq. They are trained to follow orders and do not have enough information to counter the pro-war argu-ments promoted by their superiors. Thus, even if the war in Iraq is unjust and represents a crime of aggression, the individual private cannot be held morally or legally responsible.

Delgado has some sympathy for this position, stating, "You can't blame the pawns for the strategy of the chess player." Yet he thinks this does not excuse soldiers from the responsibility to evaluate and resist illegal orders:

> One of the conclusions I came to was that a thinking, moral person cannot transfer their entire moral responsibility to someone else, especially to a president, in this case, in which you have no confidence. There is a moral culpability to say, "I'm giving up my rationality, I'm giving up my decision-making and putting it in the hands of someone else." In fact, an individual has some culpability by putting himself or herself in a situation where he or she may be called upon to participate in an unjust war. As a soldier, you accept the possibility that your commander may order you to do something illegal. You accept the possibility that you may be ordered into an illegal war merely by signing up. That was something I couldn't accept. A soldier has a responsibility to disobey unjust orders or immoral orders. The way the army interprets this is incredibly narrow. It says basically if your commander says, "Shoot this baby in the back of the head," then you say, "No."

Delgado argues that a soldier's ethical responsibility is much broader and includes an obligation to evaluate the causes of a war before participating in the killing.

In fact, Delgado believes that if soldiers investigate and determine that the war in Iraq is immoral and illegal, then they should throw down their rifles and refuse to fight. If significant numbers of soldiers took this risk, the consequences could be profound. If the administration lost the moral support of our soldiers, most citizens would ask, "What business do we have fighting this war?" The United States would be sending people who don't believe in the cause and don't want to be there. Delgado believes that there should be more options beyond CO status for soldiers who ethically disagree with a particular war. These individuals certainly shouldn't be treated as traitors and criminals.

Delgado explains,

> I think that there should be a legal means in place to serve this purpose, either a broadening of CO legislation, or perhaps a change in the way enlistments are done. Right now enlistment is universal—you agree to serve in everything. Perhaps there should be a class of soldiers, like a militia, who agrees to serve when they support the war and not serve when they don't, so those people who fully believe in the army project are free to enlist universally. But let's make room for people [like Ehren Watada] who say, "I'll fight in Afghanistan, but not in Iraq." It would be interesting to have a class of soldiers like that, similar to the colonial militia. We would have the regulars, who serve everywhere, and the militia, who serve only when they support the cause. So I'm not supporting an insurrection. I'm supporting the creation of a legal pathway for soldiers to assert their moral authority. The army says orders don't trump your moral compass. This new status would give an individual the ability to decide whether a policy is immoral or unethical. We are a democracy that believes in individuality and personal responsibility. If we vest those values and that responsibility in soldiers, how can we then complain when they take that authority and apply it to the war in general? A soldier can be told he or she has to go to war because it is an order and he or she has to obey the law. But does law trump morality? If the Iraq war is immoral or illegal or unethical, I don't think you should legally be held responsible to go.

The British military was very concerned about the legality of the invasion of Iraq. The British did not want their soldiers brought before the International Criminal Court and prosecuted for war crimes. Watada noted this difference:

> I now know that the British military was very concerned about the Iraq invasion being an illegal "war of aggression." The British military officers were very concerned that their soldiers could be prosecuted for international war crimes. Britain is part of the International Criminal Court (ICC), whereas the U.S. is not. The British military needed guarantees from their attorney general that the invasion of Iraq was legal under international law.

Some officers in the U.S. military agree with their British counterparts. A general with a degree in military ethics explained to Delgado that individual morality isn't less important in war; it's more important. Delgado wholeheartedly agrees, because

> too often I hear war supporters saying, "Well, you're a soldier so you gave
> up your right to question, you gave up your right to critical thought, you
> gave up your right to make moral judgments." And what this commander
> is saying is "no, absolutely not." In fact, when you are a soldier, you have to
> occupy yourself with morality more because you are going to be in a position
> to make those decisions. So I think that this idea that soldiers can't question
> is one hundred percent wrong and we need the opposite. We need soldiers
> to be the first line of defense against unethical behavior. Soldiers need to be
> encouraged and absolutely taught that you are the ultimate responsibility,
> you are the ultimate moral compass for yourself. When you take that away,
> atrocities become possible because everyone can say, "It wasn't me; I was
> just following orders." We don't accept that. We didn't accept the "superior
> orders" defense at Nuremberg. If in the future the Iraq invasion is declared
> to be illegal and an aggressive war, there could be an attempt to prosecute
> the participants. It won't be a defense (in this hypothetical scenario) to say,
> "Well, my superiors ordered me to participate in an illegal war, so I can't be
> held responsible."

JUS IN BELLO—JUSTICE IN WAR

As noted in chapter 2, U.S. soldiers are expected to obey the laws of war. American soldiers can be prosecuted for torturing or killing prisoners of war, not caring for the wounded, attacking civilians, and stealing. These laws, drawn from The Hague and Geneva Conventions and customary international law, are clearly explained in *The U.S. Army/Marine Corps Counterinsurgency Field Manual* and in *The Law of Land Warfare*.[17]

The *Charter of the International Military Tribunal at Nuremberg*, affirmed by a unanimous resolution of the General Assembly of the United Nations and perhaps the most definitive statement of the content of war crimes in international law, states in Principle VI(b): "War crimes: Violations of the laws or customs of war which include, but are not limited to, murder, ill-treatment of prisoners of war or persons on the seas, killing of hostages, plunder of public or private property, wanton destruction of cities, towns, or villages, or devastation not justified by military necessity."[18]

The United States is also party to twelve other conventions relating to land warfare, some of which carry very detailed provisions.[19] The U.S. Supreme Court has declared that the "purpose of the law of war" is to "protect civilian populations and prisoners of war from brutality."[20] In addition, the laws of war are found in international customary law, which, under the U.S. Constitution, is part of American law, according to the U.S. Supreme Court.[21] These laws of war constantly apply to all sides in a conflict, irrespective of whether one side has committed or is committing frequent violations of these laws.

The laws of war are thus "real law" and not just abstract idealism unrelated to the brutal reality of combat. In fact, the United States has officially long believed that the idea of war crimes in international law is not only a realistic philosophy of law but serves the best national interests of the United States as well.

However, both Watada and Delgado point out that U.S. soldiers often lack an understanding about the legality of what they are doing. Watada believes that the majority of U.S. soldiers have no knowledge of the Nuremberg decision, the *United Nations Charter*, or *The Law of Land Warfare*. He supports this claim with an explanation of his army training:

> As an enlisted soldier, I wasn't taught any lessons from Vietnam and there was no discussion of the tragedy at My Lai. As an officer we were given one class on the laws of warfare. The class was called "The Law of Land Warfare," and they did reference the My Lai massacre. But it's a whole different story in class, with a JAG (Judge Advocate General) lawyer explaining what the law is [versus what it's like in combat]. When you actually go to war it's all different. And we were not taught about the laws regarding "wars of aggression" and the fact that our participation in such a war could be illegal.

Delgado's training in the laws of war was also minimal and "didn't have much weight behind it":

> The army had more formal procedures and much more instruction in marching and floor buffing than they did in rules of engagement (ROE). I spent far more time with a floor buffer than I did with the ROE, the rules of land warfare, or the Nuremberg or Geneva Conventions. It's just not emphasized. People didn't really perceive it as that essential to basic military training. Maybe they thought, "Oh, you'll get this when you get ready to go to war." But the problem was that when we later got ready to go to war, we didn't get it, either. So it [the laws of war] was left almost intentionally nebulous. The drill sergeant was almost impatient with us—it's just common sense—don't torture people, don't kill civilians, don't blow up things you don't have to—basic common sense. The problem is in war "basic common sense" doesn't cut it because you are dealing with highly emotionally charged, really ambiguous situations. In warfare, you need some more formal guidelines.

Delgado's army training was extremely informal and incomplete. The Geneva Conventions, for example, were never discussed.

The "emotionally charged" nature of warfare inherently brings forth the aggressive component of human nature and human psychology. In such an atmosphere, even a person with a tremendous strength of character will have difficulty keeping his or her moral bearings and show-ing compassion and understanding to the enemy. Why should "rules" of war be applied to these monsters? The demonized enemy is often barely seen as human. The soldier is told that everything must be done to achieve "victory" over the terrorists and that "legal niceties" should not stand in the way. The rules of war are precisely designed to prevent this aggressive stance from spinning out of control and causing great harm and suffering to innocent civilians. If Delgado and Watada are correct, the U.S. Army training in the basic laws of war is incomplete and inad-equate. This cavalier approach toward war crimes most likely contributed to the many documented cases of abuse to Iraqi civilians and prisoners, including the torture and cruel, inhumane, and degrading treatment pho-tographed at Abu Ghraib.

Delgado notes how war has a "universalizing" effect on every indi-vidual: no matter how "moral" the person is when entering the conflict, violence brings out the harmful side of human nature:

It's almost naïve to just count on people's inner angels to keep them pure. . . . I'm talking here about war itself . . . maybe they are righteous going into it, maybe everybody is morally neutral when they sign up. But war and violence have a universal effect on almost everyone. For example, if the pro-fession of arms is inherently noble, what about the Nazi soldier? How does one, even if you are a good person, a moral person, how do you maintain your integrity being a Nazi soldier guarding a concentration camp? I am not saying that this is the same thing [as an American soldier in Iraq]. What I am saying is that when you are put in such a morally ambiguous and nebulous situation, even your own morality can slip away. Everybody in that situation turns black to a greater or lesser extent. Some people have a higher threshold. You can't kill someone else without turning black. You are a good person in peace time when you didn't kill someone. Now in Iraq, when you go to battle and kill someone, that has a tremendous effect on you as a person, no matter how nobly intended the killing was. My sergeant argued that if you keep your intentions pure while you do the killing, then you won't be marked by it. By that, he meant that if you kill without hate in your heart, you will be OK. However, from my Buddhist perspective, the squeezing of the trigger is hatred. That action itself demands some kind of hatred, or some kind of separation in your heart, that is inherently corrupt.

The U.S. military's own investigations into the abuse of Iraqi prisoners and civilians support Delgado's eye witness account at Abu Ghraib and in Iraq. The war in Iraq does seem to often erode a soldier's ethical compass, with often-disastrous results. For example, Gen. Antonio M. Taguba con-ducted an investigation into the activities of the 800th Military Police Bri-gade in Iraq. Taguba found that "numerous incidents of sadistic, blatant, and wanton criminal abuses were inflicted on several detainees." This abuse was systematic and intentional and included punching, slapping, and kicking detainees; jumping on their naked feet; forcing naked male detainees to wear women's underwear; forcing groups of male detainees to masturbate themselves while being photographed and videotaped; using military working dogs (without muzzles) to intimidate and frighten detainees; and positioning a naked detainee on an MRE box with a sandbag on his head and attaching wires to his fingers, toes, and penis to simulate electric torture.[22] An additional investigation by former Secretary of Defense James R. Schlesinger reported 300 incidents of alleged detainee abuse.[23] Also, as noted in chapter 2, a 2007 official army survey reported that 10 percent of 1,767 troops stated that they had mistreated civilians in Iraq by, for example, kicking them or needlessly damaging their possessions. Perhaps most shockingly, the army report stated, "Less than half of soldiers and Marines believed that non-combatants should be treated with dignity and respect."[24] There is clear evidence that current military training in the laws of war is inadequate.

Extensive training in the laws of war is thus critical to prevent future Abu Ghraibs. Each of us has within ourselves the potential to do bad, to do evil, to commit torture. Everyone has a breaking point. The laws of war are designed to prevent all of us from crossing that line. As Delgado summarizes,

> At some level we are all violent, we are all Abu Ghraib torturers, except some of us are able to suppress [our violent instincts] more or less completely. Others of us have lower breaking points. One of the jobs of government in society is to help people stay beneath their breaking points. When the government fails, when they set up policies that wink and nod at torture and call Arabs sub-human, they are in fact doing the opposite and pushing people toward their breaking points. These policies guarantee that the greater percentage of those at the lower breaking points will step over the line. So the fact that individuals have moral responsibility to me is inarguable. But this does not excuse the government from helping people stay within moral boundaries. And that is the dual criticism we can make of Abu Ghraib. Yes, those individuals in that unit morally failed. However, they didn't fail alone. They didn't fail without help. The government pushed them and drove them to fail.

Delgado continues,

> This [the torturer at Abu Ghraib] is me too. I could do that. . . . If you put someone in a hellish prison, they may become brutal, even if they weren't before. I try to bear that in mind and not sit back in judgment. For me, one of the saddest parts of this war is that people feel like I am judging them [when I talk about Abu Ghraib]. They feel that I am separating myself from the soldiers and saying they are bad people and I am above them. But I do

not feel that way. I am just saying, "Hey, I got through this and didn't break, and unfortunately some people did." Let's set up a system where the people who have lower breaking points are kept out of these morally ambiguous situations. At Abu Ghraib we didn't need a force of professional, full-time thugs. We needed a force of doctors, school teachers, lawyers and professors to be in that situation to bring their moral authority to bear. We needed people with the highest breaking points at Abu Ghraib, and instead we put the people with the lowest, and, of course, the results were we got what we deserved.

THE ETHICAL SOLDIER

An ethical soldier, like an ethical citizen, can be defined as someone who will assume individual moral responsibility during a time of war. The ethical soldier will thus evaluate the overall justice of the war itself (*jus ad bellum*) and will fight only in legal and moral conflicts. The ethical soldier will also adhere to all the laws of war (*jus in bello*), including the norms governing prisoners of war and the protection of civilians. The ethical soldier will not exempt himself or herself from the obligation of all citizens in a democracy to critically assess and evaluate the actions of his or her leaders. This soldier will instead apply the highest standards of decency and morality to himself or herself and his or her country.

Watada calls on all soldiers and citizens to accept this moral responsibility:

> What I am talking about is for everybody to take individual responsibility to evaluate what we are doing in Iraq and how we got there. In taking that responsibility, I found it to be an illegal invasion and occupation of a sovereign country. And I found that during our occupation of Iraq, we have committed various individual war crimes. But it is the illegality of the occupation and invasion itself that made all of those other crimes possible and will continue to make all those things possible. We are now engaged in a low-grade guerilla war. But I leave it open for every single person, be they civilian or military, to decide in their own minds what they feel is the right thing to do. If an individual feels that the right thing to do is to go to Iraq and try to do good things there, then God be with that person. I hope they come back safe. If, however, an individual feels that his or her participation is wrong and is unable to support and fight in the war, then I don't think that individual should be condemned or prosecuted for this stance.

Watada notes that there are certain state and federal laws that hold a person liable for failure to report a rape or a murder. If a person just watches the crime and walks away, he or she can be prosecuted. Iraq for him was the same type of situation. He couldn't just walk away from a crime that was being committed:

> For me, it really didn't matter that I would be prosecuted. I felt that the Iraq war was legally and morally wrong. I did not want to go through the rest of my life knowing that I had been a part of it. You either condone or enable what is going on or you stand against it. There is no fence to sit on. I tell myself to be true to myself. I couldn't just say, "Oh, I'm in the military and therefore I can't really do anything about the war. I'm just going to do my year and get out and that's my protest." I couldn't do that because for that year I would be enabling Bush. And the war would continue for another whole year with a full contingent of soldiers.

Delgado also came to the conclusion that for him there was "no fence to sit on." He saw his continued presence in the military as an implicit endorsement of the war, and he had to get out. Even though he wasn't personally torturing anyone or even pulling the trigger of a gun, he felt his presence as an army mechanic contributed to the suffering. His army work as a mechanic "freed up someone else to do immoral actions," and he thus felt like "an enabler." Delgado explains,

> I fixed a vehicle so that they could drive the vehicle into the city and do things that I wouldn't do. I'm directly making that possible. Being a mechanic frees someone else up to be an infantryman, to be an interrogator, to be a torturer. So I'm allowing them the freedom and ability to do what they have done. I also feel that membership in an organization implies a strong, silent, moral assent. Membership implies consent. For example, membership in the National Rifle Association implies agreement with its project. For me, that is a problem with the army. As long as I was in the army, and not specifically dissenting or saying that I wanted to leave, then someone could read from my membership that I agreed with what the army was doing. In other words, if I don't say no, it's as good as saying yes.

While arguing for individual moral responsibility, both Watada and Delgado insist that those soldiers who participate in the war are not war criminals. Delgado explains,

> While I do think that every soldier in Iraq is morally complicit in what is happening in Iraq, this complicity is not absolute, as there are greater and lesser degrees of involvement. For example, a medic helping people who had been injured in Germany during World War II—yes, they are participating in the [Nazi] war effort, but in a very minor way compared to the interrogators putting in the thumb screws. So there are levels of moral complicity, and it's not absolute. Mere participation in the war effort in Iraq doesn't make a soldier a war criminal.

Yet both Watada and Delgado want us to recognize that each "cog in the wheel" contributes to the entire machine's moving forward. Each individual must therefore examine and confront his or her individual level of complicity and moral responsibility.

This issue of moral responsibility for the actions of the government during war applies to all citizens, not just soldiers. Delgado points out that the monks in Myanmar can't be held responsible for what their government does because they had no hand in electing them. Myanmar is a dictatorship which crushes voices of opposition. The same can't be said about citizens in a democracy. We have the ability to speak out and to vote. It could be argued, therefore, that soldiers and citizens give their moral assent to war policies when they abstain and don't vote or when they don't protest aggressive war and war crimes. These citizens and soldiers are clearly not as morally culpable as the president who authorized the illegal invasion, torture, and renditions. Yet some degree of moral culpability does stay with the silent witness who does nothing to stop the country's illegal actions.

THE SOLDIER AS HEROIC ICON

Americans are trained from childhood to revere the armed forces. There is no other career so venerated. To a significant extent, individual soldiers are exempt from criticism or any serious ethical examination of their actions. To even raise the issue of the individual moral responsibility of the soldier, especially during a time of war, is to open oneself up to personal attack of traitorous behavior and for "not supporting the troops." "These are the men and women putting their lives on the line for the security of the country. How dare you question their moral integrity!"

Delgado hopes to deconstruct and "explode the idea of the soldier as a heroic icon." It really upsets him to see this blind obsequiousness toward the military. Delgado explains,

> People hold the idea that individuals join the army solely for patriotic reasons and that therefore everything they do is motivated by selfless, idealistic goals. This creates a climate in our culture that you can't criticize soldiers. Really, you can't. Soldiers are heroes; they are lions. That is where the debate ends. I disavow that view because I have seen too much of the reality of human nature in war and in too many soldiers. So I want people to understand that the very act of becoming a soldier is a constant moral "gray area." A soldier makes tons of decisions, right and wrong, every moment. Everybody has a mixture of good and evil, selfish and selfless actions. I want people to think about what it means to be a soldier and to be critical. It is important to

apply critical thought to the military. A soldier's action always falls within a "gray area." There is no *Saving Private Ryan* pure heroism—that's only in Hollywood. At the same time, soldiers are not demons—they are not horrible, massacring murderers.

Delgado is arguing that we apply the same ethical standards to soldiers as we do to other professions. Individuals fulfilling essential public services, such as military service, need to be held accountable for immoral and illegal behavior. He believes that it is counterproductive to place the individual soldier on a moral pedestal above others. Such adoration can lead to the creation of an environment in which immoral conduct is excused and illegal practices rationalized.

The U.S. government made this exact point at the Nuremberg Tribunal. Telford Taylor was a member of the American prosecution staff and chief counsel for the United States at the Nuremberg war crimes trials. Taylor spoke at length at Nuremberg to clarify a soldier's responsibility during an aggressive war. Taylor's comments are worth quoting at length:

> Now, needless to say, it is not the prosecution's position that it is a crime to be a soldier or a sailor or to serve one's country as a soldier or sailor in time of war. The profession of arms is an honorable one and can be honorably practiced. But it is too clear for argument that a man who commits crimes cannot plead as a defense that he committed them in uniform.
>
> It is an innocent and respectable business to be a locksmith; but it is nonetheless a crime if the locksmith turns his talents to picking the locks of neighbors and looting their homes. And that is the nature of the charge . . . that in performing the functions of diplomats, politicians, soldiers, sailors, or whatever they happened to be, they conspired, and did plan, prepare, initiate, and wage illegal wars and thereby committed crimes under Article 6(a) of the charter. . . .
>
> The military defendants will perhaps argue that they are pure technicians. This amounts to saying that military men are a race apart from and different from the ordinary run of human beings—men above and beyond the moral and legal requirements that apply to others, incapable of exercising moral judgment on their own behalf. . . .
>
> Such is not the view of the United States. The prosecution here representing the United States believes that the profession of arms is a distinguished profession. We believe that the practice of that profession by its leaders calls for the highest degree of integrity and moral wisdom no less than for technical skill. We believe that, in consulting and planning with the leaders in other fields of national activity, the military leaders must act in accordance with international law and the dictates of public conscience. Otherwise the military resources of the nation will be used, not in accordance with the laws of modern society, but in accordance with the law of the jungle.[25]

Delgado points to the dangers resulting from the different attitude that American society holds toward the doctor and locksmith compared to the soldier:

> Why isn't there the same lionization of locksmiths that there is of soldiers? No one says that to even talk critically about any locksmith is to undermine the whole institution of locksmithery. Yet this is what happens with soldiers. We are not allowed to discuss the point when a soldier crosses from morality to immorality. In fact, people don't even want to accept the possibility that a soldier could do an immoral action (unless it is really egregious). But my question is: where does that line [between morality and immorality] lie? For a locksmith, it's clear when he is breaking into a house. But with a soldier [it's more difficult]. [Is it] okay when he destroys a building? When he kicks in a door? When he hits a person? Where exactly is the line between morality and immorality? Yet it is almost impossible to discuss these issues. There is a chilling effect on any discussion of a soldier's morality. I think that the line between the moral and immoral actions of a soldier is a lot closer than we think and that we step over [that line] a lot more than we admit.

THE BUSH BETRAYAL

To many soldiers the Iraq war was just a symptom of what is really wrong with our country. Ordinary people feel that they have lost control over our collective destiny. Many citizens have concluded that the Bush administration betrayed the basic principles of justice and rights fundamental to American constitutional law and morality. Watada certainly feels that way:

> For me, as a member of the U.S. military, I felt a profound sense of betrayal, and the betrayal went all the way to the top, to the Department of Defense and the Bush administration. And I felt that I couldn't just sit on the fence where it is safe for me. I can't say that I am just doing what I'm told and I really can't decide if it's right or wrong. A lot of the American people believe that soldiers are not to think for themselves but only to do what they are told. And a lot of soldiers take that path and just do what they are told. But I felt that what the administration was doing was ethically wrong—not only with the Iraq war, but with the wire taps, the torture, the president's "signing statements," the renditions, the recess appointments, the corruption in the Iraqi construction projects, the dismal response to Hurricane Katrina, election fraud, and on and on and on. I felt that we were riding down a path leading to the destruction of our own country.

Both Watada and Delgado call on all Americans (soldiers and citizens) to speak out against the occupation of Iraq and to prevent such a violent action from happening again. Both state that "you can't just sit on the fence. You are either part of the solution or you are part of the problem." If you do nothing, your silence is in effect condoning the war in Iraq and enabling the administration to continue to violate the law.

Watada argues that we have to do more than just vote against Bush. It's not enough just to say, "Well, I didn't vote for him":

> I think that's an absolute excuse. I think as a nation we do have to own it. You can say when George Bush was elected in 2000 that we didn't know what we were getting into. But by 2004, the Iraq war was well under way; torture was well under way. We knew what was happening, and the majority of people still voted for him. People's fear and their subsequent desire for paternal governance overcame their loyalty to American ideals. The sad truth that came out of this election was that a lot of Americans don't really have very much loyalty to the American project. They don't really care that much about the Constitution. They don't really believe in a secular society. They don't really believe in a liberal, non-torturing, non-oppressive society. They are more afraid of terrorism than they are confident in the Constitution. That is what George Bush's reelection drove home to me. At that point Americans didn't care about whether the government trampled on the Constitution. They didn't care whether Bush broke the law. Fear of terrorism drove many to accept this attack and betrayal of American values. I personally felt like the country had broken up with me. The country and I went in two different directions because I wouldn't accept this betrayal.

The violent, unjust, and vindictive image that the United States represents to the majority of the world is probably not the representation of America held by most U.S. citizens. After all, the violence and the war itself are far away, halfway around the world. It is perhaps too easy to just accept that this devastation abroad is the "price for freedom" at home. Yet this betrayal of American values and international law is backfiring. It is not making us safer. Aggressive war has perpetuated the violence in an ongoing and vicious cycle.[26]

Delgado believes that nonviolent strategies against terrorism would be far more effective. Such strategies, he argues, could be based on improving the standard of living in the countries in the Middle East, encouraging homegrown democratic reform, and fostering Palestinian–Israeli peace. He sees poverty, injustice, political repression, and Western intervention as "root causes" of the support terrorist organizations receive. A strategy for combating terrorism, therefore, must address these fundamental causes. The United States instead seems to constantly pursue violent directions, which Delgado believes are totally counterproductive:

> We tell the terrorists [and the countries in the Middle East] that violence and war are illegitimate and that they have to stop the violence. And the

way we are going to teach them this is by bombing their cities, invading their countries, killing many of their citizens. This is how we will show that violence and war are illegitimate! We are asking them to renounce the very violence that we use against them. We thus do not offer a better world. The only alternative we offer them is to fight back. Perhaps we'd have more success if we were to say, "Look, we don't need to fight; there is a better way. Let's encourage democratic reforms, let's encourage economic growth, let's encourage freedom and liberty in your country." Such an approach would greatly benefit America and make us safer.

7

⟡

Britain

Resignations from the Blair Government

Principled resignation to protest morally problematic state policy is more common in Britain than in the United States. As noted in chapter 1, the list of British government leaders who resigned from office to protest Blair's decision to align with the United States and invade Iraq is lengthy and impressive. Did these principled resignations make a difference? While these actions clearly did not stop the Blair government from joining the occupation of Iraq, these acts of protest did contribute to a strong, robust, and democratic debate among the British people on the government's foreign policy decisions. In the United States, on the other hand, dissenters were tormented and branded as "disloyal" to the troops. Even those in Congress who initially opposed the war felt compelled to vote year after year to support the effort. The Bush administration manipulated the patriotic fervor that swept the country after 9/11 to gain public support for the Iraq war and effectively marginalized the principled voices of dissent. In Britain, on the other hand, voices of dissent were part of the mainstream, and, as a result, the issues surrounding the legitimacy and morality of invading Iraq were more fully debated and aired. Dissenters were not branded as "traitors." Thus, in the end, the bold resignations from the Blair government cannot be seen as simply empty and futile gestures unable to stop the occupation of Iraq. These actions, instead, were central to igniting a broad and critical national examination of the country's foreign policy in the Middle East.

These issues are explored below, first through a summary of the crisis Blair faced with the growing resignations from his government in 2003. The list of British government leaders who resigned from office to protest the Iraq war is striking and includes: Bob Blizzard, Anne Campbell, Robin Cook, John Denham, Michael Jabez Foster, Lord Hunt, Ken Purchase, Andy Reed, Carne Ross, Clare Short, and Elizabeth Wilmshurst. Most of these individuals were elected representatives to the British Parliament and remained in the House of Commons after resigning from their posts in the Blair administration. However, others who resigned, like Carne Ross and Elizabeth Wilmshurst, were members of the British civil service and not the Parliament. With their principled resignations, these civil servants gave up their careers in the government, sacrificing their financial livelihood in an attempt to protect their honor and moral integrity.

Following this summary of the 2003 crisis in the British government, I analyze and describe the decisions of four key individuals in the government to resign: Carne Ross, Clare Short, Andy Reed, and John Denham. This chapter then concludes with a review of some of the common themes that emerged in my separate discussions in London with these four public officials. All raised issues of peer pressure, humiliation and loneliness; collective responsibility and party discipline; moral numbness; and the contradictions inherent with a strategy of "working from within."

CRISIS IN THE BLAIR GOVERNMENT

When Prime Minister Tony Blair decided to join forces with Pres. George W. Bush to invade and occupy Iraq, he faced a very different political situation than the U.S. president. Bush could rely on his conservative Republican Party, which held a majority of seats in both the U.S. Senate and House of Representatives in 2003, to support his plans for war. Since Bush also had the support of conservative Democrats, he faced little opposition to his preemptive war strategies in Iraq. In Britain, however, the strongest support for the war came from the opposition Conservative Party, not Blair's Labour Party. The Conservative Party fully supported the confrontation with Iraq. The British public and the Labour Party, on the other hand, were deeply divided and uneasy about the 2003 war planning that seemed to be moving forward with such great dispatch. Furthermore, Blair's close relationship with Bush caused many in his own party to wonder how much independence the British government maintained in their "special relationship" with the United States. At one point, for example, even Nelson Mandela described Blair as "the U.S. foreign minister."[1] On February 15, 2003, the largest peacetime demonstration in British history took place as hundreds of thousands of people filled the streets of London to protest the Bush/Blair Iraq war policy. Yet Blair seemed to be winning over public opinion. In early March 2003, opinion polls showed that 50 percent of the British supported military action, while 42 percent were against.[2]

On March 18, 2003, a crucial debate and vote on Iraq took place in the House of Commons. After failing to obtain a second UN resolution (following Security Council Resolution 1441) authorizing an invasion of Iraq, Blair had decided to go ahead and support the American invasion, anyway. Blair strongly urged the Members of Parliament (MPs) to back this position and vote to support his stance on Saddam Hussein and preemptive war. The debate, disrupted by protestors shouting from the public gallery, took more than eight hours. The prime minister argued that the people of Iraq would suffer if the House refused to support his policy. He warned that retreat would send a dangerous message to other "tyrants" and leave the Iraqi people in "pitiless terror." "This is the time for this House to give a lead, to show we will stand up for what we know to be right . . . that we will confront the tyrants and terrorists who put our lives at risk . . . that we have the courage to do the right thing." Commentators thought his comments indicated that he would resign rather than pull U.K. forces out of the Gulf.[3]

Yet Blair was facing a major backbench rebellion over his plans to invade Iraq. Former Labour Defense Minister Peter Kilfoyle called the Iraq war "illegal, immoral, and illogical." If 165 Labour MPs rebelled, Blair would have to rely on the Tory votes to win the ballot on Iraq. If 245 Labour MPs voted against him, he would lose even with the Tory support. And, to Blair's dismay, he faced a slew of resignations from his government.[4]

On Sunday, March 9, 2003, Labour MP Andy Reed resigned from office, stating that he had no choice but to quit as parliamentary private secretary to the environment secretary because, as a Christian, he felt the Iraq action was an "unjust war." With this action, Reed became the first British public official to resign in protest over Blair's Iraq war policy.

On Monday, March 17, 2003, the leader of the House of Commons and former British foreign secretary, Robin Cook, resigned, stating, "Neither the international community nor the British public are persuaded that there is an urgent and compelling reason for this action in Iraq." As a result, Cook's parliamentary private secretary, Ken Purchase, automatically left the government and signed the amendment in the Commons opposing Blair's Iraq policy. Purchase told me that he had been clear with the chief whip of the Labour Party that "unless there was a second resolution from the UN," he "would not be supporting joining the U.S. to invade Iraq." The ethical dimension for Purchase was the sidelining of the UN. He stated: "I am a long-term, life supporter of the idea of the United Nations being an effective and powerful force in world affairs, and particularly enforcing agreed mandates." When Blair decided to go ahead with the invasion without the UN's authorization, Purchase felt that he was left with no choice but to resign.[5]

On Tuesday, March 18, 2003, while Blair was defending his policies to the House of Commons, two of his ministers resigned over his stand on Iraq. Home Office Minister John Denham and Health Minister Lord Hunt quit the government, along with two ministerial aides. Denham said he resigned because he believed it was crucial to have an international consensus for preemptive action. Lord Hunt told BBC Radio: "At the end of the day I don't support this action, and it would be hypocritical for me to stay in government." More resignations in opposition to the Blair Iraq policy quickly followed. Sandra Osborne, parliamentary aide to the Scotland secretary, quit her post and said that war should only be conducted with a second UN resolution. Anne Campbell, Labour MP for Cambridge, resigned from her role as parliamentary private secretary to the secretary of state for trade and industry. Bob Blizzard, Labour MP for Waveney, resigned as parliamentary private secretary to the work and pensions minister.

A further March 18 resignation would come back to haunt Blair two years later. Elizabeth Wilmshurst had worked for nearly three decades in the legal department of the Foreign and Commonwealth Office (FCO), rising to the position of deputy head of legal affairs. Wilmshurst led the U.K. delegation to set up the International Criminal Court in The Hague and served as legal counselor to the U.K.'s mission to the UN. In her resignation letter, Wilmshurst wrote: "I regret that I cannot agree that it is lawful to use force without a second [UN] Security Council resolution." In releasing her letter, however, the British government removed the next sentence, which read: "My views accord with the advice that has been given consistently in this office before and after the adoption of UN Security Council resolution 1441 and with what the attorney general gave us to understand was his view prior to his letter of 7 March." When the censored sections of Wilmshurst's letter were leaked to the public in 2005, there were widespread allegations of a cover-up. Here was documentary evidence that Attorney General Lord Goldsmith had changed his mind about the legality of the Iraq war just days before the conflict began. This seemed to confirm widespread speculation that the attorney general had been pressured by Blair to switch his view and sanction the war.[6]

On Wednesday, March 19, 2003, David Kidney, parliamentary private secretary to the environment minister, announced that he had quit his post on Tuesday evening and would vote against Blair's Iraq policy. Hastings MP Michael Jabez Foster resigned as parliamentary private secretary to the attorney general to express his opposition to the Iraq war.[7] Foster told me that this was the hardest decision he had made in more than six years in the government. But Foster continued, "[W]e should not be taking action against Iraq unless we were genuinely and immediately the subject of possible aggression. . . . I didn't buy the argument that we were under immediate attack." The day might come when Saddam would become a threat, but that time, according to Foster, was not yet here.[8]

International Development Secretary Clare Short decided in March to stay in the cabinet but remained very critical of the handling of the crisis. However, Short joined the ranks of the dissenters and resigned from the government in May 2003. She claimed that Blair did not follow through on his promises to her to strive to gain UN legal authority for the Iraq occupation and to fully utilize the UN in the Iraq reconstruction effort. When these promises were broken, Short felt that she had to resign.

Yet, despite all this opposition from his own party, Blair won the vote in the House of Commons on March 18, 2003. The amendment brought by the antiwar forces, stating that "the case for war against Iraq has not yet been established," was voted down 396 to 217. The government motion endorsing the Blair Iraq policy to "use all means necessary to ensure the disarmament of Iraq's weapons of mass destruction" was adopted by a vote of 412 to 149. Only 84 members of Blair's Labour Party broke with him to vote against this authorization for military action against Iraq.

Events in Iraq, of course, didn't unfold the way in which Blair and Bush imagined. The British and American soldiers were not greeted with flowers and cakes. Saddam Hussein did not have weapons of mass destruction or any connection to al-Qaeda. The public soon learned that Iraq never posed an imminent threat to the United States, Britain, or its neighbors. The lack of planning, corruption, disorganization, neglect, and ignorance dominating the occupying U.S./British operations in post-invasion Iraq was not only discouraging but, to many, also criminal.[9] Iraq soon spiraled into the bloody horror predicted to occur by many Middle East experts before the invasion. Civil war and sectarian strife led to the murder of thousands of innocents and the maiming of tens of thousands of other Iraqis. In addition, millions were forced to flee into exile as refugees seeking the protection of the UN or neighboring states.

The British public demanded an explanation of how this all happened; how could the Blair government be so wrong about Iraq? Why would the government take the country to war on faulty intelligence? In the attempt to "sell the war," was the Blair government's case against Saddam Hussein exaggerated and distorted? How could the terror of war be unleashed on such a flimsy basis?

In the midst of this public debate, a further tragedy occurred. In September 2002, the British government had produced a dossier alleging Iraq could deploy its weapons of mass destruction (WMD) within forty-five minutes. This claim was central to Blair's case for supporting the invasion of Iraq. In May 2003, BBC Today journalist Andrew Gilligan reported that Downing Street had "sexed up" this dossier against the wishes of the intelligence agencies. On July 10, 2003, Dr. David Kelly was named as the suspected source of this information. On July 17, 2003, Dr. Kelly was found dead. (In February 2008, proof of the role that Blair public relations officials had in drafting this dossier on prewar intelligence emerged in London. An earlier version of the document did not include the claim that Iraq could launch chemical or biological weapons within forty-five minutes of an order to use them. This charge was inserted later to bolster the argument for war. Critics charge that press officials were drafting the document that was used as a justification for going to war, not the impartial intelligence experts like Dr. Kelly.)[10]

Dr. Kelly, an expert on biological weapons, worked for the U.K. Ministry of Defense and served as a UN weapons inspector in Iraq. The revelations about Kelly's discussion with BBC journalist Gilligan about the British government's dossier on WMD in Iraq led to a political crisis in the British government and the media. Kelly was found dead days after appearing before the parliamentary committee investigating the scandal. The Hutton Inquiry, a public investigation into Kelly's death, concluded in January 2004 that he had committed suicide and had not, in fact, said some of the things attributed to him by Gilligan. Some still contend that this official account of suicide is implausible. Medical specialists, for example, question the Hutton Inquiry's conclusion that Dr. Kelly bled to death from a self-inflicted wound to his left wrist.[11]

The public demanded further investigations into the Iraq war. On February 3, 2004, the government announced an inquiry into the use of intelligence relating to Iraq's WMD. This official British inquiry into the use of intelligence on Iraq's WMD was headed by Lord Butler, and its final report is referred to as the "Butler Report." The Butler group hoped to resolve the paradox that prior to the war both the British and American governments insisted with certainty that Iraq possessed WMD yet no such weapons or programs were found by the Iraq Survey Group.[12]

In July 2004, the Butler Report concluded that the key intelligence used to justify the war with Iraq was unreliable. British intelligence (MI6) did not check its sources, relied on third-hand reporting, and over-relied on dissident and unreliable Iraqi exiles. According to the Butler Report, Iraq did not have significant, if any, stocks of chemical or biological weapons in a state fit for use or any plans for using them. Furthermore, the report states that the pre-war claim that Iraq could use weapons of mass destruction within forty-five minutes was "unsubstantiated" and should not have been made without clarification. In terms of the decision to go to war, the report concludes that there was "no recent intelligence" to lead people to conclude that Iraq was of more immediate concern than other countries.[13]

One key British official called to testify before the Butler Inquiry was Carne Ross. Ross served for more than fifteen years in the British Foreign Service. At the United Nations, Ross was the U.K. delegation's Iraq and Middle East expert. Following his secret testimony to the Butler group, Ross resigned from the Foreign Service in September 2004. Ross felt that the British government was misrepresenting the situation in Iraq and that he could no longer be a part of it. The government did not come forward with the alternatives to war and instead produced reports that were one-sided and based on unreliable information to support the Bush/Blair policy.

The Blair government continued to be dogged with revelations about the pre-war decision-making process. On May 1, 2005, the *Sunday Times of London* published the "Downing Street Memo," the secret minutes of a meeting Blair held with his government's national security and foreign policy team in July 2002. At this meeting, the head of British intelligence, reporting on a recent trip to Washington, D.C., stated that the Bush administration had months earlier decided to wage war no matter what. The issue now was how to sell the war, and Washington was engaged in a campaign to see to it that "the intelligence and facts" would be "fixed around the policy." The Iraq war was thus publicly "justified by the conjunction of terrorism and WMD." However, this was all for public consumption, as the British foreign secretary pointed out that "the case [for war] is thin. . . . Saddam was not threatening his neighbours, and his WMD capability was less than that of Libya, North Korea, or Iran." What to do? The secretary proposed that "We should work up a plan for an ultimatum to Saddam to allow back in the UN weapons inspectors . . . [to] help with the legal justification for the use of force." Blair immediately grasped the significance of this proposal and stated that "it would make a big difference politically and legally if Saddam refuses to allow in UN inspectors."[14]

These were shocking revelations. Here is documentary proof that the British and American governments had decided in early 2002 to go to war with Iraq. The subsequent actions with the UN (inspections, deadlines, and so on) were all window dressing for public consumption. Saddam, of course, didn't play along. He allowed the weapons inspectors in and foiled the Blair scenario of a legally and morally sanctioned war.

By 2007, the British people had learned enough about the pre-war machinations and could no longer support this war. These revelations, the bloody occupation, and a low-level civil war had undermined public support. In March 2007, polls showed that 82 percent of the British people thought it was wrong to have invaded and occupied Iraq.[15]

THE BRITISH VOICES

John Denham, Michael J. Foster, Ken Purchase, Andy Reed, Carne Ross, and Clare Short spoke to me about their individual decisions to resign from the British government to protest the Iraq war.[16] With the exception of Ross, all of these individuals were Members of Parliament and could remain in the Parliament while resigning from the government. Ross, on the other hand, had no job or financial safety net to protect him after he resigned from the British Foreign Service.

Resignations from the British Cabinet and government over moral principle are not uncommon in the parliamentary system of government in the United Kingdom. As opposed to the U.S. system, British Cabinet members are drawn from the House of Commons and continue to serve as MPs. The appointment of ministers to the cabinet is seen as one of the single most powerful constitutional powers of the prime minister. Cabinet members are to uphold a degree of "collective responsibility" and publicly support the policies of the government, regardless of personal reservations. However, in the case of Iraq, many individuals in the government reached a point where it was impossible to morally support the government's position on preemptive war. At that point, these individuals felt they had no choice but to resign. While giving up their government positions, these individuals could continue to serve their constituents as MPs in the House of Commons.

Each individual who broke with the Blair government struggled deeply with the moral issues surrounding the war in Iraq. As noted in earlier chapters, ethical decision-making during a time of war is complex, and the correct moral action will often depend on an individual's position in the government. Unfortunately, moral action is not simply choosing "good" over "evil." Each individual has to rationally determine his or her own correct course of action. The decision-making and actions of Ross, Short, Reed, and Denham clearly illustrate the different moral paths taken by these British leaders to protect their individual moral autonomy.

Ross came to question the morality of the entire system of diplomacy and high politics. He resigned from the Foreign Service and restructured his life to put his skills at the service of the poorest countries and peoples who lack representation in global politics. Short's struggle to find the right "ethical balance" during the rush to war with Iraq is perhaps the most poignant. She refused to take the "easy road" and tried to first work from within before ultimately deciding that she could not be associated with a government that misleads and lies. This trajectory meant that she ended up being attacked from both the left and the right. Reed's strong Christian beliefs led him to examine the Iraq war policy through the lens of Christian just war doctrine. When he quietly registered his moral objections, he became the first person in the British government to resign over the Blair Iraq strategy. And finally, Denham resigned because he felt the Iraq invasion would create greater insecurity in the world and intensify the problem of global terrorism. Yet Denham kept his disagreement within the bounds of acceptable British discourse, didn't publicly attack Blair, and was reappointed to the cabinet by Britain's new prime minister, Gordon Brown.

The difficult paths to principled resignation by Ross, Short, Reed, and Denham are now analyzed in detail. While the moral reasoning differed in each case, all four concluded that to protect their honor and moral integrity, they had to break with their government.

CARNE ROSS
FOREIGN AND COMMONWEALTH OFFICE
RESIGNATION: SEPTEMBER 2004

Carne Ross served for more than fifteen years in the most prestigious ministry in the British government, the Foreign and Commonwealth Office. He rose quickly through the diplomatic ranks and by the age of thirty had already completed foreign service in Germany and Afghanistan. For four and a half years, he served in the U.K. delegation to the United Nations Security Council. In this position, he was the U.K. delegation's Iraq and Middle East expert, holding the rank of first secretary. He was very loyal to his country during this period. In fact, his dogged pursuit of British commercial and strategic interests at the UN earned him the reputation as a "Rottweiler" among his UN colleagues. Yet Ross now looks back at that period with guilt and anger. The breach came in 2004.[17] Ross writes:

> I resigned from the British Foreign Office in September 2004. The breaking point finally came when I testified (in secret) to the official inquiry on Iraq's WMD (the Butler Inquiry, as it was known). I wrote down all that I thought about the war, including the available alternatives, its illegality and the misrepresentation of what we knew of Iraq's weapons. Once I had written it, I realized at last, after years of agonizing, that I could no longer continue to work for the government.[18]

The "years of agonizing" were partially a result of seeing the ways in which the British government was misrepresenting the situation in Iraq. The expert knowledge Ross gained on Iraq convinced him of a reasonably consistent picture from the late 1990s into 2002: Iraq was not rearming to any great extent and posed no threat to its neighbors, Britain, or the United States. While questions remained as to the disposal of past stockpiles of weapons, "containment was working." The Butler Report later confirmed that there was no evidence to suggest that Iraq was either significantly rearming or had intent to attack its neighbors.[19] Yet this was not what either the British or the American government was telling its citizens. According to Ross, the problem was not that the government was deliberately lying about Iraq's weapons. It was, rather, a situation where officials selectively chose evidence, ignored or removed contradictions to that evidence, and polished (or spun) the report. Alternatives to war were not considered. The government was thus producing reports on Iraq that were one-sided and based on unreliable information. Evidence selectivity and biased reports are a danger in any government agency (consistently positive economic reports come to mind). Yet Ross believes, "When seeking to justify military action, the government has a duty to tell the whole truth, not just a partial account of it."[20] "The governments did not manufacture lies, but neither did they tell the truth."[21]

The invasion of Iraq in March 2003 heightened the issues of individual moral responsibility for Ross. He heard colleagues be extremely critical of the war while they were deeply involved in executing it. Yet these individuals felt no responsibility for the violence and killing taking place in Iraq. The responsibility for war was simply pushed off onto the politicians and the functionaries at the top level. Ross found that most government officials simply did what they were told and did not examine the ways in which their actions supported war policies. The British Foreign Service seemed filled with a certain degree of "moral numbness" or complete indifference. "It simply wasn't our job to worry about the moral implications of what we were doing." Even worse, this "moral indifference is presented as a virtue." Those individuals who "see things as they 'really are' are the more 'practical' and 'realistic.' Those who dare to exhibit their own moral judgment or criticism are condemned as 'romantic,' 'sentimental' or just plain 'immature.'"[22] By 2004, Ross could no longer be a part of a diplomatic corps that discouraged dissent and demanded loyalty to the story line. Ross was ready to assert his own moral autonomy.

Furthermore, Ross not only had become disenchanted with traditional diplomacy but also began to question the relevance of theories of international relations used to justify power politics. In their attempts to give coherence and neatness to global affairs, international relations theories (political realism, neoconservatism, liberal internationalism, and so on) all seemed to "betray the reality, and the complexity, of what actually took place." The reality is that policy-makers are influenced by a host of cultural, political, historical, and emotional factors that can't be placed into the simplistic and "dangerously reductionist" terms offered by these theories. Policy-making "is more random, more arbitrary, just simply messier and more human than theory would have us believe."[23] While rejecting the traditional ways of viewing global politics and engaging diplomatic affairs, Ross was committed to applying his skills and knowledge to creating a more just world.

In 2005 Carne Ross founded a nonprofit agency called Independent Diplomat (ID), with the motto "a diplomatic service for those who need it most." The ID seeks to provide services to poor and neglected regions of the world so that these peoples get access to the decision-makers and international forums that make policy, such as the European Union and the United Nations. Clients of ID include the Polisario Front of Western Sahara and the governments of Kosovo, Somaliland, and the Turkish Republic of Northern Cyprus. This new undertaking has brought Ross recognition. In 2005 he was named by Britain's Joseph Rowntree Charitable Trust a "visionary for a just and peaceful world."

The guiding principle of ID is the minimization of human suffering. Ross believes that experienced and professional diplomats have a role to play in helping prevent conflict and improve the human condition. But the focus is on helping those who need it the most: the disadvantaged, politically oppressed, and economically marginalized. Ross was able to find financial backers to this new enterprise, including George Soros and the Oak Foundation. ID now has offices in London, New York, and Brussels.

Richard Whitman, a professor of politics at the University of Bath, praises the role of the Independent Diplomat. As noted above, it is rare for diplomacy and foreign policy to focus on morality and not national self-interest. According to Whitman, "What he [Ross] brings is a moral element to foreign policy. Historically, we think of diplomats as almost amoral."[24]

CLARE SHORT
MEMBER OF PARLIAMENT
SECRETARY OF STATE FOR INTERNATIONAL DEVELOPMENT
DEPARTMENT FOR INTERNATIONAL DEVELOPMENT
RESIGNATION: MAY 2003

Clare Short was elected a Labour Party MP in 1983 and served for the next twenty-three years as a Member of Parliament for Birmingham Ladywood. She was secretary of state for international development in the Blair cabinet from May 1997 until her resignation in May 2003. Following the controversy surrounding her resignation and her subsequent criticisms of the Blair government, Short decided in 2006 not to run for reelection to the Parliament and to stand down in the next general election.[25]

Short's struggle to keep a clear ethical balance during the Bush–Blair push to war with Iraq in 2003 put her in the public spotlight. In her mind, the sanctions against Iraq were morally problematic due to the harm caused to the poor people and the children of the country. While she loathed the regime of Saddam Hussein, she believed that international law required that all additional moves to alter that government had to be led by the UN. Furthermore, she thought that there were options available to tighten the pressure on the Hussein regime that could be utilized. Instead of following up on these options, Short saw Bush and Blair pursuing a "reckless" path toward war with Iraq without a clear mandate from the United Nations. As a member of the Blair cabinet, she was expected to defend the Blair war policy, which was morally troublesome. Yet instead of resigning in protest, in March 2003 she announced that she would remain in the cabinet and support the government's resolution in the House of Commons. Two months later, however, in May 2003 she did resign. Short stated in her resignation letter that Blair had broken his promises to her regarding UN involvement in the reconstruction of Iraq and had negotiated a UN Security Council resolution that "contradicts the assurances I have given in the House of Commons and elsewhere about the legal authority of the occupying powers, and the need for a UN-led process to establish a legitimate Iraqi government. This makes my position impossible."[26]

Critics seemed to "pile on" Short for pursuing these actions. In March 2003 the left criticized her decision not to resign, arguing that her presence in the government gave Blair the legitimacy he needed to pursue his war policies. Then in May 2003, Blair supporters in the Labour Party criticized her when she did decide to resign, arguing that she was unwilling to stand by the party during a critical time. In the end, a hullabaloo ensued, with many from the left and right seemingly unwilling or unable to understand or accept Short's logic for staying and then going.

Yet, in listening to Short, I was struck by her ethical search for real-world solutions to the many thorny issues surrounding the Iraq debacle. When it became clear that Bush and Blair were going ahead with the Iraq war, instead of resigning in protest, Short tried to "work from within" to help create a reconstruction program led by the UN that would benefit the people of Iraq. A public resignation at this point would have perhaps been the "easier" road. She could have walked away from it all with a clear conscience and become a public "hero" to the antiwar movement. Principled resignation to protest the rush to war would probably have been seen as a courageous and moral action by many, if not most, of the population in Britain.

To Short, however, the situation was not that simple. She had the ear of the prime minister of Britain, and through him, of the president of the United States. She could put demands on these governments to moderate the extreme unilateralism and short-sightedness of the British/U.S. foreign policy toward Iraq. Blair's foreign minister Robin Cook had already resigned to protest the hasty push to war. Short was therefore in a unique position. Blair could not afford to lose another cabinet minister. Two senior cabinet members resigning in protest over British war policies could have empowered others in the Labour Party to also speak and act against these policies. As a result, Blair seemed willing to listen to her arguments and negotiate. Short thought that perhaps by staying and continuing to "work from within," she could leverage her position to achieve key policy changes. Thus, instead of resigning, she pursued the more difficult path of attempting to restrain the Bush/Blair policies in the Middle East. Short was particularly concerned with (a) a clear UN mandate behind the military actions in Iraq, (b) the internationalization of the reconstruction of Iraq, and (c) a U.S./British commitment to the "road map" for peace between Israel and Palestine.

It is hard to criticize Short's decision to first stay and then reconsider once she realized her strategy was not working. She had to give it a try. She had to see if Blair would listen and then whether he would keep his word. Probably more than any other individual opposed to the war, she had the access and political position to be able to have her voice heard. While a flamboyant resignation in March may have been popular with those opposed to the war in Iraq, such an action was probably not the most ethical course. In her position, the moral action was to stay and fight from within until it became clear that such an approach was futile. By May 2003, after Blair broke his promises to her, the ineffectiveness of this "work from within" strategy did become clear. Thus, it was at this point that Short resigned. It had become all too clear that Short's positions on Iraq and the Middle East were being ignored. Furthermore, her continued presence in the cabinet was used to justify policies that she considered dangerous and misguided. She had to go.

Clare Short's thoughtful and dramatic journey highlights the complexity of maintaining both moral autonomy and loyalty to one's party and government. In this regard, it is worth noting the similarities and differences between the actions of Short and Colin Powell. Both Powell and Short decided not to resign in March 2003, despite their serious reservations about the invasion of Iraq. Powell, in fact, set his reservations aside and used his high position to build public support for the conflict. Short, on the other hand, did the opposite and used her high position in early 2003 to warn against the "reckless" path to war. After the war began, both Powell and Short were marginalized by their respective leaders and could not influence war or reconstruction policies in Iraq. It was at this point that Short realized that a "working from within" strategy was morally problematic, because her continued presence gave great legitimacy to the disastrous Blair war policies. Powell, on the other hand, refused to acknowledge the way in which he was used by the Bush administration to validate the problematic occupation and never considered acting to protect his moral autonomy. Thus, as opposed to Powell, in the end Short was able to keep her "ethical balance" and take the right moral actions both to stay and then to go.

ANDY REED
MEMBER OF PARLIAMENT FOR LOUGHBOROUGH
PARLIAMENTARY PRIVATE SECRETARY
RESIGNATION: MARCH 2003

In early March 2003, Andy Reed quit as parliamentary private secretary to Environment Secretary Margaret Beckett to protest the British government's decision to support a United States–led invasion of Iraq without a UN mandate. With this action, Reed became the first person in the British government to resign over the Blair/Bush Iraq strategy. He resigned without making a press statement, trying to quietly register his moral objections without becoming a "media star." Unfortunately for him, word leaked out and he was soon inundated with calls. More than 160 media organizations from around the world called his cell phone, attempting to get a statement from him. To avoid charges of opportunism and self-promotion, he simply unplugged his phone and did not return these calls.

George W. Bush has spoken often about his belief in Jesus and his strong Christian faith. The evangelical Christian movement in the United States solidly supported Bush and was a core constituency behind the invasion and occupation of Iraq. Furthermore, many fundamentalist Christians believe that Bush is carrying out God's work in the Middle East. Yet this perspective is probably a minority view within the worldwide Christian community. Many other Christians believed that the war in Iraq was a violation of the long-standing Christian "just war" tradition. The doctrine of the just war can be traced back to Augustine in *The City of God* and should be understood as part of the historical Christian debate over pacifism ("turn the other cheek").[27]

Reed's ethics flow from his strong Christian beliefs. He is not a Christian pacifist and had supported military action in Afghanistan. He evaluated the many explanations from Blair and Bush for unilaterally invading Iraq in 2003 from a Christian just war perspective. He came to the conclusion that this war was not just, that the case for war had not been made, and that the killing of civilians was therefore not justified. He met with Blair and explained his reasoning. When it was clear that the war was going forward, he decided that he had to resign. In the end, this was an easy decision for him. While he regretted the decision to leave the Blair government, morally he felt that he had no other choice. Staying in office would have meant he had to publicly support the Iraq invasion, something he could not in good conscience do.

Reed did not want to go "over the top" in his condemnation of Tony Blair. He continued to respect the prime minister and believed that Blair was doing what he thought was in the best interests of the country. Reed, therefore, wanted to avoid personal attacks which he saw as counterproductive. He thus pursued a "quiet" resignation strategy through which he could be true to his moral principles without engaging in vitriolic mudslinging. However, since he was the first government official to resign in protest of the Iraq war, the media spotlight proved hard to avoid.

JOHN DENHAM
MEMBER OF PARLIAMENT
CABINET MINISTER
RESIGNATION: MARCH 2003

John Denham was elected a Member of Parliament for Southampton Itchen in 1992. Following the election of Tony Blair and the new Labour government in 1997, Denham served as a government minister. In May 1997, he was appointed parliamentary under secretary of state at the Department of Social Security (DSS). In July 1998 he was made a minister of state at the DSS. In June 2001 he was made minister of state at the home office responsible for crime reduction, policing, and community safety. In March 2003 Denham resigned from the Blair government, as he could not support the United States–British invasion of Iraq. Denham felt that the Iraq invasion would create greater insecurity and deepen problems of extremism and terrorism. He believed that the unilateral actions of the United States seriously undermined the multilateral forces that were united on the need to confront the global threats that emerged after 9/11. Yet the United States seemed to have "thrown away the world's sympathy" and instead embarked on a path that brought it great danger.

In his resignation speech to the House of Commons on March 18, 2003, Denham stated:

> The U.S. Administration appear at times to delight in stressing their disdain for international opinion and in asserting their right to determine not only the target but the means and the timetable, their gratuitous actions apparently designed to make a common voice impossible, not least here in Europe. That has made the international coming together that we need impossible to achieve. . . . The action against Iraq is, I believe pre-emptive, and therefore demands even greater international support and consensus than other sorts of intervention. We do not have it. Such isolation entails a genuine cost and

danger. It undermines the legitimacy that we must maintain to tackle the many threats to global security. It fuels the movements that are antipathetic to our values and way of life.[28]

Yet despite these conclusions about the Iraq intervention, Denham remained extremely loyal to Tony Blair. Denham stated, "I do not blame the prime minister. . . . No one could have worked harder to forge consensus. His achievements are real, not least in persuading the U.S. administration to take the United Nations route. However, our prime minister has been ill served by those whom he sought to influence."[29] Thus, despite his resignation, Denham remained steadfast in his respect for the Labour Party and Blair. He has expressed support for those in the cabinet who did not resign in protest but instead tried to pursue good work in the many critical areas of public service—education, housing, and so on. Denham was thus careful not to publicly reprimand the prime minister or the party; he did not "burn any bridges" with his resignation. He instead kept his resignation within the bounds of the accepted discourse of British politics.

This approach has served him well. In June 2007, Britain's new prime minister, Gordon Brown, appointed Denham to a new cabinet-level post, secretary for innovation, universities, and skills. Brown hoped that his appointment of some critics of the Iraq war to his cabinet would help to heal the rifts in the party over the conflict and perhaps win back some of the disenchanted.[30]

Denham believes in the principle of "collective responsibility" within a democratic government. Policy differences will emerge within all governments. To become a part of the government requires accepting that one will not agree with all decisions on all policies. A government could not function if ministers resigned over every policy disagreement, as business would come to a halt. Collective responsibility, therefore, means supporting the party and the policy, even if you would have done things quite differently. It is only in extreme cases—like the Iraq war—when one's personal ethics are on the line that, according to Denham, resignation should be considered. His strong feeling that the invasion of Iraq would worsen the battle against terrorism caused him to step down.

PEER PRESSURE, HUMILIATION, AND LONELINESS

The journey from loyal Blair supporter to public critic was a difficult one for all of those who resigned. The pressures to remain in the government were monumental and came from not only the "Blairites" in the government but also friends and family. To decide to quit means setting aside the dozens and dozens of rationalizations as to why it is better to stay in office. Such pressures have led countless Foreign Service officers to "hold their noses" and support odious and immoral government policies. Resignation involves overcoming these peer pressures and family conflicts and facing the future on one's own—often a very lonely path. Furthermore, the Blair government was aggressive in defending its policies and disparaging opponents. It takes courage to stick one's neck out to try to stop a "patriotic" push to war.

It took Carne Ross, for example, years to come to his decision to quit the government. He agonized and wrestled with this decision because of the personal consequences. During the run up to the war he drafted many resignation letters but never submitted them. Why?

> I was afraid, basically. To be honest, I think I was afraid of being publicly humiliated. I knew what would happen to me if I stuck my head up and said what I actually thought, which was, "I don't agree with this, and I think that what our government is saying is dishonest." In those days, you could sense this incredibly powerful, almost emotional, rush to war. I was in the U.S. at the time and [the Iraq war] was very much part of the post-9/11 kind of emotion. To stand up in front of that runaway train carried a risk you would have been crushed, and I wasn't prepared to endure that.

In addition, the risks for Ross were much greater than for the members of Parliament who resigned. It is important to draw a distinction between civil servants, like Ross, and politicians. As Ross explains,

> A politician who resigns his or her place in the cabinet, or from a ministerial position, remains in the Parliament. This is substantively different from civil servants who actually resign their jobs and give up everything. I gave up everything. I gave up my salary from the day I quit and my pension, everything. I didn't get a fucking penny. And I'm still bitter about it. It was a hell of a sacrifice. I get a pension of $12,000 a year when I turn 60. So, yes, there is a big, bloody difference between an MP who leaves the cabinet and my resignation. I say this with some bitterness in my voice, and I feel it bitterly because it has cost me a lot. I went for a year without any money at all, which was one of the hardest years of my life. I had just gotten married, and we had nothing. It was very, very hard. I didn't have a nice job to walk into when I quit; I had nothing.

With her twenty-six years of government service as an MP, Clare Short will retire with a significant parliamentary pension. Her financial future and well-being is thus more secure and stable than that faced by Ross. However, when she broke with Blair, Short cut her salary in half, reduced her pension, and debilitated her future political prospects. She was ostracized and humiliated by her colleagues. After putting her whole life into building the Labour Party, she found herself suddenly completely cut off and estranged from it:

> People who were sort of buddies and friends, who previously would come and crawl all over [me] and ask [me] to come and speak at their constituency dinners, now sort of look the other way. Not all of them, of course, but a lot do. If you look at resignations in the past within the Labour Party, sometimes groups of people will fight and then work out a compromise. Certainly when I resigned it was just about the merits—the lies were indefensible, and there was no question that I had to resign. But my assumption was that there would then be a fight in the party that I would be part of.

Unfortunately, there was no real "fight" in the Labour Party, and Short felt that she had to move on. Others in the party who felt as she did refused to speak up. Short states,

> There are lots of people on Labour's back benches who are as unhappy as I am about the Iraq policy. But somehow they are willing to stay inside the tent. These MPs weren't in the government; they were back benchers. So, in their minds, they are not so implicated in the policy and can stick with the party. But they won't speak up in debates on Iraq [either] or criticize in the same kind of way as I did.

Short really felt that after her resignation, she would be able to join with others to try to hold Blair accountable. Instead, the party effectively made Short appear unreliable and untrustworthy and made it impossible for other MPs to support her principled actions. After serving in the British Cabinet, Short now found herself alone, at the bottom, out of favor and often deprecated by her former friends and colleagues.

Andy Reed and John Denham, on the other hand, pursued a quieter, less confrontational path than Short and Ross. As a result, neither Reed nor Denham experienced significant personal repercussions to their reputations or finances from their acts of resignation. Reed's decision to resign was perhaps easier than some of his colleagues because of his Christian principles and belief in just war theory. Reed states,

> Having wrestled with the arguments, for me it was reasonably clear-cut. I read as much as I could on just war. And it seemed to me that this case was clear-cut—Iraq was not a just war. And therefore, from a deep moral perspective, it was quite easy to say, "I can't support this and I have got to tell you why." I was able to do this in an amicable way with the prime minister. He was very understanding, and still is. But walking in on Monday to the Commons Tea Room to my fellow colleagues was more difficult.

Since he was not a cabinet minister, Reed had less to lose than Short.

I was a very junior parliamentary private secretary. I wasn't even a minister, so I didn't lose any money. I really didn't lose anything, because I'm not personally ambitious necessarily to be a minister. That is probably the only real cost—I will probably now never be a minister. But I don't really care about that. I just wanted the freedom at the time to be able to say "No" [to the rush to war in Iraq] publicly. I was fed up with having to tell people, "It's difficult." I just wanted to say no [to the invasion].

As noted above, Denham kept his criticisms of the government within the bounds of accepted discourse of British politics and kept the door open for future cabinet positions. His Labour Party colleagues thus continued to treat him well, and he did not face any of the ill will that was heaped on Short. As a result, Denham feels that in the British culture

there is enormous goodwill toward somebody who, as I did, resigns for reasons of principle, even if there is profound disagreement with the decision. The only response I really got was one of respect for what I had done. I wasn't criticized at all to my face. I don't know what people said behind my back. But nobody has said to me, "You shouldn't have done that," or "you should have been more loyal." Because the fact is that while there were people who fully believed the whole thing [rationale for war with Iraq], there were plenty of other people who were troubled by it. These people were having the same conversations in their minds as I was having. Therefore, plenty of people could understand entirely what I had done. So, for me, there was no personal cost (although if I had not resigned, I might have been in the cabinet by now).

Denham was back in the cabinet by late June 2007.

COLLECTIVE RESPONSIBILITY AND PARTY DISCIPLINE

British Cabinet members accept the principle of "collective responsibility." This principle means that officials are called on to defend things that they don't necessarily agree with and to defend things that aren't necessarily what they might have done in the same circumstances. For Denham, collective responsibility means

Sometimes you'll defend a policy that other ministers have carried out that you think is probably a mistake. And likewise, you expect your colleagues to do the same for you. In fact, the collective responsibility of government can't work in any other way. Otherwise, government would sort of collapse every other day, because a government in which everybody agrees on what everybody else has done has never existed. That's the reality of the business of government. [I ask] if I vote for this [policy], can I defend this particular

decision in private afterwards with sufficient conviction or sufficient justification. If a minister thinks [he or she] can't do that, then at that point the person can't continue as minister. So the issue and pressure for me was whether
I could defend this policy after the event.

When the principle of collective responsibility is combined with party
discipline, open debate and criticism can be stifled. There is more discipline in the British parties than exists in the United States. The party whip
in Parliament is the enforcer, and all MPs are supposed to vote together as
a bloc. While in the United States it is common for a member of Congress
to vote against his or her party on a particular issue, in Britain this is not
the norm. Short explains,

> Party loyalty is very important. People talk like they give their lives to the
> party and they want to be loyal to the party. I was one of those. I put my
> life into it; there is no question about it. So, on top of that deep tradition of
> loyalty, there is also all this patronage of power. If you are an older MP and
> want to go to the House of Lords, you'd better keep your nose clean. If you
> are a younger MP and you ever want to be a minister, you better not rock
> the boat. And the party leadership is quite ruthless. Some of the back bench-
> ers have been warned that if they go too far, they wouldn't be able to stand
> as a Labour MP for reelection. I'm sure in a way I sort of helped with the
> discipline in the Labour Party today because, you know, you don't want to
> end up like Clare Short!

Such pressures make it foolhardy for a cabinet minister or Labour MP
to fundamentally question the direction of the Labour government. These
same forces exist in the British civil service as well. Ross describes how
difficult it is in the Foreign Service for individuals to question the status
quo. If an individual resists the government's story, he or she will not be
promoted. The result is that individuals in the government fear going
too far in their critique of British policy.[31] Such dynamics limit the voices
of moral dissent in the formulation of foreign policy. In the case of Iraq,
individuals in the Foreign Service who objected to the justification for war
were afraid to speak out because they would be going too far by challenging the basic WMD/Iraq story line. Ross explains,

> One issue is structural. In the British Civil Service—I can't speak for the
> American State Department, but I guess they are similar—you are clearly
> instructed to believe that you are the mere exponent of other people's deci-
> sion. You are merely the implementer of politicians' choices and therefore
> ultimately not responsible for them. But also ultimately you don't have the
> freedom to question them. It is your responsibility merely to implement
> them. Second, part of the cultural context of the Foreign Service in par-
> ticular—not necessarily for all government service, but certainly part of the

Foreign Service—is that war is something that states sometimes have to do. There is a different moral and intellectual approach to war in government service than there is in the broader public. In government you are implicitly taught in various ways that governments sometimes have to do dirty work in order to protect their peoples, to protect their interests. There is a certain amorality which is acknowledged in government, sometimes even celebrated. Third, there are the more subtle forces about how groups work and being in a group where loyalty to the group is valued much more highly than questioning the collective wisdom of the group. It is very clear in institutions like the British Foreign Office that you are not likely to advance to the top if you are known as the sort of person who questions policy, whether over wars or anything else. The business of state craft is seen as such an amoral practice, that even to talk about morality in that context is viewed as naïve. I mean, you would not be having this conversation inside the foreign office. Talking about morals is not really encouraged. It is a hard-headed business where you are supposed to look at the world through cruel, cold eyes and disinterestedly, dispassionately assess what your country wants and then go out and get it. Certainly the senior officials in the Foreign Service manifest this kind of attitude through their behavior. It is not easy to be the one in the group who sticks out—regardless of whether the group is government servants or a platoon of soldiers or a group of cooks in a restaurant. It is not easy to be the one to say, "I think what we are doing is wrong." It is much, much easier to just go along with it.

MORAL NUMBNESS

Civil servants and cabinet ministers thus often enter a world of "moral numbness" in which these individuals do not accept individual responsibility for the government's decisions. An individual can feel that "well, it is the government's decision; I'm just part of this machine; I can't stop it, anyway; I'm not ultimately making the decision to go to war." By "moral numbness," I mean this dynamic which leads to an inability for individuals to accept moral responsibility for their actions. Moral numbness can also result from a belief that there are two moralities—one for individuals and another for the government (as reviewed in chapter 3). It is expected that individuals will not lie, cheat, steal, or kill. The state, on the other hand, is forced to dirty its hands (often with killing, torture, and war) in order to protect the country's political freedom and economic viability. Government employees become numb to these actions and accept them as part of the unfortunate reality of real-world politics.

Ross agrees that there are two moralities:

While I don't think it is right, I absolutely do think it [two moralities] is true. I think that exponents of government think that they are entitled to behave in an amoral fashion because they are representing government. I certainly did. I think what we did in sanctions on Iraq, for example, was morally wrong. But any moral qualms we had about it were silenced by the belief that we were entitled to do so because we worked for the government. I think that is particularly true in war-making. There is something about a collective irresponsibility of being in government as well that is at play here. It is not just about the moral rules of being in government; it is also about the irresponsibility of being in a group. The truth is if you do these things for the British government, if you stay in the British government, you are never likely to be held to account for it in any serious way.

Short notes how such a system not only promotes amoral behavior among individual civil servants and cabinet members but also undermines the standing of the state itself in international relations:

If it becomes my party [or my country], right or wrong, then it's all cynical, isn't it? If we say our lies and constantly calculate our advantage, it all becomes a dirty game. It's the opposite if a world is based on the rule of law, of international law. With international conventions that outlaw torture, for example, we are raising the standards of humanity, binding all of ourselves to better values. I know that the establishment of the International Criminal Court (ICC) was much more contentious in America. But the British just strongly supported it. A former military dictator in Bolivia asked me on a recent trip whether he would be arrested if he visited the U.K. Human rights law and the ICC are striking fear into the heart of dictators all over the world. The rule of law means murder is murder and if anyone does it, then the law will come and get them. International law can move the whole level of our civilization upward. But we have to be sincere about the rules we agree to; we have to mean them and all adhere to them and expect them to apply to everybody. Look at what's happened to America: extraordinary rendition, Guantanamo, being willing to collude in torture. America was a beacon to the world for the rule of law and a belief in human rights. It is a tragedy that this has been shredded and lost. It also means that America is massively less respected across the world than it was. In this sense America's influence has diminished as a result of cynical "noble" lies.

Members of Parliament are particularly susceptible to "moral numbness" and a lack of sense of personal responsibility for the government's actions. As one of four hundred MPs, Reed said it was too "easy to think that your actions can't change policy and that nobody will ever really notice. You almost have to pinch yourself to say, 'Well, actually, if fifty or sixty of us didn't do it, and had enough moral backbone to say that we're not going to do it, then we could change things.' . . . But [unfortunately] there is a groupthink and a tribalism that comes around which actually raises a bigger question about how democracy works."

LIES AND WORKING FROM WITHIN

Probably the key issue that caused many individuals to break with Bush and Blair was the distortion of the truth surrounding Iraq. According to Ross, for example, the internal assessments in the U.K. and the U.S. governments were consistent and clear from 1998 to 2003:

> Those assessments were that Iraq was not significantly rearming to any extent whatsoever. It wasn't a fine or close judgment at all; it was absolutely clear. We did not believe that they had significant stocks of WMD or significant rearmament of any weapon system at all, whether unconventional weapons or conventional weapons, the means to deliver them, nothing. Their air force was nothing; their army was a shadow of its former self. In our bilateral exchanges on Iraq between the U.S. and the U.K., we would say to each other that containment was succeeding. So for the government to suddenly claim that Iraq was a threat—which the U.S. did much more than the U.K.—and suggest that the Iraqis were collaborating with terrorists was clearly an overstatement of what we knew to be the case.

Civil servants and cabinet ministers were expected to stand by and support these incorrect asserts and exaggerations about Iraq.

Were Bush and Blair lying? Ross believes that it is more complicated than inventing a lie:

> I think they misstated what they knew to be the truth. I know that I am playing with words now, but I do think it is different from deliberately lying. I think by the end of it a lot of the policy experts and diplomats believed what they were saying. The evidence had been so massaged that when they read it over to themselves, they started to believe it. I talked to several of them and they don't think they did lie. But I say to them, "Look, the dossier was dramatically different from our own internal assessments, so what about that is not lying, is not fallacious?" The response: "Oh, well, you know that I know the dossier was a mistake. But the problem is really a question of editing and, you know, drafting problems." This is the way of convincing themselves that no wrong was done. The fact that they were an intimate and intrinsic part of the greatest foreign policy catastrophe in recent history doesn't seem to cause them much lack of sleep. I know and worked with most of the people involved in the Iraq dossier. You would have to ask them why they didn't resign; I don't know.

Ross has little sympathy for the position that these individuals who knew about the government's deceit should stay and work from within. He believes such an argument is

> bullshit and always has been. I used to think that, but I don't believe it anymore. I think if you are part of it, you are culpable. The idea that you, as an

official, are exercising some kind of moderating influence on government action, I think, is pretty naïve. It doesn't seem to work that way. I just don't see officials sticking up their hands in government saying, "This is wrong and we mustn't do it." That doesn't seem to happen in government.

Ross continues,

One can't have it both ways—you are either part of the war effort or you are not. If you don't like it, you should not do it. History demonstrates clearly that the American government, or any government, is not some kind of debating club where people sit down and weigh out the options and sort of disinterestedly decide what is best. And that is clearly not what happened in the Iraq case. Instead, there was a clear determination on the part of a group of people in the administration, including the president, but above all, the vice president, Rumsfeld, and others, to go to war. Powell is stupid or naïve if he believes sending a few memos from the State Department would have stopped that. And I don't think he is stupid or naïve.

Short also reached the point of revulsion at the lies and felt the limitations of a "working from within" strategy. Short states,

It's unbearable because the lies are unbearable. The policy is a disaster. The lack of truthfulness is indefensible. Occasionally, people say to me, "Wouldn't it have been better to stay? You could have gone on with what you were doing in development." And some African presidents rang me and said, "Please stay." But you can't stay in a government where a massive central part of its policy is, in your view, indefensible. If you are in the government, you have to defend it. And that is ethically impossible.

To keep Short in the government, Blair promised UN leadership on the reconstruction of Iraq and a U.S./British commitment to the "road map" for peace between Israel and Palestine. Yet Blair didn't follow through, and ultimately Short felt manipulated and deceived. Her book documenting these negotiations with Blair is titled *An Honorable Deception?* Was Blair's deception honorable? Short believes that Blair thought so:

He recently said in his resignation statement (announcing that he was going to stand down as prime minister) that he knew what he did was contentious and that some people disagreed, but that he acted with complete sincerity and did what he thought was right (or something to that effect). This is in line with what I'm saying. He convinced himself that everything he did he was doing for the right motive. Britain should stay close to America. He swallowed some of the neocon kind of view of the world. We will spread democracy and freedom and so on. Also, after being so close to Clinton, psychologically he was worried about not being close to Bush. He wanted to

stand by America in its hour of need, post–September 11, which the whole
,world felt and which, of course, has been thrown away. Blair hasn't read
much history. He doesn't do much detail. He convinces himself of something
and then he will go for it. Yet the way he did Iraq, sailing by the seat of his
pants, was a reckless way to proceed. The thing about Tony Blair is he means
it when he says it. So he convinced himself that sticking with America was
right and that getting rid of the Saddam Hussein regime was right. Yet very
early on he was dishonest with a number of things. But he thought what he
was doing was honorable, and he thought it was honorable to engage in that
kind of deceit.

A clear example of Blair's deceit was his characterization of the legality of invading Iraq and his statements about President Chirac and the
French position at the UN. The French (along with China, Russia, and
most other nations) argued that UN Resolution 1441 did not legally authorize force against Iraq and, therefore, before such action was taken, a
new resolution was necessary. Short states,

> Blair misled the country. The Blair line was that the second resolution was
> impossible because France had said it would veto any second resolution.
> That was all over the press—the headlines, the announcements, everything.
> And it is false. And then the shock of the legal advice saying it was OK to go
> to war [without the second resolution], which we now know was concocted
> in a dishonorable way. I was stunned by the attorney's legal advice. We now
> have copies of the full legal advice [prepared for the Blair government]. . . .
> [T]he full legal advice explains that the Americans assert that there is war
> authority from the first [resolution], but the British lawyers warn that a court
> of law might side against this position.

Short continues,

> [In 2003] we had had these rumors . . . that the attorney general was of two
> minds and not certain of his legal authority. The military said that we were
> not going to war without legal authority. They didn't want themselves to be
> prosecuted in an international court for crimes against peace and war crimes,
> because, unlike America, we were keen on the International Criminal Court
> and happy to submit ourselves to it. It is now clear the military needed some-
> thing. So they concocted a statement and pretended it was the legal advice
> saying unequivocally there is legal authority for war. That was right before
> the vote on the war. There was no discussion in the cabinet. But again, naïve
> little me, I just thought the attorney general of Great Britain and Northern
> Ireland were in the teeth of war and would not politically [manufacture legal
> authority] to [please Blair]. [Just as I was naïve to] believe that the president
> of the United States really meant his [commitment to the] road map [for
> peace in the Middle East].

The idea of an "honorable deception" is close to the idea of a "noble lie" put forward by some of the neoconservatives in the United States who studied the philosophy of Leo Strauss. As discussed in chapter 3, Strauss draws on Plato and puts forward the idea that a "noble lie" can unify a country and help accomplish a state's critical goals. The government is thus permitted to lie to its citizens to achieve the greater good.

This idea of a "noble lie" is rejected by Short, Ross, Reed, and Denham. Short states,

> I think lying leads to dishonor and leads to incompetence. The massive post-invasion problems in Iraq flow partly from the dishonesty. Furthermore, lies from the government to its cabinet, parliament, and people about something as profound as a war, and sacrificing the lives of your own people and the killing of others—there is nothing more profoundly dishonorable and corrosive of trust. As a consequence of the Iraq war, there has been a massive corrosion of respect for politicians and the political institutions of Britain. So I don't think there is such a thing as a noble lie.

Reed points out that there may be times that the government should not share all its intelligence, but it should never lie:

> Quite clearly, the intelligence that was used by the United States and the U.K. to justify the action in Iraq was based on false premises. I believe that you can't lie to take a country to war. That's not a "noble" lie even if you think the cause is just (which Bush and Blair thought it was). No, I don't regard it as "noble." [However,] [t]here are times when it has been necessary, during World War II, for example, [for the government to control] how much information is good for the population to know about how well or how badly the war is going.

Denham is emphatic in his opposition to a "noble lie," which he describes as "a dangerous totalitarian doctrine." Denham states,

> No, I can't think of any circumstances which would justify a noble lie in government. Politics does exist to some extent in an area where the full truth is not revealed at every moment of every day. There are ways of not saying things, for example, which might be contentious or argued about. I would accept that is sometimes necessary. But I think that is quite different from straightforwardly telling a lie and deliberately going out to deceive. . . . I think it is best to tell the truth. Now there are things that have been done in politics which are about mobilizing support and encouraging a nation. In this country before the Second World War, there wasn't a universal enthusiasm for fighting the Germans. [To some] the Nazis were somebody else's problem. To an extent, the British government consciously went out to foster a sense of British identity and British resolve in the face of the threat from Hitler. This was a reasonable and historically correct thing to do. And,

frankly, given the nature of the Hitler regime, it didn't involve telling any lies. It was more about mobilizing all the resources of a nation to strengthen a people's resolve. You are supposed to do that in a situation of war, or other severe conflict, to bring people together. But that is not the same as deliberately going out and making things up.

I asked Ross if he could ever conceive of a situation where it would be correct for the government to pursue a strategy of a "noble lie." Ross responded,

I'm doing this thought experiment to try and think of an example where a noble lie would be correct, and I'm struggling. The whole idea of the noble lie is imbued with elitism and the approach to government with which I fundamentally disagree. I find it really hard to imagine circumstances in which I could think it was right. The most clear-cut moral case in recent history is, of course, the Nazis. Where would a noble lie have been correct with the Nazis? Perhaps it would have been correct to have exaggerated the extent of Nazi rearmament in the 1930s to mobilize the public to fight Hitler. But, in fact, what happened was the British government downplayed the extent of Nazi rearmament in the 1930s because of appeasement. An additional lie they told was that they failed to report the extent of genocide of the Jews during the war for fear that it would incite sympathy for the Germans because Britain was such an anti-Semitic nation. No, I'm skeptical of it. The noble lie is so intrinsically this view that we, the bureaucrats and politicians, can decide what is best for the citizens (who are viewed as a kind of ragged proletariat). I therefore don't really agree with it.

ETHICS AND FOREIGN POLICY

As Britain's foreign minister, Robin Cook attempted to define an "ethical foreign policy." This project ran into a variety of difficulties, including the problem of defining what was meant by "moral" and "ethical." There are tremendous differences in the British and American public as to the content of correct moral action. The claim to ethical or moral values alone doesn't help. The real issue is what the content to those ethics and morals is: what are the values being promoted? But the discussion of values is equally contested, as shown in debates over the meaning of "democracy" and "freedom."

Because of these difficulties, Ross prefers to deal as closely as possible with the nuts and bolts of a situation. Carl Popper's guidelines about what the goal of policy should be provide Ross with clear guidance. Popper

avoids discussion of the word *morality*. He doesn't call it a moral approach. He just says that governments cannot know what is best for their people.

They cannot know what individuals want, and I agree with that view. Instead, he says that government should work to minimize suffering because suffering is actually something they can know and measure, and working to minimize suffering is a much more realistic and moderate goal. He doesn't couch this proposal in moral terms, and I think that actually should be the goal of foreign policy, too, and others would argue that that is a moralist way of seeing the world. I think it is actually a very realistic way of seeing the world and, actually, a world that would bring greater justice and stability, peace and all the rest of it to us, whilst on the way addressing some pretty horrible situations.

Ross continues,

The problem today is that from World War II we've adopted a good versus evil framework. One of the troubling things about the world today is it is not easy to draw moral distinctions. I don't think it is easy to be black and white about things like the Iraq war or terrorism. And that is why World War II is not very helpful in terms of moral instruction today. Even the moral ambiguities of World War II haven't been fully explored. For example, the British philosopher A.C. Grayling attempts to make a moral reckoning of the bombing of German and Japanese cities.[32] The book is carefully argued and ultimately comes down against the bombing of these cities. It is very interesting that even sixty years later, it is difficult and complicated to fully analyze these bombing campaigns. In fact, there has been no moral reckoning about whether it was right or not. Those who spoke out against these actions at the time were pretty much universally condemned. I don't think moral choices are ever particularly clear at the time you have to make them. I didn't feel that my resignation was a particularly moral choice. Others might want to put it in those terms, but I didn't. I just felt I couldn't go back and work with these people. I felt bitter and angry about the whole thing.

Short believes that ethics are key to foreign policy and central to a democracy. She maintains that it is possible to uphold decency in government:

I think no one should compromise their ethical autonomy. That doesn't mean people won't be tempted to tell little lies, or fiddle their travel expenses, or all those little things that human beings do. But you have to have rules that constrain us all. We have this ministerial code that says partly that we must always be honest with Parliament and so on. This has clearly been breached in the Iraq case. But the enforcement mechanism is the prime minister. So, of course, if Blair is leading it, there is not going to be any enforcement. Without those standards, we are all lost. When there are no standards, there is no difference between us and any ugly government. And then the whole of humanity can go careening down, which is the danger we are in right now, riding on this Iraq whirlwind. We are killing each other at a time when, because of all the environmental threats, we need unprecedented international cooperation. So fairness and honesty aren't just morally preferable. Honesty and fair rules are the only way that humans can trust each other, cooperate, and ultimately survive.

Denham rejects the view put forward by some political realists that states should simply define their actions around their security and economic interests. Such an approach sees values and ethics as simply devices to justify the national interest. Denham states,

> I take the view that in a democracy a government's aim is to act in the collective interest of the people who elected them. When you say that states "have an interest," you are saying the people of the country have an interest—and that is something which governments legitimately seek to pursue. And this responsibility is not just in terms of narrow security, but in terms of economy, energy supplies, and the rest of it. The question is what qualifies as the collective interest. I try to operate from two criteria. First, it regards a basic sense of doing what is right. When I was in favor of intervention in Bosnia, it was because people were being killed on our continent. It wasn't really affecting the lives of most British people, so there wasn't a broader "national interest" argument. Essentially, the reason for intervention was that people were dying in front of our eyes, and it was going to get worse, and we needed to do something about it. So there is a question of doing what is right. Second, in the modern, highly globalized world, ignoring basic values of ethics, morality, and good government is not a good way of defending a nation's interests. Realpolitik [power politics] actually means taking into account the proper principles of good government. Ethics and national interests go together. You can't neatly divide them up; they are intertwined.

When Reed recently traveled to Kyrgyzstan and Uzbekistan, he was asked, "How can you come here and criticize us as a totalitarian government, when you are locking people up for twenty-eight to ninety days without a trial?" These types of questions exposed Reed to how the denial of basic human rights in the name of combating terror is viewed abroad. The United States and Britain point the finger at other states for violating human rights in the name of security. Those words ring hollow and hypocritical when we then do the very same thing ourselves.

Arguments for torture, for example, often sound so very sensible. Yet these acts of torture have caused great harm to the overall struggle against extremist terrorist violence. Reed explains,

> In terms of torture: You quite clearly have to be better than those that you are purporting to be saving from torture. Abu Ghraib and other such situations are horrendous. Any moral superiority you bring, by trying to save people from the awfulness of the Saddam regime, is undermined. It only takes a few examples of torture and we lose the support of the majority of Iraqi people. Suddenly we become the "Western monsters" the Iraqis had been told to

expect. Again, it can be used the other way around as propaganda. I'm sure
we did it during the Second World War and exposed how terrible the German monsters were. The SS practices torture, and suddenly all the Germans
are the same and we turned them into monsters. So, in terms of the Middle
East, you can understand how people feel. The United States, and the West
in particular, is seen as overly aggressive and too apologetic for Israel. It
then all becomes a conspiracy against Muslim peoples. These are conclusions
drawn from our actions, and not by what we say or believe.

Human rights are often seen as providing a framework to move beyond individual national self-interest toward a more cosmopolitan-based
framework of justice for all people. Human rights could thus merge the
national interest with a global human interest. From his Christian ethical
perspective, Reed believes that this global human rights framework is essential and that states are moving in this direction:

> The [human rights] framework has to be global and accept all fundamental
> human rights, including [social] rights to housing and education. From a
> Christian perspective, these rights should already be in place. We are made
> in God's image. Globally, we are all equal and we are our brother's keeper.
> It is thus morally wrong to ignore global problems of suffering. [However,]
> we still have got a long way to go to understand that every individual has a
> basic human right to existence—never mind whether that life is torture-free
> and all the rest. We have not even gotten to the basic understanding of [the
> necessity of] sharing the globe's resources, as a fundamental human right.
> For example, as a consequence of our actions, Bangladesh may disappear
> under water in the next thirty years. Yet we don't take the moral responsibil-
> ity of our actions. Sometimes the problems seem just too big. We don't think
> our individual action is going to make enough of a difference. We rely on
> the government or other agencies. But, yes, clearly there has to be a global
> understanding of basic human rights and then apply them in everything
> that we do.

Ross believes that human rights based on the alleviation of suffering provide an essential legal and moral framework for international relations:

> If you take as your guidebook the suffering of others, the legal framework
> of human rights is a very clear measure of that. There are clear international
> legal agreements outlining how people should be treated. This is absolutely
> intrinsic and crucial. The body of human rights law and the growth of un-
> derstanding of human rights has been an incredibly positive and important
> development in the world—even if it hasn't delivered human rights protec-
> tion to everyone. It has provided a central moral framework for understand-
> ing what is going on. The idea of mass human rights abuse now is widely
> understood. It has taken a while, but it is real progress in the international
> debate.

INDIVIDUAL MORAL RESPONSIBILITY

Too many of us go about our days oblivious to the moral implications of our government's actions on the planet. We do not feel a sense of personal responsibility for policies that may lead to human rights abuses abroad. The welfare of people halfway around the world is a low priority compared to making sure we can take care of ourselves and our families. There is only so much that an individual can do in life.

Ross rejects this exculpatory logic and believes that the citizens of Britain and America are responsible for their government's actions in Iraq. Ross explains,

> There is a very troubling dissociation between the government and the people they represent. The people, the voting public, do not really feel responsible for the actions of their government. Take the true example of a thousand-pound bomb manufactured in the United States, delivered by the United States to Israel, and then dropped on Palestinian civilians in the Gaza Strip. American citizens clearly feel no direct responsibility for that whatsoever. Likewise, very few British people feel real responsibility for the actions of the British army in Iraq. They see it as Blair's war, and he gets the blame for it. The corollary of an elite that takes upon itself the freedom to do these things in government is a public that feels no responsibility for these actions. I don't approve of that.

But is it realistic to expect working-class people, some struggling to survive, to act on these foreign policy issues that seem so distant to their personal reality? Isn't it reasonable for the general public to put their trust in the government to provide security and direct foreign affairs? Ross doesn't let any of us off the hook:

> I don't think it is that hard to speak up. I understand the difficult situation of the hard-working folk who are holding down two jobs and have got two kids at home. But what about everybody else? I can sympathize with the difficulties of the working class, but even they, too, have a responsibility to exercise their choices. These government policies are done in their name and for their security. What are they, dumb animals? I don't buy it.

Ross concludes,

> There are loyalties to the truth and to moral conscience, and that is really the only thing. Ultimately, I believe that even the law is not something that should supersede one's own moral conscience, and there I am at one with the neocons. They believe that, too. In an extreme situation, I would consider breaking the law. Arguably, I am breaking the law by speaking out now because of the Official Secrets Act. In extremis, many people would break the law to protest or try to stop something they felt was extremely morally offensive.

8

⟨∞⟩

Individual Moral
Responsibility in
a Time of War

As seen throughout this book, individual Foreign Service officers and
members of the military successfully maintained their honor and
moral autonomy while remaining loyal to their country. For these individuals, defending the national interest meant opposing the war policies
of the particular administration in power. The decision to stay in the government or to resign in protest was really secondary. The key issue was to
act, to not lose one's voice, and to not personally contribute to the harm.

With their resignations, Brady Kiesling, John Brown, and Ann Wright
restored their personal moral integrity and regained their public voice
to oppose government policies they considered immoral and unethical.
Ehren Watada and Aidan Delgado concluded that the best way to honor
their oath to uphold the Constitution and the law was to break with a war
they determined was illegal. Watada and Delgado felt that morally they
could not hide behind "superior orders" and participate in a war of aggression. While Wayne White was able to maintain his voice and successfully challenge and change unethical policies in the government, Colin
Powell had difficulty maintaining his ethical balance in the Bush administration. And in Britain, Carne Ross, Clare Short, Andy Reed, and John
Denham decided that they could not be a part of the Blair push to war in
Iraq, resigned from the government, and asserted their moral autonomy.

Yet, as with the Vietnam War, the antiwar voices were, for the most
part, ignored during the initial intervention and occupation in Iraq. In
fact, the same political pressures that were present in America during the
Vietnam War in the 1960s and 1970s are tragically present in the twenty-
first century. To this day, the United States still hasn't adequately grappled

with the forces of escalation that led to unnecessary and prolonged blood-shed in Vietnam. In order to understand U.S. actions in Iraq since 2003, it is necessary to gain an appreciation of the power of these dynamics on U.S. foreign policy.

Political scientists have documented three intersecting "logics" that pulled the United States deeper and deeper into the war in Vietnam: the logic of domestic politics, the logic of international credibility, and the logic of sunken costs.[1] The logic of domestic politics is the belief that a president cannot appear to be weak on defense. Those politicians who *exaggerate* the threat of the enemy have historically been rewarded at the polls, while those who are perceived as "weak" are punished by the voters. This has led to huge military budgets that have little (if any) re-lationship to actual threats to the security of the United States. Domestic politics seems to demand that a president pump up military spending, never admit "defeat," and never appear to "appease" the enemy. The logic of international credibility demands that the United States be per-ceived abroad as strong and untouchable. To back down in war before achieving "victory" is seen as dangerous to America's global standing as a world power. Our credibility is said to suffer if we don't achieve the war's objectives. If we are perceived as weak, we would have difficulty persuading, intimidating, or coercing other nations to follow our priori-ties. To avoid this loss of international credibility, the United States must "stay the course" in a war.

Finally, the logic of sunken costs is probably the most important factor contributing to the creation of a spiraling dynamic pulling the United States further and further into conflicts well beyond the initial intentions of civilian leaders. Sunken costs refers to the blood and money invested in the war. After the blood of U.S. soldiers is shed in the conflict, the pres-sure on our leaders is to redeem those lives. As more lives are lost—hun-dreds, thousands—these pressures to redeem the mounting deaths rise exponentially, and the administration sends in more troops, which leads to further loss of life, which leads to more troops being sent, and on and on. This dynamic of sunken costs is almost impossible to break. As the sunken costs rise, few leaders have the courage to look into the eyes of the dead soldiers' parents and tell them that we made a mistake and we are ending the conflict. Few leaders are willing to accept an analysis that leads to the conclusion that those lives should have been spared. It takes a brave leader to call for a major change of course in a war that has taken the lives of so many of America's sons and daughters.

It is, of course, the soldiers fighting in these wars who suffer the most. As Chris Hedges writes,

The violence of war is random. It does not make sense. And many of those who struggle with loss also struggle with the knowledge that the loss was futile and unnecessary. This leaves psychological wounds among survivors as well as veterans. Many of the soldiers who fought in Vietnam must grapple with the realization that there was no higher purpose to the war, that the sacrifice was a waste. It is easier to believe the myth that makes such loss noble and necessary, despite the glaring contradictions.[2]

Yet the responsibility to stop this escalation dynamic does not rest solely with the country's leaders. In a democracy, all citizens have a duty to take responsibility for the direction of their country's domestic *and* foreign policies. Opinions can be expressed through voting, speaking out, writing letters to Congress and local papers, signing petitions, organizing and participating in demonstrations, civil disobedience, and so on. We have the ability to seek the truth and apply moral reasoning to foreign policy. In this information age, we have the means to gather the relevant information and assess the moral case for the war in Iraq. We are not simply lumps of coal or dumb animals.[3] We have the ability for moral reasoning and should apply it to the decisions that the government takes in our name. As the Dalai Lama wrote,

> [I]t all starts with the individual, with asking what the consequences are of your actions. An ethical act is a nonharming act. And if we could enhance our sensitivity to others' suffering, the less we would tolerate seeing others' pain, and the more we would do to ensure that no action of ours ever causes harm.[4]

When a citizen comes to the conclusion that the government's policies are immoral, he or she has a duty to sort out the correct path to take to oppose those policies. There is no one correct passageway. Rather, the appropriate ethical action will depend on a citizen's position in society, as there are levels of moral responsibility in a time of war.

Unfortunately, those who challenge the country's war policy are often ignored, silenced, or attacked. For example, in the war's first year I gave two presentations on Iraq, one at a local community club and the other at my school. In both lectures, I divided the time equally. Half the time went to presenting the utilitarian ethical framework used by the Bush administration to support the war in Iraq. The other half of the time was spent on ethical criticisms of the war, presenting the documentation of those who felt the war was not a "just war." I concluded by giving my opinion—which was that, in the end, after weighing both sides, I felt that the war could not be legally or morally justified. In both situations, the reaction by some to my talk was virulent and condemnatory. To a few vocal colleagues and students, the conclusion to my talk on campus was inappropriate and out of line. I was accused of using my position of authority to indoctrinate students toward my political views. At the end of the talk at the community center, the room exploded in indignation. Individuals yelled from the back of the room, "The U.S. does not torture." Others shouted, "The bodies of the victims from Saddam were warm when we found them after the invasion." These incensed individuals disrupted the event and ended the discussion.

These hurtful experiences were discouraging. But more important than my personal feelings is the sad reality that the hostility and belligerence on display in some of these encounters accurately reflect the level of civil discourse across the country. The Iraq war has created a divided citizenry. America has separated into opposing antagonistic camps overtly hostile to each other. This political polarization occurred quickly after the Iraq invasion and deepened as the war progressed.

Many professors retreat when confronted with these emotional and irrational political attacks. Many teachers, for example, have traditionally found it much easier to frame the myriad of issues surrounding "justice" by talking about history. It is safer and easier to talk about individual moral responsibility during the Holocaust and World War II, or even the Vietnam War, than it is to discuss the current Iraq war. To criticize the president in a time of war is seen as just too political and dangerous. Some actually consider such discussion to be traitorous, disloyal, and "a part of aiding a surrender to terror."[5] Yet all citizens in a democracy, including teachers, have a moral and political duty to question and debate issues of killing, war, and torture. Teaching is not about proselytizing to one's political views, but a responsible professor will apply his or her training to the "big questions" confronting our society and will not hide from the challenges of complexity or controversy.

LESSONS

In the spirit of encouraging an open and honest dialogue over war policies in Iraq and the Middle East, I offer the following key "lessons" drawn from my discussions with the Foreign Service officers and military personnel who struggled with these issues.

1. The Danger of Loyalty Becoming a Vice Instead of a Virtue

The privileging of loyalty over all other values has had devastating consequences on the political system and the foreign policy of the United

States. In the Bush administration, it is hard to detect any other value favored as highly as loyalty. Key administration officials demonstrated incompetence and ignorance, but as long as they remained loyal to the president, they were protected and often promoted. Loyalty in this case became a vice instead of a virtue. While the Bush administration is an extreme example, the dangers from the privileging of loyalty over all other values have long permeated the entire government.

As one of many values, loyalty is a desirable quality for an individual in the government to maintain. Individuals in the Foreign Service and military are expected to be faithful to the country and to the president. The government would certainly have trouble functioning if it were filled with "disloyal" employees. However, the problem is that loyalty is placed above all other norms. Honesty, competence, critical thinking, compassionate behavior, and selflessness are all important values as well and often should win out.

The dangers of loyalty as the primary virtue became abundantly clear during the rush to war in Iraq. Out of misplaced "loyalty" to the administration, many Foreign Service officers kept their criticisms of Iraq policy to themselves and didn't challenge the inferior quality of the intelligence used to promote the war. Military officers didn't speak up with their misgivings about the poorly thought through Rumsfeld war plan. Lawyers bent over backward to twist the laws to somehow authorize aggressive war and torture. Many citizens set aside their qualms about invading Iraq and chose to support the president as a sign of loyalty to the country during a difficult time.

To prevent these dangers from spiraling out of control again in the future, loyalty must be balanced with other equally important behavioral norms and values. The key issue for citizens, civil servants, and military personnel is to have personal integrity and to act ethically in every circumstance. This means being honest to one's personal moral convictions while carrying out the government's orders, and when the two conflict, often one's personal moral convictions should carry the day. The tremendous pressures to loyally support the state in a time of war must be balanced with other virtues, including maintaining one's voice and moral autonomy. A patriotic defense of the public good in a time of war demands nothing less.

2. The Danger of Ignoring the Ethical Dimension to Policy Decisions

In describing his view of the decisions and debates leading to the invasion of Iraq, Colin Powell states emphatically, "This was a policy dispute, not an ethical dispute." Powell's argument that a decision to go to war, no matter how just the cause, is simply a matter of policy and not ethics is stunning and revealing. On a mundane level, of course, Powell is right. Policy disputes and decisions were arrived at within the Bush administration over war, the Geneva Conventions, cruel and degrading treatment of prisoners, torture, and wiretapping. These are certainly policy decisions.

Yet it is simply astonishing to hear Powell claim these policy decisions did not involve ethical choices and thus he wasn't concerned about losing his ethical balance. Powell seems to be saying that the Iraq war did not involve personal ethical choices for him because the morally profound decisions to go to war and suspend the Geneva Conventions were the responsibility of the president alone. Even as secretary of state, he is simply to "follow orders" and carry out the decisions of the man elected president by the American people. From this perspective, Powell never has to take personal moral responsibility for the direction of the country's foreign policy. He never has to even think about resigning over principle because he absolves himself ahead of time from any ethical or moral duty to the country. Instead, as explored in chapter 4, he pushes all the moral responsibility up to the president and simply follows orders.

Too many of us in our jobs become loyal employees, simply carrying out our instructions from superiors. It is easy to convince oneself that the ultimate outcome and moral responsibility for policy lie with those with more power and authority. As noted in chapter 3, the training for service in the military and the government emphasizes the duty to follow and obey elected leaders, which greatly facilitates the tendency for individuals to absolve themselves of personal accountability for the ethics of our foreign policy. Successful diplomats and soldiers carry out the orders they receive from the elected civilian leadership. Success is measured by obedience and not by critical thinking and moral questioning. This has led thousands of individuals to compromise their moral integrity and participate in and defend sordid foreign policy interventions that have caused extreme suffering to countless innocent civilians.

A key factor limiting an individual's sense of personal moral responsibility is the government's bureaucratic structure. Modern bureaucracies of state dilute individual moral responsibility by spreading policy implementation over "many hands," as discussed in chapter 2. The "many hands" involved in decision-making and policy implementation further distance the individual government employee from a sense of moral responsibility for policy outcomes. In such a structure, few feel ultimately that policy outcomes are their individual responsibility. Bureaucracies function through an impersonal division of labor, which makes the contribution of one person seem unimportant and insignificant. Individual Foreign Service officers and soldiers can reason that "the decision was not mine" and thus believe that their actions are not harming anyone. With so many people involved in the operations of foreign policy, no one person in particular feels responsible. No one has to face the consequences of, or assume full responsibility for, his or her individual actions. Distance from the target (Iraq) also reduces sympathy and responsibility. For all of these reasons, many individuals thus do not assume personal responsibility for policy that they oppose. Overcoming these pressures is not only the first step for an individual to reclaim his or her moral autonomy. It is also essential for an effective democratic check on the abuse of power by the executive branch of the government.

3. The Danger of Great Power "Humanitarian" Intervention

When the Bush administration decided on "regime change" in Iraq, it was simply following a long-established pattern in U.S. foreign policy. In a little more than one hundred years, the United States has overthrown fourteen governments for ideological, political, and economic reasons. These violent actions were most often justified on humanitarian grounds. In the short term, these operations were thought by many to have "worked," as the old "tyrant" was overthrown and a new pro–United States regime was installed. However, in the long term, these interventions had unintended and disastrous consequences for both the people of the country experiencing the upheaval and for the security of the United States itself.[6]

The dangers of covert and overt intervention in the affairs of other nations abroad are now abundantly clear to even the casual reader of history. Examine, for example, the many ways in which Iran–United States relations remain hostile to this day, due in large part to the 1953 CIA-organized coup overthrowing the democratically elected Iranian leader Mohammad Mossadegh. U.S. "regime change" inspired thousands to join a violent Islamic movement to bring down the Shah of Iran and install the theocracy that currently controls Iran.

The United States had mixed motives in all of these "regime change" interventions, and none can be viewed as solely, or even primarily, humanitarian. Yet humanitarian language and values were used to sell the violence to the American people. This was certainly the case with the Iraq war. In addition to preventing the spread of weapons of mass destruction and stopping al-Qaeda, regime change in Iraq was said to be needed to bring down the brutal regime of Saddam and build democracy in Iraq.

Yet there was always a problem with this "humanitarian" justification of the war in Iraq. The traditional understanding of humanitarian intervention, according to Terry Nardin, is to thwart specific crimes against humanity or to rescue victims of those crimes. This is a conservative doctrine based on specific crimes being committed and not the character of a particular regime. The idea is to stop violence perpetuated against the victims. Because war causes horrible suffering to innocents, humanitarian intervention is only justified to either (a) end continuing atrocities or (b) prevent a massacre or genocidal act that is in preparation and is imminent. Again, since such interventions involve the killing and maiming of often thousands of totally innocent civilians, humanitarian wars are not allowed to address past wrongs. Such violence is only justified to prevent ongoing or imminent acts that shock the conscience of humanity. The threshold of humanitarian intervention is extremely high precisely because these arguments have been used time and again by the great powers to advance the state's power position in international politics. Economic and political goals are continuously disguised in the trappings of humanitarianism to win public support for the brutal endeavor.[7]

It is thus impossible to accept the "humanitarian" interventionist argument for invading Iraq to overthrow a tyrant, free twenty-five million Iraqis, and install a democracy. These types of arguments for invading Iraq were made by both neoconservative politicians and liberal academics and polemicists in the United States and Britain.[8] Carne Ross, responding with force and disdain to the "liberal hawks," stated,

> Well, they are not the ones doing the dying, are they? That's my response. I have a great deal more respect for Iraqis who share that argument. Frankly, it is for them to make that argument, not us. I met a lot of Iraqis before the war. I was in touch with a lot of Iraqis, and very few of them argued for a violent overthrow of Saddam, very few of them. While they wanted him gone, they predicted that violent chaos—which we now see—would be the result of an outside invasion. The terrible violence today in Iraq was predicted. The Iraqis themselves would warn us of it. The humanitarian argument for invading Iraq was an incredibly kind of "white man's burden," post-colonialist way of looking at the world—we are going to help liberate Johnny Iraqi from his long night of horror. While in theory this may sound good, life is just so much more complicated. Our leaders did not bother to look at the complexities or, frankly, the peaceful alternatives. Nobody ever talks about the peaceful alternatives. Wolfowitz, Rumsfeld, and the rest—none of them talk about the fact that there was actually a peaceful alternative which involved cutting off Saddam's illegal oil revenues. Instead, we were allowing Saddam to continue by legally and illegally buying his oil. We could have cut off the illegal supplies that were going directly to his regime, and we did nothing about it. I and other officials repeatedly argued that something should be done about it and nothing ever was. The British government did not sit down and go through the policy options in any careful manner. Instead, they were swept along toward war without properly considering the alternatives. I know that to be true.

4. The Danger of Ignoring the Human Costs of War

At the beginning of the war, the Bush administration successfully banned all news coverage of flag-draped coffins returning to military installations such as Dover Air Force Base in Delaware and at interim stops such as Ramstein Air Base in Germany. On ABC News, top-tiered anchor Charles Gibson told Ted Koppel, embedded with the Third Infantry Division, that it would be "simply disrespectful" to show either the American or Iraqi dead. In the aftermath of the 2004 election, the media clamped down even further on graphic and accurate presentations of the war. Kevin Sites, an employee of NBC News, caught on video a marine shooting an apparently unarmed wounded insurgent prisoner in a mosque in Fallujah. When NBC ran the report, Sites made no judgment, pending the marines' own investigation of this case, and cautioned that a war zone is "rife with uncertainty and confusion." Despite this, Sites was branded a traitor, an antiwar activist, and even an "enemy combatant" by the powerful right-wing media. A website established by relatives of marines thanking the cameraman for bringing them news from Iraq had to be shut down after Sites received death threats. In an earlier incident, the *New York Post* demonized and smeared an Associated Press television cameraman as having "a mutually beneficial relationship with the insurgents" because his camera had captured the horrific images of four American contract workers slaughtered in Fallujah.[9] As noted in chapter 6, Aidan Delgado was furiously attacked by conservative pundits and bloggers when he spoke out against the racist and aggressive behavior of U.S. soldiers toward civilians that he had witnessed in Iraq.[10] When *The New York Times* in January 2007 published a photo of a U.S. soldier lying mortally wounded on the ground, the paper was heatedly charged by some political conservatives with showing disrespect for the troops. Michael Massing surmises, "Most Americans simply do not want to know too much about the acts being carried out in their name, and this serves as a powerful deterrent to editors and producers."[11]

Throughout the occupation, the U.S. military has gone to great lengths to control graphic images from the war zone. For example, in the summer of 2008, Zoriah Miller, a freelance photographer in Iraq, was forbidden to work in Marine Corps–controlled areas of the country after posting photos on the Internet of several dead marines killed in a suicide attack. The marine commander in Iraq sought to have Miller barred from all U.S. military facilities throughout the world. There have been numerous other incidents of journalists banned from covering the U.S. military in Iraq. In 2004, Stefan Zaklin, formerly of the European Pressphoto Agency, was barred from working with the military after he published a photo of a dead army captain lying in a pool of blood in Fallujah. In 2005, Chris Hondros, of Getty Images, was kicked out of his embed unit after he published a photo of a screaming, blood-spattered little girl. Her unarmed parents had been killed by a U.S. Army unit. In 2007, two *New York Times* journalists were disembedded after the paper published a photo of a mortally wounded soldier shot through the head. The overall impact of this active official military and government suppression of the images of the war is startling. According to *The New York Times,* "after five years and more than 4,000 American combat deaths, searches and interviews turned up fewer than a half-dozen graphic photographs of dead American soldiers." The human dimensions of the war have been scrupulously censored and sanitized.[12]

It is hard to face the reality of the human cost of our intervention in Iraq. Examine, for example, the following eye-witness accounts. Jon Lee Anderson, reporting for *The New Yorker,* described 12-year-old Ali Ismael Abbas as so badly burned in a U.S. missile attack on Baghdad that his entire torso was black, his arms so mutilated that they "looked like something that might be found in a barbecue pit." Ali's pregnant mother, his father, and his six brothers and sisters were all killed by the blast. The bodies of his family members, unrecognizable in the morgue, had become a collection of some grotesquely mutilated charred body parts with some red flesh. "[His mother's] face had been cut in half, as if by a giant cleaver, and her mouth was yawning open. . . . The body of his brother was all there, it seemed, but from the nose up his head was gone, simply sheared off, like the head of a rubber doll. His mouth, like that of his mother, was open, as if he was screaming."[13]

Staff Sergeant David Bellavia, a fervent supporter of the Iraq war, recounts in his memoir that while his platoon was on just its second patrol in 2004 in Iraq,

> a civilian candy truck tried to merge with a column of our armored vehicles, only to get run over and squashed. The occupants were smashed beyond recognition. Our first sight of death was a man and his wife both ripped open and dismembered, their intestines strewn across shattered boxes of candy bars. The entire platoon hadn't eaten for twenty-four hours. We stopped, and as we stood guard around the wreckage, we grew increasingly hungry. Finally, I stole a few nibbles from one of the cleaner candy bars. Others wiped away the gore and fuel from the wrappers and joined me.[14]

This stark reality of war is minimally reported and, for the most part, ignored inside America. The gruesome details of war are not carried in the mainstream media, and the administration has fought hard to keep the devastating impact of the war from the eyes of the general public. The Bush administration may have felt that when confronted with the reality of war, the majority of the American people would reject military solutions. Consider how most human beings react to the following eye-witness account: "We pass a bus, smashed and burned, with charred human remains sitting upright in some windows. There's a man in the road with no head and a dead little girl, too, about three or four, lying on her back. She's wearing a dress and has no legs." This man and little girl were killed by the U.S. artillery bombardment of Nasiriyah. On the highway outside the city, marines find torched vehicles with "charred corpses nearby, occupants who crawled out and made it a few meters before expiring, with their grasping hands still smoldering."[15]

It is a fact of tremendous significance that since the beginning of the Iraq war, there has been no official attempt to accurately determine the number of dead and injured Iraqi civilians. Unofficial estimates by academics and NGOs range from 85,000 to more than 700,000. A study by the World Health Organization in January 2008 indicated with a 95 percent degree of certainty that between 104,000 and 223,000 civilians had died.[16] Unfortunately, an accurate number of civilian casualties will never be known. The American people can thus go about their lives oblivious to the true level of devastation inflicted on this poor country. Both the numbers killed and the images and descriptions of the ghastly nature of the fighting in Iraq are hidden from most citizens.

Nobel Peace Prize Laureate Oscar Arias writes,

> War, and the preparation for war, are the two greatest obstacles to human progress, fostering a vicious cycle of arms buildups, violence, and poverty. In order to understand the true human cost of militarism, as well as the true impact of unregulated arms sales in the world today, we must understand that war is not just an evil act of destruction, it is a missed opportunity for humanitarian investment. It is a crime against every child who calls out for food rather than for guns, and against every mother who demands simple vaccinations rather than million dollar fighters. Without a doubt, military spending represents the single most significant perversion of global priorities known today.[17]

When provided with accurate information, the American people have historically displayed very good instincts about foreign policy. This was certainly the case with the Vietnam War. When the truth about the loss of American and Asian lives became clear, most Americans sought to end that bloody quagmire. When American voters are denied this information and instead simply told to trust their leaders and fight on to victory, democratic control of foreign policy breaks down. The danger of hiding the true costs of war from the public is that it undermines democracy and the ability to hold individuals in the government accountable for their actions.

5. The Importance of an "Ethic of Principled Resignation"

After the Vietnam War, scholars identified the many ways in which group loyalty ill-served the country during that catastrophic intervention.[18] Instead of individual accountability, America has fostered a political tradition that breeds conformity over conviction, group loyalty rather than individual accountability. A government employee is evaluated by the willingness to play ball rather than for his or her candor and commitment to principle. As a result, key individuals didn't speak up and voice their opposition to war policies in Vietnam and instead chose to quietly go along with the team.[19]

As discussed in chapter 2, if the United States had a tradition of an ethic of principled resignation, many of these government employees may have spoken up and challenged Johnson's and Nixon's war policies. Even the threat of resignation might have had an impact on policymakers during that war. Instead of challenging war policies, misgivings were submerged and, for the most part, not voiced. The privileging of an ethic of loyalty over candor and principle helped to create the phenomenon of groupthink inside the government during the Vietnam War. As a result, alternative peaceful paths to ending that conflict were never seriously debated. These destructive patterns of groupthink and conformity have unfortunately been repeated during the Iraq war and occupation.

An ethic of principled resignation, on the other hand, would serve to support habits of personal integrity and moral autonomy. Such an ethic is based on the idea that the primary duty of all government employees and all citizens is to individual conscience. From the very beginning of his or her government career, the individual government employee would understand that he or she was expected to always voice his or her objections to immoral policies. The employee is never to "go along to get along." And, as already noted, the mere threat of resignation over principle could serve as a deterrent to egregious actions by the state. With an ethic of principled resignation in place, serving one's country would no longer be placed in opposition to critical thinking in policy formation. Public dissent by both Foreign Service officers and soldiers to objectionable policies would be seen as normal and refreshing behavior.

Instead of being ostracized and punished, Foreign Service officers and military personnel who refuse to promote policies they consider immoral should not be punished. The establishment of an "ethic of principled resignation" would highlight the importance of individual moral autonomy in policy-making. Such actions can expose unconscionable government policy, draw the public's attention to an insufficiently debated issue, supply the public with "inside" information necessary to an informed debate, and potentially even reverse the objectionable policy through the democratic political process.[20]

Weisband and Franck assert that if America had a tradition of acting on principles of moral autonomy, it would have a positive impact on our democracy. An ethic of principled resignation could serve to support individuals acting to protect their moral autonomy. All military and government employees would do their duty first to their conscience and, after that, to the public and the president. If this were the tradition, it is possible to imagine how different presidents' decisions around war and intervention would have been more forcefully challenged.[21]

"They've said I am an enemy of the people," says the doctor in Henrik Ibsen's play *An Enemy of Society* after being hounded for threatening to expose an embarrassing truth about the city's profitable medicinal baths. "Well, then, I'll be an enemy of the people."[22] A tradition of support for an ethic of principled resignation could help prevent those who exposed the truth about Iraq (Watada, Delgado, Wright, Kiesling, and others) from being labeled unpatriotic and an "enemy of the people." It would help us all assert our individual moral responsibility in a time of war.

6. The Importance of Individual Moral Autonomy

It is unhealthy for an individual to submerge his or her ethical disagreements and defend an immoral policy in order to keep a job. The psychological toll in such a situation can be acute and lead to physical damage and serious health problems. Asserting one's moral autonomy, on the other hand, can be liberating to one's body and soul. I was struck by how many of the individuals interviewed for this book linked health troubles to the demands of conformity inside the government. Once these individuals later reclaimed their moral integrity, their bodies healed and their overall health dramatically improved. For example, Brady Kiesling's depression, brought on by being required to defend the war in Iraq, ended only after he resigned and voiced his opposition to these policies. Similar pressures caused Ann Wright to experience severe health problems which ultimately led her to be medically evacuated from Mongolia. Ann's health noticeably improved only after she resigned and regained her moral integrity and public voice.

Determining the correct action to take to protect one's moral autonomy is difficult. How does one determine that the government's actions are "immoral"? As Peter Singer points out, ethics is not an issue of personal tastes, like choosing chocolate over vanilla ice cream. It is not enough to declare oneself a Christian, Muslim, secular humanist, Buddhist, or postmodernist. Such pronouncements don't take the discussion of the morality of U.S. foreign policy very far. For example, there is no one "Christian" or "Muslim" position on the many issues swirling around the war in Iraq. In addition, ethical reasoning is not about simply stating a position on a moral issue and a different person stating his or her disagreement. Reducing ethics in this manner leaves no room for debate and no way to judge between the many ethical "tastes." While treating Christian views, Islamic law, utilitarianism, and all other outlooks with respect, ethical reasoning involves the search for the overlapping consensus that exists between these views. In addition, ethical reasoning involves discussion over these different secular and religious moral perspectives in order to judge which views are defensible and which are not acceptable. Ethical reasoning is challenging and involves much more than simply stating one's particular religion or moral framework.[23]

It is critical in a democracy for all citizens to be engaged in this process of ethical reasoning. Every leader in the world today makes the claim that his or her policies are based on a moral and ethical vision. Even Adolf Hitler claimed to have ethics on his side and defined his racist vision within the context of "human rights."[24] It is thus incumbent upon individual citizens to engage in ethical reasoning and judge the actions of their government accordingly. It is particularly essential for every individual in a democracy to use his or her ethical reasoning to evaluate the morality of a leader's decision to go to war.

Such a process includes establishing the line at which each of us is able to say to our government, "Not in my name." In a democracy, citizens have a duty to make value judgments about the morality of the state's policies and to act on those conclusions. Goethe's hero Faust declared: "Two souls, alas, are housed within my breast, and each will wrestle for mastery there."[25] To acquiesce to torture and aggressive war is to succumb to Faust's dark soul and accept the unspeakable. Sophocles writes in *Antigone* that "what a person can do, a person should do."[26] And what we can do is reclaim our individual moral integrity and soul by refusing to conform and blithely accept destructive and avoidable war policies.

THE DEATH THREAT

I had just returned to my office after speaking at a rally in February 2003 against the planned U.S. invasion of Iraq and found the following seething male voice on my answering machine: "I want to know what branch of the military you served in. I think you are a traitor. I want to be the first person to put a rope around your neck and hang you in the middle of St. Petersburg [Florida] for what you told those kids down there."

In a panicked state, I quickly called both the city and campus police. I was told that unless the death threat was in writing, there was nothing that the police could do. They did try to trace the call but, since another call had been recorded after this one, it couldn't be tracked.

Suddenly I felt quite vulnerable. Who would make such a call? Is this just a crank call that can be ignored? Clearly, the person knows how to find me. Will he follow me? Slash my tires? Rough me up? Unfortunately, there are a lot of passionate people in this country with guns. How seriously should I take this menacing threat? Remembering back to the days of Nixon and COINTELPRO,[27] I realized that the government has not shied away in the past from infiltrating rallies, disrupting events, intimidating speakers. Has the Bush administration now joined Nixon in such illegal and immoral actions? These were among the many thoughts that kept spinning around my mind as I attempted to come to grips with my first (and hopefully last) death threat. I methodically went through the possibilities and discussed security options with authorities—parking in different spaces, removing my phone number and address from all listings, assigning campus security to watch my office, and so on. I didn't think I was too rattled, but after getting home and decompressing, my partner found me crying in the shower.

I decided not to tell the students about this incident. For many of these young people, this rally was their first attempt in the political process at trying to change public policy. These students were part of the unprecedented global antiwar demonstration which took place in sixty countries, involved eight hundred cities, and included more than ten million people around the world. This outpouring of protest was all designed to *prevent* a war from breaking out. Never before in history had such an event occurred before a war had actually begun. The global turnout, in fact, even surpassed the high numbers achieved at the height of the antiwar movement during the American–Vietnam War. Despite this huge success, the odds of impacting either the Democratic Party or the Bush administration were minimal (and the invasion and occupation of Iraq proceeded as planned in March 2003). Many students, realizing the negligible impact of their actions, were already discouraged. I did not want to add to their dismay by scaring them with stories of harassment and death threats.

The hateful message, however, did keep going around and around in my brain. Why would someone consider me a traitor for opposing this war? Why would his level of anger rise to the point of issuing a death threat? Why would he consider it abusive for a professor of political science to express his opinion about the pending war in Iraq?

There were numerous grave risks to individuals who spoke out or protested the war in Iraq in 2003 and 2004. After public opinion turned against the war in 2006, it was easy to forget the real dangers to those who expressed opposition to the foreign policy of the Bush administration at the beginning of the war. George Bush, Dick Cheney, and Colin Powell had notoriously linked Saddam Hussein not only to stockpiles of weapons of mass destruction but also to al-Qaeda and the monstrous attacks on innocent Americans on September 11, 2001. Those who opposed the war were thus attacked not only as unpatriotic but also as giving aid and comfort to the terrorists. Antiwar organizers were threatened and accused of treason. Local nonviolent protest groups were infiltrated. Commencement speakers who dared to criticize the war were booed, heckled, and accused of supporting the enemy.[28] Entertainers who spoke out against the war received death threats, and the right-wing media and extremists organized and supported boycotts of their products. As noted earlier, Ari Fleischer, the president's press spokesman, threatened Americans to "watch what they say, watch what they do."[29] All of this had a chilling effect on free speech in America.

Yet the moral responsibility of a professor of political science in a time of war cannot be either silence or gratuitous sycophancy. One of the common sentiments expressed by all the Foreign Service officers and military personnel interviewed for this book was a plea for all of us—teachers, soldiers, government officials, students, and citizens—to find our voices and assert our individual moral autonomy in a time of crisis and violence.

Unfortunately, when a president is mobilizing the country for war and asking for obedience, too many of us lose our voice. Loyalty to the troops and the country is thought to imply acquiescence to the president's war policies. Yet it is exactly at this time—when a president is attempting to take the nation to war—that open and honest debate is most needed. The antiwar movement did mobilize and voices of opposition to the invasion of Iraq were spoken. It is encouraging and inspiring to see that during this dangerous time individual Foreign Service officers and members of the military were able to reclaim their moral integrity and express their ethical disagreements with the rush to war in Iraq.

The Iraq war is the central moral issue of our time because, as with all warfare, it involves the intentional murder of human beings. As discussed in chapter 3, the key ethical issue is: When does the government have the right to take another person's life? Unfortunately, as with the Vietnam War, the United States did not exhaust all nonviolent options before invading Iraq. As documented throughout this book, Iraq presented no threat, and there was time to pursue other nonviolent strategies to contain Saddam. Furthermore, since Saddam was not committing genocide or other crimes against humanity in 2002–2003, the invasion cannot be viewed as humanitarian. A world in which the strongest state proclaims a unilateral right to intervene to prevent potential future acts of aggression or genocide is a planet of perpetual war and never-ending suffering.

The UN structure for peace is fundamentally based on the most essential human right, the right to life. No person or nation has the right to use other human beings as means to some greater end—democracy, freedom, justice, and so on. When a government violates this principle, its actions become both illegal and immoral. For many in America and Britain, this was the critical ethical line that was crossed with the invasion of Iraq.[30]

Dostoyevsky hammers home on this most fundamental moral principle, the sanctity of life. No individual, terrorist group, political organization, or government has the right to abuse other human beings for some higher purpose. In *The Brothers Karamazov*, Ivan has the following exchange with his religious brother Alyosha:

"Tell me straight out, I call on you—answer me: imagine that you yourself are building the edifice of human destiny with the object of making people happy in the finale, of giving them peace and rest at last, but for that you must inevitably and unavoidably torture just one tiny creature, that same child that was beating her chest with her little fist, and raise your edifice on the foundation of her unrequited tears—would you agree to be the architect on such conditions? Tell me the truth."

"No, I would not agree," Alyosha said softly.

"And can you admit the idea that the people for whom you are building would agree to accept their happiness on the unjustified blood of a tortured child, and having accepted it, to remain forever happy?"

"No, I cannot admit it, Brother."[31]

Most of us would probably respond as Alyosha and never agree to the torture of an innocent child. Most of us can probably not even imagine such an action. But, tragically, this is exactly the utilitarian calculation that often leads to war and torture. It becomes a mathematical question. If the torture of the child (or any human being) saves ten lives, is it then justified? Or does the torture need to save one hundred lives to be justified? One thousand lives? Or is democracy for twenty-five million Iraqis worth the deaths of tens of thousands of innocent children and elderly civilians? If one agrees with Dostoyevsky that the torture and killing of any human being is a moral line that should never be crossed, then this type of inhumane mathematical calculation in itself is also immoral.

Dostoyevsky is unrelenting in his condemnation of the "lesser-of-two-evils" defense that many academic liberal interventionists (liberal hawks) used to justify the Iraq invasion. In *Crime and Punishment*, to justify killing an old pawnbroker and stealing her money, Raskolnikov overhears a student telling a young officer, "Kill her, take her money, on condition that you dedicate yourself to the service of humanity and the common good: don't you think that thousands of good deeds will wipe out one little, insignificant transgression? For one life taken, thousands saved from corruption and decay."[32] Hundreds of thousands of Iraqis killed or maimed in the war, but ultimate freedom for twenty-five million.

Tragically, the United States and other governments embraced this "lesser-of-two-evils" logic to legitimate aggressive action and launch a preventive war on a weaker state without properly considering the alternatives. As the diplomats interviewed in this book document, there were peaceful alternatives. To their great credit, these individuals kicked and screamed and heroically tried to stop the senseless killing.

The actions of these individuals demonstrate that not everyone loses his or her moral autonomy during a time of war. In fact, many are willing to take a stand, revolt against the accepted policy, and act to change what is perceived as an immoral action. The Reverend Dr. Martin Luther King, Jr., also challenged an entire generation to rethink basic premises about loyalty, patriotism, and service, even as the country was sinking deeper into war. It is unfortunate, as Taylor Branch notes, that many of his ideas seem so alien, unmanly, and embarrassing to many Americans today. At the height of the Vietnam War, Dr. King lamented the ways in which Americans gave up their moral autonomy and accepted the violent direction of the Johnson administration. Dr. King endorsed a strategic alternative to violence: "We will stop communism by letting the world know that democracy is a better government than any other government and by making justice a reality for all of God's children." Dr. King, dramatically embracing Kantian principles, stated: "I'm committed to nonviolence absolutely. I'm just not going to kill anybody, whether it's in Vietnam or here." He urged his staff to rise above fear and hatred alike. "We must not be intimidated by those who are laughing at nonviolence now," he told his staff on his last birthday. Only hours before his death, Dr. King startled an aide by declaring: "In our next campaign, we will have to institutionalize nonviolence and take it international."[33]

Dr. King reminds us of the impact and importance of moral autonomy in a time of war. He stresses that the best way to safeguard democracy is to practice it. Our values are the essence of our strength. The accepted trade-off between freedom and security behind many current policies (arbitrary arrests, coercive interrogations, torture, and so on) is therefore misguided and weakens our country. But, perhaps most importantly, Dr. King shows us that it is possible to act to uphold deontological principles of human rights even when the country turns to fierce violence. It is hard to envision Dr. King supporting a framework of either "dirty hands" or cold utilitarian calculations that sacrifice the rights and lives of individuals for "democracy" or some other greater good. Such policies have clearly not served us well in the current "Global War on Terror." In fact, one could argue that U.S. success and respect in the world hinge on the incorporation of Dr. King's perspective into the fight against those who practice terrorism.

In reclaiming my moral autonomy during the rush to war in Iraq, I came to the belief that no government has the right to kill innocents for some "greater good." The "right to life" is beyond the power of the government to abrogate for abstract foreign policy objectives. We criticize terrorists for killing innocents for their self-proclaimed beneficent goals. The same moral criterion should apply to our own conduct as well.[34] A compassionate new world order cannot be built through torture and war. There is a relationship between means and ends. With the exception of acts of self-defense, the killing of one innocent person to benefit others is a violation of the foundational principle of the entire human rights project launched following World War II. The vast majority of Americans supported the invasion and occupation of Iraq in 2003, believing it to serve a greater good. Yet even with majority approval, the killing of innocent people for an abstract national interest is illegal and immoral. It is the line at which I break with my government.

Notes

CHAPTER 1: INTRODUCTION

1. Whereas it is commonly believed that there is some distinction between the terms "ethical" and "moral," to many philosophers they are synonyms, with the former derived from the Greek and the latter from the Latin. I will thus use "moral" and "ethical" as essentially equivalent terms.

2. Dennis F. Thompson, *Political Ethics and Public Office* (Cambridge, Mass.: Harvard University Press, 1987), 5–6.

3. Bernard Williams, *Moral Luck* (Cambridge: Cambridge University Press, 1981), 44–45.

4. Mark Danner, "We Are All Torturers Now," *New York Times*, January 6, 2005, 27(A).

5. CBS News, "CIA Chief: No 'Imminent Threat,'" February 5, 2004. http://www.cbsnews.com/stories/2004/02/24/iraq/printable601876.shtml (accessed July 18, 2007).

6. The "Downing Street Memo" is a summary of a secret July 23, 2002, meeting of the United Kingdom Labour government, including defense and intelligence figures, discussing U.S. policy toward Iraq. This document has been called the "smoking gun" memo, as it includes the following: "Bush wanted to remove Saddam, through military action, justified by the conjunction of terrorism and WMD. But the intelligence and facts were being fixed around the policy." The "Downing Street Memo" is available at: http://www.timesonline.co.uk/tol/news/uk/article387374.ece (accessed July 14, 2007).

7. The "Butler Intelligence Report," titled "Review of Intelligence on Weapons of Mass Destructions," is available at: http://www.butlerreview.org.uk (accessed July 16, 2007).

8. Paul Pillar, "Policy, and the War in Iraq," *Foreign Affairs* 85, no. 2 (March/ April 2006): 15.

9. For a clear discussion of the impact of Abu Ghraib and Guantanamo, see Aryeh Neier, "How Not to Promote Democracy and Human Rights," in Richard Wilson, ed., *Human Rights in the 'War on Terror'* (Cambridge: Cambridge University Press, 2005). See also David Cole and Jules Lobel, *Less Safe, Less Free* (New York: The New Press, 2007), 23–69.

10. "Autonomy in Moral and Political Philosophy," *Stanford Encyclopedia of Philosophy*, published July 28, 2003. http://plato.stanford.edu/entries/autonomy moral (accessed February 28, 2008).

11. Edward Weisband and Thomas M. Franck, *Resignation in Protest: Political and Ethical Choices Between Loyalty to Team and Loyalty to Conscience in American Public Life* (New York: Grossman Publishers, 1975), 3. Weisband and Franck use the term "ethical autonomy" to describe this norm. I use "moral autonomy" throughout this text.

12. Social psychologist Irving Janis first identified the phenomenon of "groupthink" in 1972. Groupthink is said to occur when a group makes faulty decisions due to group pressures to conform. Groupthink often leads to deterioration in moral judgment, a demonization of other groups, ignorance of alternative approaches, and ultimately irrational actions. Irving L. Janis, *Victims of Groupthink* (New York: Houghton Mifflin, 1972), 9.

13. Henry David Thoreau, "Civil Disobedience," in *Civil Disobedience and Other Essays* (New York: Dover Publications, 1993 [1849]), 3.

14. Karl Jaspers, *The Question of German Guilt*, trans. E. B. Ashton (New York: Dial Press, 1947), 69–70.

15. See, for example, Gary Rosen, ed., *The Right War? The Conservative Debate on Iraq* (New York: Cambridge University Press, 2005); Thomas Cushman, "The Human Rights Case for the War in Iraq: A Consequentialist View," in Richard Wilson, ed., *Human Rights in the 'War on Terror'* (Cambridge: Cambridge University Press, 2005).

16. See, for example, Philippe Sands, *Lawless World: America and the Making and Breaking of Global Rules from FDR's Atlantic Charter to George W. Bush's Illegal War* (New York: Viking, 2005); Helen Duffy, *The 'War on Terror' and the Framework of International Law* (Cambridge: Cambridge University Press, 2005); Richard A. Falk, *The Costs of War: International Law, the UN, and World Order After Iraq* (New York: Routledge, 2008); Philippe Sands, *Torture Team: Rumsfeld's Memo and the Betrayal of American Values* (New York: Palgrave Macmillan, 2008); Jane Mayer, *The Dark Side: The Inside Story of How the War on Terror Turned into a War on American Ideals* (New York: Doubleday, 2008).

17. Socrates, in Plato, *The Republic*, Book Eight, quoted in Jonathan Glover, *Humanity: A Moral History of the Twentieth Century* (New Haven, Conn.: Yale University Press, 1999), 379. See also Francis Cornford, trans., *The Republic of Plato* (Oxford: Oxford University Press, 1945), 267. Cornford's translation reads: "Constitutions cannot come out of stocks and stones; they must result from the preponderance of certain characters which draw the rest of the community in their wake."

18. Thoreau, "Civil Disobedience," 2.

CHAPTER 2: THE MORAL
OBLIGATIONS OF CIVIL SERVANTS AND SOLDIERS

1. CNN, "Audit: U.S. Lost Track of $9 Billion in Iraq Funds," January 31, 2005. http://edition.cnn.com/2005/WORLD/meast/01/30/iraq.audit (accessed on November 8, 2007).

2. Peter Slevin, "Wrong Turn at a Postwar Crossroads? Decision to Disband Iraqi Army Cost U.S. Time and Credibility," *Washington Post*, November 20, 2003, A01. http://www.washingtonpost.com/ac2/wp-dyn/A63423-2003Nov19?language =printer (accessed November 8, 2007).

3. See, for example, Thomas E. Ricks, *Fiasco: The American Military Adventure in Iraq* (New York: Penguin Books, 2006), 74–80; Lawrence J. Korb, "The Cost of Failing to Plan," Center for American Progress, March 19, 2004. http://www.american progress.org/issues/2004/03/b38979.html (accessed November 8, 2007); Anthony Zinni, "They've Screwed Up," CBS News, May 21, 2004. http://www.cbsnews .com/stories/2004/05/21/60minutes/main618896.shtml (accessed November 8, 2007).

4. Associated Press, "Wolfowitz Comments Revive Doubts Over Iraq's WMD," *USA Today*, May 30, 2003, http://www.usatoday.com/news/world/iraq/ 2003-05-30-wolfowitz-iraq_x.htm (accessed October 9, 2007).

5. Eric Schmitt, "Pentagon Contradicts General on Iraq Occupation Force's Size," *New York Times*, February 28, 2003. http://www.globalpolicy.org/security/ issues/iraq/attack/consequences/2003/0228pentagoncontra.htm (accessed November 8, 2007).

6. Thomas Nagel, "Ruthlessness in Public Life," in Stuart Hampshire, ed., *Public and Private Morality* (Cambridge: Cambridge University Press, 1978), 76.

7. Nagel, "Ruthlessness in Public Life," 75.

8. Joel L. Fleishman, "Self-Interest and Political Integrity," in Joel L. Fleishman, Lance Liebman, and Mark H. Moore, eds., *Public Duties: The Moral Obligations of Government Officials* (Cambridge: Harvard University Press, 1981), 53–54.

9. Fundamentalists of any religion or dogma do not experience such feelings of inadequacy. Fundamentalists are not "uncertain" about right and wrong and often claim to know the best foreign policy for our country.

10. In December 1966, President Johnson's intimate friend and press secretary, Bill D. Moyers, resigned to become publisher of the Long Island newspaper *Newsday* (see *The New York Times*, December 15, 1966, A1). Moyers had apparently become disillusioned with the Vietnam War. Yet it does not seem to be the case that Moyers resigned to protest the war. Furthermore, he did not become a vocal opponent to the war, despite his private doubts. Moyers explains his resignation as follows: "I left the White House in early 1967 for journalism and put those years and events behind me, except to reflect on how they might inform my reporting and analysis of what's happening today. I was chastened by our mistakes back then, and I am chagrined now when others repeat them." Bill Moyers, *Moyers on Democracy* (New York: Doubleday, 2008), 303.

11. Edward Weisband and Thomas M. Franck, *Resignation in Protest: Political and Ethical Choices Between Loyalty to Team and Loyalty to Conscience in American Public Life* (New York: Grossman Publishers, 1975), 188.

12. Amy Gutmann and Dennis Thompson, *Ethics & Politics: Cases and Comments*, 3rd edition (Chicago: Nelson-Hall Publishers, 1997), 141.

13. J. Patrick Dobel, *Public Integrity* (Baltimore: The Johns Hopkins University Press, 1999), 95.

14. Dobel, *Public Integrity*, 96.

15. See "The Paradox of Access" in Dobel, *Public Integrity*, 99–105.

16. James C. Thomson, Jr., "How Could Vietnam Happen? An Autopsy," *Atlantic Monthly* (April 1968), 49.

17. Dobel, *Public Integrity*, 99.

18. Albert O. Hirschman, *Exit, Voice, and Loyalty: Responses to Decline in Firms, Organizations, and States* (Cambridge: Harvard University Press, 1970), 101.

19. See, for example, the documentation at the PEW Global Attitudes Project, available at: http://pewglobal.org/reports/display.php?ReportID=256 (accessed November 9, 2007); and the World Public Opinion available at: http://www.world publicopinion.org/pipa/articles/home_page/394.php?lb=hmpg1&pnt=394&nid =&id (accessed November 9, 2007).

20. Hirschman, *Exit, Voice, and Loyalty*, 104–105.

21. Weisband and Franck, *Resignation in Protest*, 12.

22. Thompson, *Political Ethics and Public Office*, 75.

23. See Thompson, *Political Ethics and Public Office*, 40–65.

24. Ferdinand Kuhn, Jr., "Britain Is Shocked," *New York Times*, February 21, 1938.

25. "First Lord Quits British Admiralty," *New York Times*, October 2, 1938.

26. Aristotle, *Nicomachean Ethics* (350 BC), trans. W. D. Ross (Raleigh, N.C.: Alex Catalogue/E-book, 2000), Book II, 2, p. 14. Emphasis added.

27. Leavenworth is home to the Combined Arms Center, a research center that includes the Command and General Staff College for midcareer officers, the School of Advanced Military Studies for the most elite, and the Center for Army Lessons Learned.

28. Elisabeth Bumiller, "At an Army School for Officers, Blunt Talk About Iraq Strategy," *New York Times*, October 14, 2007, A1.

29. David S. Cloud, "Ex-commander Calls Iraq War 'Nightmare,'" *New York Times News Service*, October 13, 2007. http://boston.com/news/world/articles/2007/10/13/ex_commander_calls_iraq_war_nightmare (accessed October 24, 2007).

30. Lt. Col. Paul Yingling, "A Failure of Leadership," *Armed Forces Journal*, May 2007. http://www.armedforcesjournal.com/2007/05/2635198 (accessed October 24, 2007).

31. Bumiller.

32. Bumiller.

33. Michael Walzer, *Just and Unjust Wars: A Moral Argument with Historical Illustrations*, 3rd ed. (New York: Basic Books, 1977), 299–300.

34. Interview with Ehren Watada, September 12, 2007.

35. Jack Goldsmith, *The Terror Presidency: Law and Judgment Inside the Bush Administration* (New York: Norton & Company, 2007), 60.

36. *The U.S. Army/Marine Corps Counterinsurgency Field Manual* (Chicago: University of Chicago Press, 2007), 351–352.

37. Interview with Ehren Watada, September 12, 2007.

38. Douglas Jehl, Steven Lee Myers, and Eric Schmitt, "The Struggle for Iraq: Investigation; Abuse of Captives More Widespread, Says Army Survey," *New York Times*, May 26, 2004.

39. Chris Hedges and Laila Al-Arian, "The Other War: Iraq Vets Bear Witness," *The Nation*, July 30, 2007. http://www.thenation.com/doc/20070730/hedges (accessed February 7, 2008).

40. Thomas E. Ricks and Ann Scott Tyson, "Troops at Odds with Ethics Standards," *Washington Post*, May 5, 2007. http://www.washingtonpost.com/wp-dyn/content/article/2007/05/04/AR2007050402151_pf.html (accessed October 26, 2007).

41. Aidan Delgado, *The Sutras of Abu Ghraib: Notes From a Conscientious Objector in Iraq* (Boston: Beacon Press, 2007), 71–72.

42. Delgado, *The Sutras of Abu Ghraib*, 78.

43. Walzer, *Just and Unjust Wars*, 38–39.

44. Paul Christopher, *The Ethics of War and Peace*, 3rd ed. (Upper Saddle River, N.J.: Prentice Hall, 2004), 242.

45. Robert Nozick, *Anarchy, State, and Utopia* (New York: Basic Books, 1974), 100. Quoted in Walzer, 40.

46. Quote from Walzer, *Just and Unjust Wars*, 38.

47. J. Joseph Miller, "*Jus ad bellum* and an Officer's Moral Obligations: Invincible Ignorance, the Constitution, and Iraq," *Social Theory and Practice*, Vol. 30, No. 4 (October 2004), 464.

48. Miller, *Jus ad bellum*, 464.

49. Miller, *Jus ad bellum*, 483–484.

50. Kendrick Clements, "William Jennings Bryan," in Edward S. Mihalkanin, ed., *American Statesmen, Secretaries of State from John Jay to Colin Powell* (Westport, Conn.: Greenwood Press, 2004), 74.

51. Michael Kazin, *A Godly Hero: The Life of William Jennings Bryan* (New York: Knopf, 2006), 123–127.

52. Nancy Mitchell, *The Danger of Dreams: German and American Imperialism in Latin America* (Chapel Hill: The University of North Carolina Press, 1999), 167–168.

53. Kazin, *A Godly Hero*, 217–218.

54. Clements, *American Statesmen*, 80.

55. Kazin, *A Godly Hero*, 236–238.

56. Clements, *American Statesmen*, 80.

57. Weisband and Franck, *Resignation in Protest*, 28.

58. Weisband and Franck, *Resignation in Protest*, 29–30.

59. *The New York Times*, June 10, 1915, p. 10. Quoted in Weisband and Franck, *Resignation in Protest*, 65.

60. Weisband and Franck, *Resignation in Protest*, 66.

61. Weisband and Franck, *Resignation in Protest*, 66–67.

62. Kazin, *A Godly Hero*, 254–255; Ronald Steel, "All You Need Is Love," *The New York Review of Books*, June 22, 2006, 38–39.

63. Kazin, *A Godly Hero*, 260.

64. Cyrus Vance, *Hard Choices: Critical Years in America's Foreign Policy* (New York: Simon and Schuster, 1983), 408.

65. Vance, *Hard Choices*, 409.

66. Vance, *Hard Choices*, 409–410.

67. Vance, *Hard Choices*, 410.

68. Daniel Ellsberg, *Secrets: A Memoir of Vietnam and the Pentagon Papers* (New York: Penguin Books, 2002), 88–90. Mark Perry, *Four Stars* (Boston: Houghton Mifflin Company, 1989), 148–160. This summary of Gen. Harold Johnson's struggle with principled resignation is taken directly from Ellsberg's *Secrets* and Perry's *Four Stars*. See also Lewis Sorley, *Honorable Warrior: General Harold K. Johnson and the Ethics of Command* (Lawrence: University Press of Kansas, 1998), 208–226.

69. Ellsberg, *Secrets*, 91.

70. Ellsberg, *Secrets*, 94–95.

71. Perry, 156. Also quoted in Ellsberg, *Secrets*, 97.

CHAPTER 3: ETHICAL THEORY AND WAR

1. There is a family of theories within the consequentialist ethical framework, including utilitarianism, ethical egoism, rule consequentialism, and negative consequentialism. The focus here is on the views and approaches of utilitarian thinkers and writers. See John Stuart Mill, *Utilitarianism* (Indianapolis: ITT Bobbs-Merrill, 1985 [1863]).

2. Michael J. Smith, *Realist Thought from Weber to Kissinger* (Baton Rouge: Louisiana State University Press, 1986), 6–7.

3. Dean Acheson, "Homage to Plain Dumb Luck," in R. A. Divine, ed., *The Cuban Missile Crisis* (Chicago: Quadrangle Books, 1971). Quoted in C. A. J. Coady, "Politics and the Problem of Dirty Hands," in Peter Singer, ed., *A Companion to Ethics* (Oxford: Blackwell Publishing, 1993), 373.

4. George F. Kennan, *Realities of American Foreign Policy* (Princeton: Princeton University Press, 1954), 47, 48, 103.

5. Kennan, *Realities*, 48.

6. Smith, *Realist Thought*, 188.

7. Anatol Lieven and John Hulsman, *Ethical Realism: A Vision for America's Role in the World* (New York: Pantheon Books, 2006), 62–83; quote, p. 83.

8. Hans J. Morgenthau, *Human Rights and Foreign Policy* (New York: Council on Religion and International Affairs, 1979), 13.

9. Isaiah Berlin, "A Special Supplement: The Question of Machiavelli," *The New York Review of Books*, Vol. 17, No. 7, November 4, 1971.

10. Niccolò Machiavelli, *The Prince*, trans. N. H. Thompson (New York: Dover Publications, 1992), 40, 43.

11. Niccolò Machiavelli, *Discourses on Livy*, trans. Harvey C. Mansfield and Nathan Tarcov (Chicago: University of Chicago Press, 1996), 301.

12. Machiavelli, *The Prince*, 23.

13. Berlin, "A Special Supplement."

14. See Paul Rynard and David P. Shugarman, *Cruelty & Deception: The Controversy Over Dirty Hands in Politics* (Australia: Pluto Press, 2000).

15. Jean-Paul Sartre, "Les mains sales," in *No Exit and Three Other Plays* (New York: Vintage Books, 1955), 223–224.

16. See Stuart Hampshire, "Public and Private Morality," in Stuart Hampshire, ed., *Public and Private Morality* (Cambridge: Cambridge University Press, 1978), 49–50.

17. Machiavelli, *The Prince*, 46.

18. Immanuel Kant, *Groundwork of the Metaphysic of Morals*, trans. H. J. Paton (London: Hutchinson & Co., 1948), 70, 96. Italics in original.

19. Chris Brown, "International Social Justice," in David Boucher and Paul Kelly, eds., *Social Justice: From Hume to Walzer* (London: Routledge, 1998), 111.

20. Immanuel Kant, *Perpetual Peace: A Philosophical Sketch*, in Hans Reiss, ed., *Kant's Political Writings* (Cambridge: Cambridge University Press, 1970), 98–99. Italics in original.

21. William F. Felice, *Taking Suffering Seriously: The Importance of Collective Human Rights* (Albany, N.Y.: SUNY Press, 1996), 17–34.

22. The International Bill of Human Rights encompasses the *Universal Declaration of Human Rights*, the *International Covenant on Civil and Political Rights*, and the *International Covenant on Economic, Social and Cultural Rights*.

23. William F. Felice, *The Global New Deal* (Lanham, Md.: Rowman & Littlefield Press, 2003), 186.

24. Michael J. Smith, "Ethics and Intervention," *Ethics and International Affairs*, 1989, Vol. 3, 21–22.

25. Smith, "Ethics and Intervention," 22.

26. Smith, "Ethics and Intervention," 23–24. Smith's argument resonates with John Rawls' discussion of "reflective equilibrium" in his *A Theory of Justice* (Cambridge, Mass.: Harvard University Press, 1971), 48–53.

27. Michael Walzer, "Political Action: The Problem of Dirty Hands," *Philosophy and Public Affairs*, Vol. 2, No. 2 (Winter 1973): 164.

28. Walzer, "Political Action," 168.

29. Walzer, "Political Action," 171.

30. Walzer, "Political Action," 168.

31. Walzer, "Political Action," 178.

32. Walzer, "Political Action," 179–180.

33. Edward Weisband and Thomas M. Franck, *Resignation in Protest: Political and Ethical Choices Between Loyalty to Team and Loyalty to Conscience in American Public Life* (New York: Grossman Publishers, 1975), 4.

34. Bernard Williams, *Moral Luck* (Cambridge: Cambridge University Press, 1981), 57.

35. Williams, *Moral Luck*, 66.

36. Williams, *Moral Luck*, 58.

37. Williams, *Moral Luck*, 62.

38. See "The National Security Strategy of the United States of America 2002." http://www.whitehouse.gov/nsc/nssall.html (accessed February 11, 2007).

39. Carne Ross presents a thoughtful discussion of Leo Strauss and the noble lie. See Carne Ross, *Independent Diplomat: Dispatches from an Unaccountable Elite* (Ithaca, N.Y.: Cornell University Press), 71, 80–81.

40. "Cheney Offended by Amnesty Criticism," CNN.com, May 31, 2005. http://www.cnn.com/2005/US/05/30/cheney.amnestyintl./index/html (accessed June 6, 2006).

41. Walzer, "Political Action," 170.

42. Walzer, "Political Action," 172.

43. Walzer, "Political Action," 178.

44. Neoconservatism should not be confused with those international relations theories often called either "liberal internationalism" or "idealism." While both neoconservatives and idealist/liberal internationalists focus on ethics in the formulation of foreign policy, the values promoted by each side are in fundamental opposition. Most idealist/liberal internationalists, for example, believe in multilateralism, international law, diplomacy, cosmopolitan ethics, international human rights, and the global human interest. Idealist/liberal internationalists do not believe that "democracy" and "freedom" can be brought about through military force and empire building.

45. Interview with Peter Singer, September 14, 2006.

46. See, for example, Thomas Cushman, "The Human Rights Case for the War in Iraq: A Consequentialist View," in Richard Wilson, ed., *Human Rights in the 'War on Terror'* (New York: Cambridge University Press, 2005); Michael Ignatieff, "The American Empire: The Burden," *The New York Times Magazine*, January 5, 2003; and Kate Zernike, "Threats and Responses: Liberals for War," *The New York Times*, March 14, 2003.

47. See, for example, "Prison Interrogators Got F.B.I. Warnings," *The New York Times*, February 24, 2006; Adam Liptak, "Interrogation Methods Rejected by Military Wins Bush's Support," *The New York Times*, September 8, 2006.

48. Isaiah Berlin, *Four Essays on Liberty* (Oxford: Oxford University Press, 1969), 132.

49. Ari Fleischer, White House Press Briefing, September 26, 2001. http://www.whitehouse.gov/news/releases/2001/09/20010926-5.html.

CHAPTER 4: STAYING IN

1. In July 2007, "Individual Moral Responsibility in a Time of War" was the working title of this manuscript *How Do I Save My Honor?*

2. Thomas L. Friedman, "The Powell Perplex," *The New York Times*, December 19, 2000, A31. Also quoted in Karen DeYoung, *Soldier: The Life of Colin Powell* (New York: Knopf, 2006), 298.

3. David Rothkopf, *Running the World: The Inside Story of the National Security Council and the Architects of American Power* (New York: Public Affairs, 2005), 396–397. See also DeYoung's summary of Rothkopf, *Soldier*, 322.

4. Karen DeYoung, *Soldier: The Life of Colin Powell* (New York: Knopf, 2006), 326–332.

5. DeYoung, *Soldier*, 335.

6. Colin L. Powell, *My American Journey* (New York: Random House, 1995), 308.

7. This account is taken directly from Karen DeYoung, *Soldier*, 364–372.

8. DeYoung, *Soldier*, 369.

9. Colin L. Powell, "Draft Decision Memorandum for the President on the Applicability of the Geneva Convention to the Conflict in Afghanistan," January 26, 2002. Reproduced in *The Torture Papers: The Road to Abu Ghraib*, Karen J. Greenberg and Joshua L. Dratel, eds. (New York: Cambridge University Press, 2005), 122–125.

10. DeYoung, *Soldier*, 371.

11. Quote in Thomas E. Ricks, *Fiasco: The American Military Adventure in Iraq* (New York: Penguin Press, 2006), 27.

12. DeYoung, *Soldier*, 396.

13. DeYoung, *Soldier*, 401–402.

14. DeYoung, *Soldier*, 429. See also Bob Woodward, *State of Denial* (New York: Simon & Schuster, 2006), 106.

15. See Nicholas Lemann, *The New Yorker*, October 18, 2004. "By August [2002], Powell had come around to the view that the war couldn't be headed off. He decided that the best chance was to influence how it was done, not whether."

16. Steven R. Weisman, "Powell Calls His U.N. Speech a Lasting Blot on His Record," *New York Times*, September 9, 2005, A10.

17. Sarah Baxter, "Powell Tried to Talk Bush Out of War," *The Sunday Times (UK)*, July 8, 2007. http://timesonline.co.uk/tol/news/world/us_and_americas (accessed October 4, 2007).

18. DeYoung, *Soldier*, 12.

19. DeYoung, *Soldier*, 430–431.

20. Interview with John Brady Kiesling, September 30, 2005.

21. See Dennis Jett, "The Failure of Colin Powell," *Foreign Service Journal*, February 2005, 24.

22. Charles Lewis and Mark Reading-Smith, "False Pretenses," The Center For Public Integrity. http://www.publicintegrity.org/WarCard/Default.aspx?src=home &context=overview&id=945 (accessed February 14, 2008).

23. Weisman, "Powell Calls His U.N. Speech a Lasting Blot on His Record," A10.

24. See comments of Colin Powell, Aspen Ideas Festival, "Order, Law, and Governance in the 21st Century," July 7, 2006, p. 21. http://www.aspeninstitute.org/atf/cf/%78DEB6F227-659B-4EC8-8F84 (accessed October 4, 2007).

25. Bob Woodward, *Plan of Attack* (New York: Simon & Schuster, 2004), 178.

26. Thomas Powers, "What Tenet Knew," *The New York Review of Books*, July 19, 2007, 70–74.

27. Paul R. Pillar, "Intelligence, Policy, and the War in Iraq," *Foreign Affairs*, March/April 2006, Vol. 85, No. 2, p. 16.

28. "Regional Consequences of Regime Change in Iraq," *Report of the Select Committee on Intelligence on Prewar Intelligence Assessments About Postwar Iraq*, 110th Congress, 1st Session. Quotes pp. 22–23. http://intelligence.senate.gov/prewar.pdf (accessed December 28, 2007).

29. CBS News, "The Man Who Knew," February 4, 2004. http://www.cbsnews.com/stories/2003/10/14/60II/printable577975.shtml (accessed October 6, 2007).

30. Hans Blix, *Disarming Iraq* (New York: Pantheon Books, 2004), 91.

31. Fairfax Digital, "Iraq Invasion Violated International Law: Blix," August 7, 2003. http://www.smh.com.au/articles/2003/08/07/1060145783214.html (accessed March 1, 2008).

32. Blix, *Disarming Iraq*, 210–211.

33. Quote of Senate Select Committee on Intelligence from Thomas E. Ricks, *Fiasco: The American Military Adventure in Iraq* (New York: Penguin Press, 2006), 90.

34. Thomas Powers, "What Tenet Knew," *The New York Review of Books*, July 19, 2007, 73. See also Joseph Lelyveld, "The Good Soldier," *The New York Review of Books*, November 2, 2006, 4–8.

35. See comments of Colin Powell, Aspen Ideas Festival, "Order, Law, and Governance in the 21st Century," July 7, 2006, p. 21. http://www.aspeninstitute.org/atf/cf/%78DEB6F227-659B-4EC8-8F84 (accessed October 4, 2007).

36. Quoted in Blix, *Disarming Iraq*, 272.

37. Powell, *My American Journey*, 148.

38. Powell, *My American Journey*, 148.

39. Powell, *My American Journey*, 149.

40. Walter Isaacson, "Colin Powell," *GQ*, October 2007, 276.

41. Powell, *My American Journey*, 207–208.

42. Powell, *My American Journey*, 434.

43. DeYoung, *Soldier*, 230, 510.

44. Unless otherwise noted, all quotes from Wayne White are from my interview with him on August 14, 2007, in Skytop, Pennsylvania.

45. Wayne White, "Warnings Unheeded," transcript of testimony delivered to Ad Hoc Senate Hearing on Pre-War Iraq Intelligence & Related Matters, Washington, D.C., June 26, 2006. http://www.mideasti.org/articles/doc535.html (accessed November 30, 2007).

46. White, "Warnings Unheeded."

47. White, "Warnings Unheeded."

48. Greg Miller, "Democracy Domino Theory 'Not Credible,'" *Los Angeles Times*, March 14, 2003. http://www.commondreams.org/headlines03/0314-06.htm (accessed December 1, 2007).

49. Miller, "Democracy Domino Theory 'Not Credible.'"

50. See Thomas E. Ricks, *Fiasco: The American Military Adventure in Iraq* (New York: Penguin Press, 2006), 86–88.

51. Miller, "Democracy Domino Theory 'Not Credible.'"

52. U.S. Central Command (CENTCOM) is responsible for U.S. security interests in twenty-five nations that stretch from the Horn of Africa through the Arabian Gulf region into Central Asia.

53. White, "Warnings Unheeded."

54. "Rumsfeld Blames Iraq Problems on 'Pockets of Dead-Enders,'" *USA Today*, June 18, 2003. http://www.usatoday.com/news/world/iraq/2003-06-18-rumsfeld_x.htm (accessed December 1, 2007).

55. White, "Warnings Unheeded."

56. White, "Warnings Unheeded."

CHAPTER 5: GETTING OUT

1. Associated Press, "Rice Reminds Iraq-War Diplomats of Oath, Duty," November 2, 2007. http://www.msnbc.msn.com/id/21603235 (accessed November 19, 2007).

2. Associated Press, "Rice Reminds Iraq-War Diplomats of Oath, Duty."

3. Associated Press, "Diplomats Explain Refusal to Serve in Iraq," *St. Petersburg Times*, January 9, 2008, A10. Other concerns raised by the 4,300 respondents included safety and security issues, pay disparities, and the leadership of Secretary of State Condoleezza Rice and her top deputies.

4. Unless otherwise noted, all quotes from John Brady Kiesling are from my interviews with him on September 30 and October 2, 2005.

5. John Brady Kiesling, "U.S. Diplomat's Letter of Resignation," *The New York Times*, February 27, 2003. http://www.nytimes.com/2003/02/27/international/27WEB-TNAT.html?ex=1223870400&en=571b1104fc20ad64&ei=5070 (accessed October 11, 2008).

6. Eric Boehlert, "Odd Man Out," Salon.com, March 19, 2003. http://www.salon.com/news/feature/2003/03/19/_kiesling (accessed August 2, 2007).

7. John Brady Kiesling, *Diplomacy Lessons: Realism for an Unloved Superpower* (Washington, D.C.: Potomac Books, 2006), 1–2.

8. Unless otherwise noted, all quotes from John Brown are from my interview with him on October 1, 2005.

9. John Brown, "Why I Resigned," *Foreign Service Journal*, September 2003, 14.

10. Brown, "Why I Resigned," 16.

11. "John Brown's Public Diplomacy Press & Blog Review" is available free by requesting it at the USC Center of Public Diplomacy. http://uscpublicdiplomacy.com/index.php/newsroom/johnbrown_main.

12. Unless otherwise noted, all quotes from Ann Wright are from my interviews with her on August 22, 2005.

13. U.S. Army Specialist Casey Sheehan, Cindy Sheehan's son, was a casualty of the Iraq War. In his honor, the antiwar protesters outside President Bush's ranch in Crawford, Texas, named their encampment Camp Casey.

14. Truthout 2007: Freedom and Democracy Awards Citations. http://www.truthout.org/article/truthout-2007-freedom-and-democracy-awards (accessed October 11, 2008).

15. Chalmers Johnson, *The Sorrows of Empire* (New York: Henry Holt and Co., 2004), 224.

16. "Rumsfeld Made Iraq Overture in '84 Despite Chemical Raids," *The New York Times*, December 23, 2003.

17. Joost R. Hiltermann, *A Poisonous Affair: America, Iraq, and the Gassing of Halabja* (New York: Cambridge University Press, 2007), 1–21, 46–51, 126–129; quote p. 17. Samantha Power, *A Problem from Hell: America and the Age of Genocide* (New York: Basic Books, 2002), 171–245; quote p. 226.

18. Secretary Colin L. Powell, "Remarks at Halabja Mass Grave Site Ceremony," September 15, 2003. http://www.state.gov/secretary/former/powell/remarks/2003/24100.htm (accessed December 29, 2007).

19. Colin L. Powell, "Remarks at Stakeout after His Visit to the Halabja Memorial Museum," September 15, 2003. http://www.state.gov/secretary/former/powell/remarks/2003/24689.htm (accessed December 29, 2007).

20. On September 6, 2002, in an interview with the *New York Times*, Andrew Card said: "From a marketing point of view, you don't introduce new products in August." Mr. Card was responding to the question of " . . . why the administration waited until after Labor Day to try to sell the American people on military action against Iraq."

21. Secretary of Defense Rumsfeld's one-time assistant, Ken Adelman, wrote in 2002: "I believe demolishing Hussein's military power and liberating Iraq would be a cakewalk." "Cakewalk in Iraq," *Washington Post*, February 13, 2002. http://www.washingtonpost.com/ac2/wp-dyn/A1996-2002Feb12 (accessed on August 8, 2007).

22. See Deputy Secretary of Defense Paul Wolfowitz Interview with Sam Tannenhaus, *Vanity Fair*. "News Transcript," U.S. Department of Defense, May 09, 2003. http://www.defenselink.mil/transcripts/transcript.aspx?transcriptid=2594 (accessed August 8, 2007).

23. General Eric Shinseki, then-army chief of staff, told Congress in February 2003 that the occupation of Iraq could require "several hundred thousand troops." Deputy Secretary of Defense Paul Wolfowitz called this estimate "wildly off the mark" and put the figure at only 100,000. Secretary of Defense Donald Rumsfeld took the unusual step of announcing that General Shinseki would be leaving when his term as army chief of staff ended. See Eric Schmitt, "Pentagon Contradicts General on Iraq's Occupation Force's Size," *New York Times*, February 28, 2003.

24. See Dave Moniz, "Ex-Army Boss: Pentagon Won't Admit Reality in Iraq," *USA Today*, June 2, 2003; CBS News, "Sources: Army Secretary Was Fired," April 26, 2003. http://www.cbsnews.com/stories/2003/04/25/national/main551191.shtml (accessed July 23, 2007).

25. Edward Weisband and Thomas M. Franck, *Resignation in Protest: Political and Ethical Choices Between Loyalty to Team and Loyalty to Conscience in American Public Life* (New York: Grossman Publishers, 1975).

26. See William F. Felice, *The Global New Deal: Economic and Social Human Rights in World Politics* (Lanham, Md.: Rowman & Littlefield, 2003).

CHAPTER 6: THE ETHICAL SOLDIER

1. Title 10, U.S. Code; Act of May 5, 1960, replacing the wording first adopted in 1789, with amendment effective October 5, 1962. http://www.army.mil/cmh-pg/html/faq/oaths.html (accessed December 5, 2007).

2. DA Form 71, August 1, 1959, for officers. http://www.army.mil/cmh-pg/html/faq/oaths.html (accessed December 5, 2007).

3. Unless otherwise indicated, all quotes from Ehren Watada are from my interview with him on September 12, 2007.

4. Mike Barber, "Unit Gets Ready for Iraq—Without Watada," *Seattle Post-Intelligencer*, June 23, 2006.

5. See Norman Solomon, "Making an Example of Ehren Watada," Common Dreams News Center, February 6, 2007. www.commondreams.org (accessed September 10, 2007).

6. Richard Falk, *The Costs of War: International Law, the UN, and World Order after Iraq* (New York: Routledge, 2008), 3.

7. Hal Bernton, "Federal Judge Tells Military to Halt Watada Court-Martial," *The Seattle Times*, October 6, 2007.

In late October 2008, a federal judge ruled that Watada cannot face a second court-martial on three of the five counts filed against him, citing constitutional protections against being tried twice for the same crime. Judge Settle, however, left open the possibility of a second prosecution on two other counts. Hal Bernton, "Watada Won't Be Retried on 3 of 5 Counts," *The Seattle Times*, October 21, 2008.

8. Unless otherwise indicated, all quotes from Aidan Delgado are from my interview with him on October 27, 2007.

9. Aidan Delgado, *The Sutras of Abu Ghraib: Notes from a Conscientious Objector in Iraq* (Boston: Beacon Press, 2007), 52.

10. Delgado, *Sutras*, 56.

11. Delgado, *Sutras*, 78–79.

12. According to Delgado, "hajji" was the anti-Arab, anti-Muslim epithet of choice for soldiers in Iraq: "In Arabic, a *hajji* is one who has gone on the Hajji, the pilgrimage to Mecca that is one of the five pillars of Islam. It is often used as a mild honorific, especially to describe an older man. In army usage it means 'gook' or 'Charlie' or 'nigger.'" Delgado, *Sutras*, 72.

13. Francisco de Vitoria, *On the Law of War*, in Gregory M. Reichberg, Henrik Syse, and Endre Begby, eds., *The Ethics of War: Classic and Contemporary Readings* (Oxford: Blackwell Publishing, 2006), 318–319. Emphasis in original.

14. Hugo Grotius, *On the Law of War and Peace*, in Gregory M. Reichberg, Henrik Syse, and Endre Begby, eds., *The Ethics of War: Classic and Contemporary Readings* (Oxford: Blackwell Publishing, 2006), 419.

15. *Principles of International Law Recognized in the Charter of the Nuremberg Tribunal and Judgment of the Tribunal*, 1950 U.N. GAOR, 5th Sess., Suppl. No. 12 (A/1316), in W. Michale Reisman and Chris T. Antoniou, *The Laws of War: A Comprehensive Collection of Primary Documents on International Laws Governing Armed Conflict* (New York: Vintage Books, 1994), 335–336.

16. The Nuremberg Principles were drafted during the Nuremberg trials of Nazis after World War II to determine what constitutes a war crime. The International Law Commission of the United Nations later affirmed that these principles constituted international law. The three broad categories of crimes include: (1) crimes against peace—the planning and waging of a war of aggression; (2) war crimes—concerning the treatment of prisoners of war and other customs of war; and (3) crimes against humanity—murder and other inhumane acts against civilian populations.

17. See U.S. Department of the Army, *The Law of Land Warfare* (Field Manual No. 27-10, 1963), which serves as one of the major resources for educating U.S.

military personnel on the laws of war. Included in this section are both direct quotations and the official interpretation of the various Geneva and Hague Conventions.

18. *Principles of International Law Recognized in the Charter of the Nuremberg Tribunal and Judgment of the Tribunal,* 1950 U.N. GAOR, 5th Sess., Suppl. No. 12 (A/1316), in W. Michale Reisman and Chris T. Antoniou, *The Laws of War: A Comprehensive Collection of Primary Documents on International Laws Governing Armed Conflict* (New York: Vintage Books, 1994), 336.

19. See listing in U.S. Department of the Army, *The Law of Land Warfare,* 5 (Field Manual No. 27-10, 1963).

20. This court statement is from a 1946 case involving the conviction of a Japanese commander for failing to restrain his troops from committing war crimes against civilians. *Yamashita v. Styer,* decided February 4, 1946 [327 U.S. 1], in *Principles of International Law Recognized in the Charter of the Nuremberg Tribunal and Judgment of the Tribunal,* 1950 UN GAOR, 5th Sess., Suppl. No. 12 (A/1316), in W. Michale Reisman and Chris T. Antoniou, *The Laws of War: A Comprehensive Collection of Primary Documents on International Laws Governing Armed Conflict* (New York: Vintage Books, 1994), 347.

21. See *The Paquete Habana,* 175 U.S. 677, 700, 20 S.Ct. 290, 299, 44 L.Ed. (1900), in Burns H. Weston, Richard A. Falk, and Anthony D'Amato, *International Law and World Order,* 2nd edition (St. Paul, Minn.: West Publishing Company, 1990), 133. In this decision, the Supreme Court states: "International law is part of our law . . . where there is no treaty, and no controlling executive or legislative act or judicial decision, resort must be had to the customs and usages of civilized nations."

22. "Article 15-6 Investigation of the 800th Military Police Brigade (The Taguba Report)," in Mark Danner, *Torture and Truth: America, Abu Ghraib, and the War on Terror* (New York: New York Review of Books, 2004), 292.

23. "Final Report of the Independent Panel to Review DOD Detention Operations" (The Schlesinger Report), in Mark Danner, *Torture and Truth: America, Abu Ghraib, and the War on Terror* (New York: New York Review of Books, 2004), 336.

24. Thomas E. Ricks and Ann Scott Tyson, "Troops at Odds with Ethics Standards," *Washington Post,* May 5, 2007.

25. Telford Taylor, *The Anatomy of the Nuremberg Trials* (New York: Knopf, 1992), 252–253.

26. See David Cole and Jules Lobel, *Less Safe, Less Free: Why America Is Losing the War on Terror* (New York: The New Press, 2007).

CHAPTER 7: BRITAIN

1. BBC, "Mandela Condemns U.S. Stance on Iraq." http://news.bbc.co.uk/1/hi/world/africa/2710181.stm.

2. BBC, "Key Vote after Blair Appeal," March 18, 2003. http://news.bbc.co.uk/2/hi/uk_politics/2860717.stm (accessed September 15, 2007).

3. BBC, "Key Vote."

4. BBC, "Key Vote."

5. Interview with Ken Purchase, June 12, 2007, London.

6. Colin Brown, "Iraq War: The Smoking Gun?", *The Independent/UK*, March 24, 2005. See also BBC, "Wilmshurst Resignation Letter," March 24, 2005. http://new .bbc.co.uk/go/pr/fr/-/1/hi/uk_politics/4377605.stm (accessed September 16, 2007).

7. BBC, "List of Labour Resignations," March 19, 2003. http://news.bbc .co.uk/2/hi/uk_news/politics/2860583.stm (accessed September 15, 2007).

8. Interview with Michael J. Foster, June 12, 2007, London.

9. See Thomas E. Ricks, *Fiasco: The American Military Adventure in Iraq* (New York: Penguin Press, 2006); Rajiv Chandrasekaran, *Imperial Life in the Emerald City* (New York: Knopf, 2006).

10. "British Iraq Dossier Surfaces, Without Crucial Weapons Claim," *The New York Times*, February 19, 2008, A13.

11. The Hutton Report is available at "The Hutton Inquiry Website" at http://the-hutton-inquiry.org.uk/. See also BBC News, "Timeline: Hutton Report," January 28, 2004. http://news.bbc.co.uk/2/hi/uk_news/politics/3099378.stm (accessed September 25, 2007). See also David Halpin, C. Stephen Frost, and Searle Sennett, "Our Doubts about Dr. Kelly's Suicide," *The Guardian*, January 27, 2004. http://www .guardian.co.uk/theguardian/2004/jan/27/guardianletters4 (accessed February 16, 2008).

12. The Iraq Survey Group (ISG) was the fact-finding mission sent by the United States, United Kingdom, and others after the 2003 invasion of Iraq to find the weapons of mass destruction (WMD) developed under Saddam Hussein. The fourteen-hundred-member international team, organized by the Pentagon and CIA, hunted for suspected stockpiles of WMD, including chemical and biological agents. David Kay, the head of the ISG, resigned on January 23, 2004, and stated that he believed the WMD stockpiles would not be found in Iraq. Kay commented, "I don't think they existed." The final report of the ISG in September 2004 also found that Saddam ended his nuclear program in 1991, and the ISG found no evidence of any effort to restart the program.

13. The Butler Report is available at http:/www.butlerreview.org.uk/ (accessed September 25, 2007). See also BBC News, "At-a-Glance: Butler Report." http://newsvote.bbc.co.uk/2/hi/uk_news/politics/3892809.stm (accessed September 25, 2007).

14. See Mark Danner, *The Secret Way to War: The Downing Street Memo and the Iraq War's Buried History* (New York: New York Review of Books, 2006).

15. Elizabeth Palmer, "Britain's Walking Iraq Casualty," CBS News London, March 19, 2007.

16. Unless otherwise indicated, all quotes in the text from John Denham, Michael J. Foster, Ken Purchase, Andy Reed, Carne Ross, and Clare Short are drawn from the transcriptions of my one-on-one interviews with each of them individually.

17. Nicholas Wood, "Recovering Diplomat Finds Work as Envoy of the Voiceless," *New York Times*, March 3, 2007.

18. Carne Ross, *Independent Diplomat: Dispatches from an Unaccountable Elite* (Ithaca, New York: Cornell University Press, 2007), 190.

19. Ross, *Independent Diplomat*, 72–73.

20. Ross, *Independent Diplomat*, 76.
21. Ross, *Independent Diplomat*, 80.
22. Ross, *Independent Diplomat*, 139.
23. Ross, *Independent Diplomat*, 145–146.
24. Wood, "Recovering Diplomat."
25. Henry Deedes, "Short Set to Stand Down After 23 Years as an MP," *The Independent*, September 13, 2006.
26. Clare Short, *An Honourable Deception? New Labour, Iraq and the Misuse of Power* (London: The Free Press, 2004), 215.
27. See, for example, Michael G. Cartwright, "Biblical Arguments in International Ethics," in Terry Nardin and David R. Mapel, *Traditions of International Ethics* (Cambridge: Cambridge University Press, 1992), 270–296. Of particular relevance to Christian pacifism is Cartwright's discussion of "The Historic Peace Churches," 280–283.
28. John Denham's speech to the House of Commons after resigning from the government, March 18, 2003. www.johndenham.org.uk/Resignation%20sppech.htm (accessed August 29, 2007).
29. Denham speech, March 18, 2003.
30. "New British Leader Appoints Critics of War to Cabinet," *The New York Times*, June 29, 2007, A12.
31. Ross, *Independent Diplomat*, 139–141.
32. A. C. Grayling, *Among the Dead Cities: The History and Moral Legacy of the WWII Bombing of Civilians in Germany and Japan* (New York: Walker & Company, 2007).

CHAPTER 8: INDIVIDUAL MORAL RESPONSIBILITY IN A TIME OF WAR

1. I am grateful to Professor Miroslav Nincic for introducing me to these three intersecting logics during my time at New York University. See also Miroslav Nincic, *Democracy and Foreign Policy: The Fallacy of Political Realism* (New York: Columbia University Press, 1992).
2. Chris Hedges, *War Is a Force That Gives Us Meaning* (New York: Anchor Books, 2003), 134.
3. See comments by Carne Ross in chapter 7.
4. Dalai Lama, "Religious Freedom," in Kerry Kennedy Cuomo, *Speak Truth to Power* (New York: Crown Publishers, 2000), 35.
5. Gov. Mitt Romney, Address to CPAC, February 7, 2008. http://www.humanevents.com/article.php?id=24893 (accessed February 21, 2008).
6. Stephen Kinzer, *Overthrow: America's Century of Regime Change from Hawaii to Iraq* (New York: Times Books, 2006). Kinzer documents U.S. actions to bring about "regime change" in the following fourteen countries: Hawaii, Cuba, Puerto Rico, the Philippines, Nicaragua, Honduras, Iran, Guatemala, South Vietnam, Chile, Grenada, Panama, Afghanistan, and Iraq.

7. Terry Nardin, "Humanitarian Imperialism," *Ethics and International Affairs*, Vol. 19, No. 2, 2005, 21–26.

8. See Paul Berman, *Terror and Liberalism* (New York: Norton, 2003); Thomas Cushman, ed., *A Matter of Principle: Humanitarian Arguments for War in Iraq* (Berkeley: University of California Press, 2005).

9. Frank Rich, *The Greatest Story Ever Sold: The Decline and Fall of Truth from 9/11 to Katrina* (New York: Penguin Press, 2006), 76, 105, 154.

10. Or examine the photos of the war that the mainstream media have deemed too brutal and graphic for wide distribution. Some soldiers have set up websites to bring home the true human cost of war. Aidan Delgado's website, for example, displays some of these images (http://www.aidandelgado.com).

11. Michael Massing, "Iraq: The Hidden Human Costs," *The New York Review of Books*, December 20, 2007, 82.

12. Michael Kamber and Time Arango, "4,000 U.S. Deaths, and a Handful of Images," *The New York Times*, July 26, 2008, A(1). See also Clark Hoyt, "The Painful Images of War," *The New York Times*, August 3, 2008.

13. Jon Lee Anderson as quoted in Paul Savoy, "The Moral Case Against the Iraq War," *The Nation*, May 31, 2004.

14. David Bellavia, *House to House: A Soldier's Memoir* (New York: Free Press, 2008). Quoted in Massing, "Iraq: The Hidden Human Costs," 82.

15. Evan Wright, *Generation Kill: Devil Dogs, Iceman, Captain America, and the New Face of American War* (Berkeley: Berkeley Caliber, 2008). Quoted in Massing, "Iraq: The Hidden Human Costs," 84.

16. Lawrence K. Altman and Richard A. Oppel, Jr., "W.H.O. Says Iraq Civilian Death Toll Higher Than Cited," *The New York Times*, January 10, 2008, A12.

17. Oscar Arias Sánchez, "Disarmament," in Kerry Kennedy Cuomo, *Speak Truth to Power* (New York: Crown Publishers, 2000), 46.

18. See David Halberstam, *The Best and the Brightest* (New York: The Modern Library, 2001).

19. Edward Weisband and Thomas M. Franck, *Resignation in Protest: Political and Ethical Choices Between Loyalty to Team and Loyalty to Conscience in American Public Life* (New York: Grossman Publishers, 1975).

20. Weisband and Franck, *Resignation in Protest*, 26.

21. Weisband and Franck, *Resignation in Protest*, 20.

22. Henrik Ibsen, *An Enemy of Society*, trans. William Archer (Boston: Walter H. Baker and Co., 1900), 110.

23. Peter Singer, *Practical Ethics*, 3rd Edition (Cambridge: Cambridge University Press, 1993), 1–15; Peter Singer, *The President of Good & Evil: The Ethics of George W. Bush* (New York: Dutton, 2004), 3.

24. Adolf Hitler, *Mein Kampf* (Boston: Houghton Mifflin Company, 1971), 402.

25. (Johann) Wolfgang von Goethe, *Faust*, Part one. http://www.hermetic.com/sabazius/goethe.htm (accessed February 21, 2008).

26. Sophocles, *Antigone*, adapted by Lewis Galantiere (New York: Random House, 1946), 47.

27. The FBI's Counter Intelligence Program (COINTELPRO) was charged with investigating and disrupting dissident political organizations within the United

States, including such nonviolent civil rights groups as Martin Luther King, Jr.'s Southern Christian Leadership Conference. FBI agents were directed to "expose, disrupt, misdirect, discredit, or otherwise neutralize" the activities of these organizations and their leaders. See "Intelligence Activities and the Rights of Americans," Book II, *Final Report of the Select Committee to Study Governmental Operations with Respect to Intelligence Activities,* United States Senate, April 26, 1976. http://www .icdc.com/~paulwolf/cointelpro/churchfinalreportIIa.htm (accessed November 6, 2007).

28. See, for example: "Dixie Chicked in the Heartland," Salon.com, May 22, 2003. http://dir.salon.com/story/opinion/feature/2003/05/22/hedges/index. html (accessed November 6, 2007).

29. Ari Fleischer, White House Press Briefing, September 26, 2001. http://www .whitehouse.gov/news/releases/2001/09/20010926-5.html.

30. See Paul Savoy, "The Moral Case Against the Iraq War," *The Nation,* May 31, 2004.

31. Fyodor Dostoyevsky, *The Brothers Karamazov* (New York: Farrar, Straus & Giroux, 1990), 245–246. Also quoted in Savoy, "The Moral Case."

32. Fyodor Dostoyevsky, *Crime and Punishment,* trans. Jessie Coulson (New York: Norton, 1989), 56.

33. Taylor Branch, "Globalizing King's Legacy," *The New York Times,* January 16, 2006, A19.

34. Savoy, "The Moral Case."

Index

Abu Ghraib, 2, 3, 4, 86, 91, 175, 200n9; and Delgado, Aidan, 8, 30, 126, 130–31, 138–40

Acheson, Dean, 42

Afghanistan, 8, 55, 99, 103, 155, 214n6; and just war, 160; prisoners in, 28–29; and Watada, Ehren, 128, 135

aggressive war. *See* war

al-Qaeda: Geneva Conventions and, 71–72; linking Iraq to, 12, 78, 83, 86–88, 127, 151; politics of linking Hussein to, 55, 99, 109–12, 185, 193–94

American Foreign Service Association, 98

Amnesty International, 55

Anderson, Jon Lee, 188

Annan, Kofi, 81

Arias, Oscar, 189

Aristotle, 24

Bellavia, David, 188

Berlin, Isaiah, 45, 63

Blair, Tony, 2, 9, 23, 76, 78, 147–77, 179

Blix, Hans, 78, 80–81, 111

Blizzard, Bob, 2, 148, 150

Branch, Taylor, 196

Bremer, Paul, 11–12

Britain, 147–77; Butler Report, 3, 152, 155–56, 213n13; civil service, 2, 148, 166–67; Downing Street Memo, 3, 73, 109, 153, 199n6; House of Commons, 2, 148–49, 150–51, 154, 158, 161; Hutton Inquiry, 152, 213n11; intelligence (MI6), 152–53; parliamentary system, 2, 58, 154, 163

Brown, Gordon, 9, 155, 162

Brown, John H., 3, 8, 91, 97–124, 179

Bryan, William Jennings, 2–3, 6, 33–36, 58

Brzezinski, Zbigniew, 37

Buddhism, 8–9, 112–13, 129–30, 138

Bundy, McGeorge 12

Bureau of Intelligence and Research (INR). *See* U.S. State Department

Bush doctrine, 54

Bush, George W., 27, 68, 131; al-Qaeda to Iraq, linking, 111, 193–94; Arab democracy and, 89; Blair, Tony, and, 148, 158–60, 170; Christian faith of, 160; ethics of loyalty and, 11–12; Iraq regime change and, 108, 185; Powell, Colin, and, 71–74,

Hedges, Chris, 180–181
Herbert, Bob, 131
Hiltermann, Joost, 108
Hondros, Chris, 188
Hirschman, Albert, 21–22
honorable deception, 170–72
Hulsman, John, 43–44
human rights, 105, 168, 175–77,
    196–97; ethical theory and, 41–42,
    47–50, 52, 54–56, 64, 192; Iraq and,
    108; Singer, Peter, and, 62–63;
    torture and, 3–4; U.S. military and,
    27
humanitarian intervention, 85–86,
    105–10, 114, 185–86
Humphrey, Hubert, 21
Hunt, Lord, 2, 148, 150
Hussein, Saddam, 110, 127, 186, 193;
    Britain and, 149–53, 158, 171;
    humanitarian intervention and,
    59–60, 106–8; nuclear weapons and,
    79; neoconservatives and, 55; UN
    sanctions and, 72–74.; intelligence
    on, 3, 57, 90; nonexistent links to al-
    Qaeda (*See* al-Qaeda); U.S. support
    of (*See* Iraq). *See also* weapons of
    mass destruction
Hutton Inquiry. *See* Britain

Ibsen, Henrik, 191
Independent Diplomat (ID), 157
International Atomic Energy Agency
    (IAEA), 80
International Criminal Court, 70, 135,
    150, 168, 171
Iraq: Anfal operation, 107–8; casualties
    of war, 189; Halabja campaign,
    107; intervention against (*See*
    humanitarian intervention); nuclear
    capability, 79–81, 88; sanctions
    against. *See* UN Iraq sanctions;
    Survey Group, 152, 213n12; U.S.
    support of Saddam Hussein,
    107–9. *See also* weapons of mass
    destruction
Israel-Palestine conflict. *See* Middle
    East

Jaspers, Karl, 5
Johnson, General Harold, 6, 33, 38–39
Johnson, Lyndon, 16, 38–39
jus ad bellum, 30–33, 51–52, 126, 131–36,
    140
jus in bello, 28–30, 32–33, 52, 126,
    136–40
just war, 3, 41, 47, 54, 181; Walzer,
    Michael, and, 26, 50–52, 56. *See also*
    Christian ethics; *jus ad bellum*; *jus
    in bello*

Kant, Immanuel, 4, 47–50, 62, 196
Kazin, Michael, 36
Kelly, David, 152
Kennedy, John F., 42
Kennan, George F., 43
Kidney, David, 150
Kiesling, John Brady, 3, 8, 15, 91,
    97–124, 179, 191; Powell, Colin,
    and, 75, 99, 101
Kilfoyle, Peter, 149
King, Jr., Martin Luther, 196
Kissinger, Henry, 12
Koppel, Ted, 187
Kosovo, 113–14, 157
Kyrgyzstan, 99, 103, 175

Labour Party, 148–49, 151, 157–59,
    161–62, 164–66
Law of Land Warfare, 136–37,
    211n17
Laws of War. *See* U.S. Army
Leahy, Patrick, 100
liberal internationalism, 156, 206n44
liberal hawks, 186, 195
Lieven, Anatol, 43–44
loyalty, ethic of, 6, 11, 16, 78, 84,
    118–20, 182–83, 190
Lusitania, 34

Machiavelli, 44–47, 51, 53, 60–61
Mandela, Nelson, 148
many hands, 1, 184
Marshall, George, 75
Massing, Michael, 187
McNamara, Robert, 12, 16, 21, 38, 58

About the Author

William F. Felice is professor of political science and head of the international relations and global affairs discipline at Eckerd College. Dr. Felice was named the 2006 Florida Professor of the Year by the Carnegie Foundation for the Advancement of Teaching. In addition, Felice has received Eckerd College's John M. Bevan Teaching Excellence and Campus Leadership Award, and he has been recognized by the students as Professor of the Year and by the faculty as the Robert A. Staub Distinguished Teacher of the Year.

Felice is the author of *Taking Suffering Seriously: The Importance of Collective Human Rights* (1996), *The Global New Deal: Economic and Social Human Rights in World Politics* (2003), and numerous articles on the theory and practice of human rights. He has published articles in the *Cambridge Review of International Affairs, Ethics and International Affairs, Human Rights Quarterly, International Affairs, Social Justice,* and other journals.

Felice received his Ph.D. from the Department of Politics at New York University. He has served as a trustee on the board of the Carnegie Council for Ethics in International Relations. He was also the past president of the International Ethics Section of the International Studies Association.